Rebel Journ

The Writings of Wilfi

This book is an anthology of the writings of Wilfred Burchett, perhaps the greatest journalist and war correspondent Australia has ever produced. He was also one of the most controversial figures of the Cold War, both here and overseas. Burchett published more than 30 books, and this volume brings together extracts from most of these, spanning the entire breadth of his career, from World War II, through Hiroshima, Eastern Europe, Korea, Russia, Laos, Cambodia, China, Vietnam, Angola, Rhodesia (Zimbabwe) and other areas from which Burchett reported. The book presents these documents of reportage mostly in chronological order, and thus serves not only as a significant historical overview of the period, but also as a reader in Cold War journalism.

George Burchett is an artist and translator. In 2005 he co-edited, with Nick Shimmin, *Memoirs of a Rebel Journalist: The Autobiography of Wilfred Burchett*.

Nick Shimmin completed a doctorate at the University of Lancaster in 1989 on the Manx writers T.E. Brown and Hall Caine. Since that time he has worked in sales and marketing and as a subtitling editor at the Special Broadcasting Service.

Rebel Journalism

The Writings of Wilfred Burchett

EDITED BY GEORGE BURCHETT AND
NICK SHIMMIN

CAMBRIDGE
UNIVERSITY PRESS

CAMBRIDGE UNIVERSITY PRESS
Cambridge, New York, Melbourne, Madrid, Cape Town,
Singapore, São Paulo, Delhi, Tokyo, Mexico City

Cambridge University Press
The Edinburgh Building, Cambridge CB2 8RU, UK

Published in the United States of America by
Cambridge University Press, New York

www.cambridge.org
Information on this title: www.cambridge.org/9780521718264

First published 2007

A catalogue record for this publication is available from the British Library

Library of Congress Cataloguing in Publication data
National Library of Australia Cataloguing in Publication data
Rebel journalism : the writings of Wilfred Burchett.
Includes index.
ISBN 978-0-52171-826-4 (pbk.).
1. Burchett, Wilfred, 1911–1983.   2. Foreign correspondents – Australia.   3. War
correspondents – Australia. I. Burchett, G.H. (George Harold). II. Shimmin,
Nicholas L.
070.4332092

ISBN 978-0-521-71826-4 Paperback

Contents

List of Photographs

Acknowledgements

This book is a further acknowledgement of those few remaining journalists who are still prepared to make huge sacrifices to deliver what they believe to be the truth.

It is dedicated to Vessa Burchett (1919–2007), Wilfred's wife, companion, colleague and first reader, a witness to many of the events covered in this book, mother of three of his four children (including one of the editors), a remarkable woman, of great courage and spirit, the *yin* to Wilfred's *yang*.

We would also like to acknowledge the support of the following people who have assisted or promoted Wilfred's work and the development of this project:

Deborah Franco, Ilza Burchett, Graham Burchett, Cambridge University Press in Australia (particularly Paulina de Laveaux, Adam Ford, Sandra McComb), Ragnar van Leyden, Simon Nasht, Penny Allen, Jon Rose, Hollis Taylor, Lady Borton, John Maynard, Dr Nguyen Thi Tinh, Stephen Sewell, John Pilger, Trinh Ngoc Thai, Ben Kiernan, Gavan McCormack, Christopher Reed, Kelly Gaudry, Stuart Macintyre, Tom Heenan, Stephanie Alexander, David Bradbury, Mark Davis, Kate Barton, Brendan Doyle, Steve Mori, Rainer Burchett, Peter Burchett, Anna Burchett, Patrick Griffiths, Thao Griffiths, Amanda Jane Duthie, Gerry Herman, and UNSW Press in Sydney.

The photograph of Wilfred Burchett with Allied pressmen at Panmunjom, Korea, 1952 is reproduced with the permission of Norman McSwan. All other photographs are courtesy of The Estate of Wilfred Burchett.

And our thanks to everyone else who has supported us in promoting Wilfred's work and legacy.

Foreword

by John Pilger[1]

In the late spring of 1980, shortly before I was due to leave for Cambodia, I received a phone call from Paris. A familiar, husky voice came quickly to the point. 'Can you postpone?' he said. 'I've heard about a Khmer Rouge list and you're on it. I'm worried about you.'

That Wilfred Burchett was worried about the welfare of another human being was not surprising; the quintessence of the man lay in what he did not say. He neglected to mention not only that *he* was on the same 'list', but that a few weeks earlier, at the age of seventy and seriously ill, he had survived a bloody ambush laid for him by Khmer Rouge assassins, who wounded a travelling companion. (Wilfred's intelligence was as reliable as ever; I narrowly escaped a similar ambush at the same place he was attacked.) I have known other brave reporters; I have not known another who, through half a century of risk-taking, demonstrated as much concern for others and such valour on behalf of others.

He took risks to smuggle Jews out of Nazi Germany, to drag American wounded to safety during the Pacific war, and to seek out prisoners of war in Japan in 1945, to tell them help was coming; the list is long. He sustained a variety of bombardment, from Burma to Korea, to Indochina, yet he retained a compassion coupled with an innocence bordering at times on naïveté. None of these qualities were shared with the vociferous few who worked to bring him down.

---

[1] This foreword is a revised version of the author's essay in B. Kiernan (ed.), *Burchett: Reporting the Other Side of the World 1939–1983* (London: Quartet Books; Sydney: Australasian Publishing Company, 1986).

Wilfred's politics were both instinctive and shaped by the harsh poverty of his upbringing more than by intellectual fashion. Shortly before he died he told me he had never become a communist. 'How could I be a communist?' he said. 'There were so many parties, each drawing on different circumstances, different conditions. Which one was I to choose? I chose none, because I wanted to remain just *me* . . .' If anyone made real the romantic notion of the Australian iconoclast it was Wilfred Burchett. And although his innate decency and affable personality eschewed doctrine (many of Wilfred's friends were non-socialists, even anti-socialists) at times he seemed more diplomat than journalist. Wilfred would have explained this as being part of the 'icebreaker', or go-between, role he adopted and which was, as he put it, 'a useful and honourable thing to do'. If he repeated official explanations uncritically (as during the disastrous land-reform campaigns in North Vietnam in the 1950s), the instances of him going against the doctrines of those he supported are numerous; in any case, he was seldom as close to governments on the 'other side' of the Cold War as many Western journalists are to governments and institutions, almost instinctively. Perhaps, like all originals, Wilfred Burchett was also something of an enigma.

What is beyond question is that the abiding strength of Wilfred's character – courage – allowed him to surrender commitment to a 'cause' when that cause no longer deserved his support. Although this withdrawal sometimes suffered from delayed action, as in the case of the Khmer Rouge, he would not hesitate to say that he had been wrong. 'You've got to be able to look your children in the eye and look at yourself and not be ashamed,' he said. 'You have to know when to let go . . . The question journalists, and politicians, have to ask themselves is, "Do you get off in time, or do you follow a line out of blind loyalty?" It takes courage to say, "Look, I'm wrong on this; I'm letting go."'

In China his friendship with foreign minister and later premier Zhou En-lai and other vintage revolutionaries was 'let go' with much heart-searching and sadness when he perceived the Chinese leadership's hostility to the Vietnamese at the very climax of Vietnam's struggle for independence. He was forced to abandon his old confrere Prince Sihanouk, whom he had supported for twenty-five years, when Sihanouk allied himself with the forces of Pol Pot: 'The wrench,' as the historian Ben Kiernan has written, 'must have hurt'. I remember well his agonizing over Sihanouk who, he felt, had betrayed him personally, not to mention his own people. At the end of his life it was the Vietnamese who remained alone in his pantheon. Having shared something of the Vietnamese experience, I can understand that. 'They have never let me down,' he once said in a mellow mood, allowing a glimpse of his vulnerability.

Paradoxically, Wilfred was vulnerable because he was, in the strictly professional sense, such a fine journalist. His two greatest 'scoops' left no doubt about that, while adding a precarious dimension to his life. The first was Hiroshima. He was the first Western reporter to reach Hiroshima after the atomic bomb had been dropped on 6 August 1945. He had been warned by an official of the Japanese press agency that 'no one goes to Hiroshima: everyone is dying there'. He ignored this of course. He feigned illness at Allied press headquarters in Yokohama, in order to slip away from the press 'pack', and with his beef ration he bought a ticket to Hiroshima.

The journey, mostly in darkness, demonstrated the Burchett courage. Here was a European alone in a train filled with soldiers, armed and sullen and almost certainly bitter at the moment of defeat. At two o'clock in the morning he reached Hiroshima and was promptly thrown into prison. 'There was some shouting by the police and the interpreter became pale as she translated my rare interventions,' he wrote. The 'shouting', he later learned, was about whether or not he was to be shot. It was only a senior officer of the 'Thought Police' who decided the foreigner should live. 'Show him,' he said, 'what his people have done to us.'

What Wilfred saw was published all over the front page of the London *Daily Express* beneath the headline, I WRITE THIS AS A WARNING TO THE WORLD. 'In Hiroshima, thirty days after the first atomic bomb destroyed the city and shook the world,' he reported, 'people are still dying mysteriously and horribly – people who were uninjured in the cataclysm – from an unknown something which I can only describe as the atomic plague ...'

In comprehending and identifying an 'atomic plague', he had rumbled the *experimental* nature of this first use of a nuclear weapon against people. 'It was a considerable ordeal to reach Hiroshima,' wrote the distinguished American journalist T.D. Allman in his eulogy for Wilfred, 'but it was an infinitely greater accomplishment, back then, to *understand* the importance of Hiroshima.'

Wilfred returned to Tokyo in time to attend a press conference especially convened to deny and discredit his story. He later wrote,

> A scientist in brigadier-general's uniform explained that there could be no question of atomic radiation or the symptoms I had described, since the bombs had been exploded at such a height as to avoid any risk of 'residual radiation'. There was a dramatic moment as I rose to my feet [Wilfred's sense of the 'dramatic moment' was highly tuned], feeling my scruffiness put me at a disadvantage with the elegantly uniformed and be-medalled officers. My first question was whether the briefing officer had been to Hiroshima. He had not . . . He discounted the allegation that any who had not been in the city at the time of the blast were later affected. Eventually the exchanges narrowed down to my asking how he explained the fish still dying when they entered a stream running through the centre of the city. . . The spokesman looked pained. 'I'm afraid you've fallen victim to Japanese propaganda,' he said, and sat down.

Wilfred had blown a momentous cover-up. Reporters flown to Hiroshima were kept away from the hospitals he had seen and where there was clear evidence of the 'atomic plague'. Burchett had his accreditation withdrawn and was issued with an expulsion order (from Japan), although it was later rescinded. Strict censorship was introduced. Japanese film of the victims of the 'atomic plague' was confiscated, classified 'top secret' and sent to Washington; it was not released until 1968. Three times as many people died from the effects of radiation in the five-year period after the two atomic bombs fell on Japan than on the days of the explosions; and the victims continue to die from it at a rate of at least a thousand a year. Wilfred Burchett was never forgiven for understanding and telling this truth, and telling it first. Moreover, as Phillip Knightley has pointed out, he 'went totally against everything else being written from Japan at that time, the "they-had-it-coming-to-them" and "I-saw-the-arrogant-strutting-Japs-humbled" type of story'.

He was, for a brief time, a universal hero. This is Jim Vine reporting in the Brisbane *Courier Mail* on 11 September 1945:

> A pocket-handkerchief-size Australian, Wilfred Burchett, left all other
> correspondents standing in covering the occupation of Japan.
>
> Armed with a typewriter, seven packets of K rations, a Colt revolver,
> and incredible hope, he made a one-man penetration of Japan, was
> the first correspondent into atomic-bomb-blasted Hiroshima, and 'lib-
> erated' five prison camps . . .
>
> After Hiroshima, Burchett embarked on his one-man liberation tour
> of prison camps, visiting two on the West Honshu coast and three on
> the inland sea, before official rescue parties reached them.
>
> At Tsuruga camp he sprang a masterly piece of bluff which caused
> hundreds of Japanese to lay down their arms and gave the inmates
> their first steak dinner in three and a half years.
>
> Here the inmates were alarmed at the increasing concentration of
> Japanese soldiers, all fully armed. Burchett sent for the camp com-
> mandant, known as 'The Pig', refused to answer his salute and bow,
> and, with delighted American marines for an audience, upbraided him
> soundly for not seeing that the surrender terms were carried out . . .

However, Western establishment forces never forgave him for
his revelation of the truth of an 'atomic plague'; and he was to
pay a high price for reporting from the 'other side' during the
Cold War. For seventeen years, he and his children were denied
passports by the Australian government. No charges were brought
against him; no 'crime' was ever stated. In a letter in April 1956
to Brian Fitzpatrick of the Australian Council for Civil Liberties,
Harold Holt, then Minister of Immigration and later Australian
Prime Minister, wrote that Wilfred Burchett 'left Australia fifteen
years ago. He has not since returned, his wife is not an Australian . . .
in addition his activities since his departure forfeited any claim he
might have had to the protection he would receive as the holder of
an Australian passport.' When later, an Australian judge described
the smearing of Wilfred as a 'miscarriage of justice', he spoke the
truth.

In his eulogy to Wilfred, T.D. Allman posed the question, 'What
is objectivity?' He answered this by saying that objective journalism
'not only gets the facts right, it gets the meaning of events right and

is validated not only by "reliable sources" but by the unfolding of history'. He then asked whether or not Wilfred Burchett was being objective

> when he perceived a great threat to civilization in Nazi Germany, when he perceived a great moral test for the whole world in the persecution of the Jews ... when he saw Hiroshima as the gravest threat to the survival of humanity itself ... when he refused to see the Cold War as a clear-cut battle between Western good and Communist evil ... when he said the Communist Chinese were not the pawns of Moscow ... when he said that the revolutionary ferment of Asia and Africa after World War Two was not the product of some conspiracy to take over the world, but the product of the legitimate yearnings of the Third World for freedom, dignity and progress ... We all, I think, know the answers to these questions.

I never discerned in him any bitterness, although God knows he must have felt it at times. He was almost always broke, yet he laboured at his work, 'pounding on my ancient typewriter', as he used to say, with unflagging cheerfulness and optimism which endeared him to so many people in so many countries – countries where, until shortly before he died, he had followed his old-fashioned dictum of being 'on the spot'.

I once asked him about his optimism and the scars that did not show.

We were in Vietnam at the time and he was pounding on that ancient typewriter, surrounded by screwed-up balls of paper (I think he was writing his thirtieth book at the time), festoons of washing and cans of beer cooling on equally ancient air-conditioners.

'To be happy,' he said, 'you've got to learn to slay only one bloody dragon at a time.' This was followed by a burst of impish laughter, and a beer, and another, and another ... Wilfred was kinder to his 'bloody dragons' than he was to himself. Alas.

John Pilger, July 2007

Foreword

by Gavan McCormack

One of the paradoxes of 20th century Australia was that the man who stirred greater public hatred and abuse than any other should also have been one who embodied its supposed core values: independent-mindedness, multiculturalism (long before the word became familiar), pragmatism, love of argument and of food, and a preference always for the common man and the underdog against authority.[1]

Born into a family of dissenting, cosmopolitan farmers and laborers, Wilfred Burchett grew up in an atmosphere of deep respect for learning and self-improvement. Before he became reporter and foreign correspondent, he was a cow cocky (dairy farmer), carpenter, cane cutter and vacuum cleaner salesman. He educated himself, learned languages, and travelled widely, keeping his eyes and mind open. He mixed easily and in later life earned the gratitude and respect of people from Vietnam's Ho Chi Minh and Cambodia's Prince Sihanouk to American General William Dean (when Dean was a prisoner in Korea), and Henry Kissinger (who sought his advice and help in negotiating an end to the war in Vietnam). But in Australia he was Public Enemy Number One, for much of his life subject to the unique sanction of exclusion from his own country.

---

[1] For details and documentation, see my essays: Gavan McCormack, 'An Australian Dreyfus? The Strange Case of Wilfred Burchett, Journalist,' *Australian Society* (Melbourne), Vol. 3, Number 8, 1 August 1984, pp. 6–12; Gavan McCormack, The New Right and Human Rights: "Cultural Freedom" and the Burchett Affair,' *Meanjin* (Melbourne, University of Melbourne), 1986, No. 3, pp. 389–422; Gavan McCormack, 'Korea: Wilfred Burchett's Thirty Years' War' in B. Kiernan (ed.), *Burchett: Reporting the Other Side of the World 1939–1983* (London, Quartet Books; Sydney, Australasian Publishing Company, 1986), pp. 162–211.

His was a peculiar kind of Australian bush socialism, not informed by any formal ideology or membership of any party but grounded in a moral sense of the dignity of the common man and of the righteousness of struggle against oppression. 'Authorities' are uncomfortable with such people, and the family attracted their attention long before Wilfred ventured onto the world stage. In the 1920s, the Ballarat sermons of Wilfred's father George were reported as subversive (of the empire) for their references to human equality, and the same term was applied in the 1930s to Wilfred's Poowong Discussion Club (comprised of poor farmers, the local butter factory manager, a blacksmith and a school teacher in 'back-block' rural Victoria) when it began hosting discussions with visiting speakers on subjects including life in the Soviet Union.

In 1938, Wilfred journeyed to Nazi Germany. The experience of fascism so horrified him that he mobilized his Poowong group to become immigration sponsors, opening a rescue line for German Jews that was in due course responsible for funnelling thirty-six of them to Poowong and Melbourne. But suspicions were stirred, and surveillance initiated, for what was an 'uneducated' Australian farmer doing in Berlin? One letter he wrote describing the horrors of Nazism, confiscated by the Australian censor, was not delivered until 47 years later, in 1985.

Few people – perhaps none – accumulated so voluminous an intelligence file across so many government departments, and no such file could be more revealing of the foibles, obsessions, cruelty, and petty-mindedness of a generation of Australian politicians and bureaucrats. He was accused of:

a. being a paid agent of the KGB, and of the Chinese, North Korean, Vietnamese and possibly other intelligence or military organizations;
b. of interrogating and/or brainwashing and/or torturing Australian and/or British and American POWs in Korea during the Korean War (1950–1953);
c. of cooperating in, or actually masterminding, a campaign by China and North Korea during the Korean War falsely alleging the American use of germ warfare;
d. of being a blackmarketeer, an alcoholic, and attractive to women [*sic*].

The charges were unproven, contradictory and improbable, when not positively absurd. Or – as in the alleged attractiveness to women – hinting at deep personal bitterness or jealousy on the part of those campaigning against him.

After long pleading with the Australian government to let him know details of the charges against him so that he could rebut them and return to his own country, in 1974 Burchett launched a court action for defamation. He won, but it was the most Pyrrhic of victories. The court of first instance held that he had been defamed, but that the defamation was protected by parliamentary privilege, and the Court of Appeal then ruled that although he had suffered 'a substantial miscarriage of justice' he was not entitled to any redress because his counsel had failed to protest in the appropriate way and at the appropriate time. Since costs were awarded against him, and he could not pay, his attempt to clear his name in effect made his exile permanent.

His gravest offense may have been his refusal to toe any official or government line. Such was the fear and loathing this inspired that, on a 1951 visit to his home town, Melbourne, the Lord Mayor cancelled a Burchett lecture on world developments, expostulating that 'the letting of the town hall for a meeting in support of peace would be against the principles of the United Nations'. Later, when some of the family chose to live alongside Port Phillip Bay in a Melbourne suburb, government spies speculated that the choice might have been designed to facilitate communication with 'the enemy' (by submarine).

No single episode in his life caused him such trouble as the decision to report the Korean War (1950–1953) peace talks and the POW issues *from the other side*, as a journalist whose accreditation came from the press department of the Chinese Ministry of Foreign Affairs. What he reported was diametrically opposed to the way the political and military leadership of the West saw the war and tried, falsely, to present it. When the false, garbled, and malicious stories of his activities in Korea are discounted, what remains is the portrait of an honest man who tried to tell the truth, who was almost alone in seeing the war primarily from the viewpoint of the suffering Korean people rather than of great powers or his own or any other government, and who, by helping to crack the censorship and lies propagated by other journalists when they were told to by 'responsible military authorities,' may well have helped shorten the war.

My attempt just over twenty years ago to reopen the debate on Burchett in Australia was dismissed with characteristic Cold War smear – that I was teaching 'a neo-Stalinist version of post-war Asian history' to my students and 'doctoring history.'[2] Prize-winning opinion leaders and media groups showed no sense of the fair play that was supposed to be embedded in the national character. Hopefully, with the publication of the present collection of essays, together with the recent publication of a new edition of Wilfred Burchett's autobiography and a new critical biography, those Cold War prejudices can be transcended at last and a new generation will take a dispassionate look at the life and work of the 20th century's Public Enemy Number One.

Professor Gavan McCormack
Canberra, 25 June 2007

---

[2] Robert Manne, *Left Right Left, Political Essays 1977–2005*, (Melbourne, Black Inc, 2005).

Introduction

In the 21st century it is perhaps harder than ever to operate as a good investigative journalist. The age of 'embedded' correspondents and massive government and corporate advertising produces writing which is influenced or controlled to a greater or lesser extent by the powers which dominate world events. So for journalists in both the corporate and public sector it is often a case of toeing the editorial or government line or losing their jobs. Likewise, for broadcasters and newspapers it is often necessary to promote or be silent about the policies and ideology of the incumbent government and its institutional supporters or lose public funding or political advertising revenue. The internet has countered this by giving genuinely independent investigative journalists a platform, but it remains, as yet, a small one.

In this environment it is instructive to have access to a body of work from a genuinely independent reporter, one who had his own ideas and politics which were clearly expressed throughout his career. The writing of Australian journalist Wilfred Burchett looms large in any history of 20th century reportage, and not just as a result of one of the great scoops of the century, his solo journey to Hiroshima after the first bomb was dropped. Burchett covered most major world conflicts over four decades from World War II onwards, and this book attempts to represent this immense breadth of reporting by including chapters from most of his published books over the entire period of his working life. The chapters are presented chronologically according to the events being described, but the selection is bookended by Burchett's two discourses on Hiroshima: his first celebrated scoop and his reflection on nuclear war in his last book.

The fact that Burchett travelled the world covering so many of these extraordinary world-changing events means that such an overview of Burchett's writing can serve as a reader in the Cold War and its journalism. Such an idea would be anathema to Burchett's critics, however, because he did not report these events dispassionately. When he saw injustice and hardship, he criticised those he believed responsible for it. He was never shy about expressing preference, and readers are left in no doubt that Burchett preferred his revolutionaries in sandals rather than in boots, in tropical jungles rather than on the frozen banks of the Yalu River, and that his heroes – Ho Chi Minh, Chou En-lai, Sihanouk of Cambodia, Souphanouvong of Laos, Castro and a few others – were men he had met in the flesh and with whom he established a close personal rapport. He could be highly subjective, but he was never ideological. His political choices were his personal choices, not dictated by allegiance to a political party.

Inevitably though, his support for many of the socialist and Communist regimes who were being characterised as 'evil' by the mainstream Western media led to Burchett himself being demonised by those same media. Nevertheless, much of what Burchett reported, which was dismissed by his opponents at the time, has since proven accurate, and though his political sympathies led him to mistakes and errors of judgement, he admitted most of these and moved on to correct the record (a clear example of this is his writing about the Khmer Rouge and China – see Chapters 28 and 29). This book naturally includes examples of Burchett's more polemical and misguided work, but the overwhelming majority of the chapters here demonstrate an accurate insight into current events sadly lacking in so many of his contemporaries. The presence of errors and revisions in no way discredits his work; it simply highlights the difference between the vulnerable immediacy of journalism as opposed to the relative security of historical distance.

The insight on display partly explains the resonance of Burchett's work with new audiences. The recent publication of the unexpurgated version of his autobiography provoked strident responses in the press and on the internet, reminiscent of the Cold War-era reactions Burchett encountered during his life. The reasons for this continued impact are not hard to find. Readers of the present volume will be startled by the similarities between much of what Burchett describes and many of the events they are reading about in the news. Parallels with the US-led invasion and occupation of Iraq are immediately apparent while reading his accounts of the Vietnam War (Chapter 19, for example, in describing the motivations of the Vietnamese, gives as good an insight into the attitudes of the Iraqi resistance as any contemporary account). Issues such as military abuse, government censorship, imperialist intentions, public perceptions of military conflicts, attacks on civilians, corruption and many more are as crucial in this book as they are in the more informed coverage of the Iraqi occupation. This too confirms the relevance of the present volume as a contribution to the study of journalism and the issues it confronts, which are ongoing and not confined to any one historical period.

Nick Shimmin, June 2007

The Atomic Plague [1945]

On 6 August 1945, as I shuffled along in the 'chow line' for lunch with fifty or so weary marines at a company cookhouse in Okinawa, a radio was spluttering away with no one paying attention to it as usual . . . I strained my ears to pick up a few snatches from the radio – enough to learn that the world's first A-bomb had been dropped on a place called Hiroshima.[1]

Wilfred Burchett's international reputation as a journalist and war correspondent was built upon one of the great scoops of 20th century reportage. After the second atomic bomb was dropped on Japan in August 1945 and the Japanese had announced their surrender, the Americans issued accreditation to several hundred correspondents to report on the signing of the surrender documents. All the accredited journalists dutifully made their way to the USS *Missouri*, but Burchett 'slipped the leash' and in the small hours of the morning of 2 September 1945, he boarded a train for Hiroshima.

The story of his journey to the bomb site and his efforts to get the despatch to London is one of the epic tales of modern journalism. General MacArthur had not yet sent official US Army journalists to the bomb site to manufacture a propaganda story (they arrived while Burchett was there), and so the following report was the first independent account of the results of the nuclear attack to appear anywhere in the world.

The impact of the following article on world opinion and the subsequent debate about nuclear weapons cannot be overestimated.

* * *

The Atomic Plague
'I Write This as a Warning to the World'
Doctors Fall as They Work

Poison gas fear: All wear masks

Express Staff Reporter Peter Burchett [*sic*] was the first Allied staff reporter to enter the atom-bomb city. He travelled 400 miles from Tokyo alone and unarmed carrying rations for seven meals – food is almost unobtainable in Japan – a black umbrella, and a typewriter. Here is his story from –

HIROSHIMA, Tuesday.

In Hiroshima, 30 days after the first atomic bomb destroyed the city and shook the world, people are still dying, mysteriously and horribly – people who were uninjured by the cataclysm – from an unknown something which I can only describe as atomic plague.

Hiroshima does not look like a bombed city. It looks as if a monster steamroller had passed over it and squashed it out of existence. I write these facts as dispassionately as I can in the hope that they will act as a warning to the world. In this first testing ground of the atomic bomb I have seen the most terrible and frightening desolation in four years of war. It makes a blitzed Pacific island seem like an Eden. The damage is far greater than photographs can show.

When you arrive in Hiroshima you can look around and for 25, perhaps 30, square miles you can hardly see a building. It gives you an empty feeling in the stomach to see such man-made devastation.

I picked my way to a shack [*sic*] used as a temporary police headquarters in the middle of the vanished city. Looking south from there I could see about three miles of reddish rubble. That is all the atomic bomb left of dozens of blocks of city streets, of buildings, homes, factories and human beings.

Still They Fall

There is just nothing standing except about 20 factory chimneys – chimneys with no factories. I looked west. A group of half a dozen gutted buildings. And then again nothing.

The police chief of Hiroshima welcomed me eagerly as the first Allied correspondent to reach the city. With the local manager of Domei, a leading Japanese news agency, he drove me through, or perhaps I should say over, the city. And he took me to hospitals where the victims of the bomb are still being treated.

In these hospitals I found people who, when the bomb fell, suffered absolutely no injuries, but now are dying from the uncanny after-effects.

For no apparent reason their health began to fail. They lost appetite. Their hair fell out. Bluish spots appeared on their bodies. And the bleeding began from the ears, nose and mouth.

At first the doctors told me they thought these were the symptoms of general debility. They gave their patients Vitamin A injections. The results were horrible. The flesh started rotting away from the hole caused by the injection of the needle.

And in every case the victim died.

That is one of the after-effects of the first atomic bomb man ever dropped and I do not want to see any more examples of it. But in walking through the month-old rubble I found others.

The Sulphur Smell

My nose detected a peculiar odour unlike anything I have ever smelled before. It is something like sulphur, but not quite. I could smell it when I passed a fire that was still smouldering, or at a spot where they still recovering bodies from the wreckage. But I could also smell it where everything was still deserted.

They believe it is given off by the poisonous gas still issuing from the earth soaked with radioactivity released by the split uranium atom.

And so the people of Hiroshima today are walking through the forlorn desolation of their once proud city with gauze masks over their mouths and noses. It probably does not help them physically. But it helps them mentally.

From the moment that this devastation was loosed upon Hiroshima the people who survived have hated the white man. It is a hate the intensity of which is almost as frightening as the bomb itself.

'All Clear' Went

The counted dead number 53,000. Another 30,000 are missing, which means 'certainly dead'. In the day I have stayed in Hiroshima – and this is nearly a month after the bombing – 100 people have died from its effects.

They were some of the 13,000 seriously injured by the explosion. They have been dying at the rate of 100 a day. And they will probably all die. Another 40,000 were slightly injured.

These casualties might not have been as high except for a tragic mistake. The authorities thought this was just another routine Super-Fort raid. The plane flew over the target and dropped the parachute which carried the bomb to its explosion point.

The American plane passed out of sight. The all-clear was sounded and the people of Hiroshima came out from their shelters. Almost a minute later the bomb reached the 2,000 foot altitude at which it was timed to explode – at the moment when nearly everyone in Hiroshima was in the streets.

Hundreds upon hundreds of the dead were so badly burned in the terrific heat generated by the bomb that it was not even possible to tell whether they were men or women, old or young.

Of thousands of others, nearer the centre of the explosion, there was no trace. They vanished. The theory in Hiroshima is that the atomic heat was so great that they burned instantly to ashes – except that there were no ashes.

If you could see what is left of Hiroshima you would think that London had not been touched by bombs.

Heap of Rubble

The Imperial Palace, once an imposing building, is a heap of rubble three feet high, and there is one piece of wall. Roof, floors and everything else is dust.

Hiroshima has one intact building – the Bank of Japan. This in a city which at the start of the war had a population of 310,000.

Almost every Japanese scientist has visited Hiroshima in the past three weeks to try to find a way of relieving the people's suffering. Now they themselves have become sufferers.

For the first fortnight after the bomb dropped they found they could not stay long in the fallen city. They had dizzy spells and headaches. Then minor insect bites developed into great swellings which would not heal. Their health steadily deteriorated.

Then they found another extraordinary effect of the new terror from the skies.

Many people had suffered only a slight cut from a falling splinter of brick or steel. They should have recovered quickly. But they did not. They developed an acute sickness. Their gums began to bleed. And then they vomited blood. And finally they died.

All these phenomena, they told me, were due to the radio-activity released by the atomic bomb's explosion of the uranium atom.

Water Poisoned

They found that the water had been poisoned by chemical reaction. Even today every drop of water consumed in Hiroshima comes from other cities. The people of Hiroshima are still afraid.

The scientists told me they have noted a great difference between the effect of the bombs in Hiroshima and in Nagasaki.

Hiroshima is in perfectly flat delta country. Nagasaki is hilly. When the bomb dropped on Hiroshima the weather was bad, and a big rainstorm developed soon afterwards.

And so they believe that the uranium radiation was driven into the earth and that, because so many are still falling sick and dying, it is still the cause of this man-made plague.

At Nagasaki, on the other hand, the weather was perfect, and scientists believe that this allowed the radio-activity to dissipate into the atmosphere more rapidly. In addition, the force of the bomb's explosion was, to a large extent, expended into the sea, where only fish were killed.

To support this theory, the scientists point to the fact that, in Nagasaki, death came swiftly, suddenly, and that there have been no after-effects such as those that Hiroshima is still suffering.

[*The Daily Express*, London, 5 September 1945.]

With Mick Griffith to the Plaine des Lacs [1941]

In 1937 Burchett boarded a ship to England and in 1938 he travelled to Nazi Germany and experienced first hand the horrors of fascism while helping Jews escape its terror. On returning to Australia he bombarded the newspapers with letters warning against the danger posed by German and Japanese militarism, but they were ignored. The mood at the time was one of appeasement and conciliation, but when Hitler attacked Poland and Chamberlain declared war on Germany, Burchett was suddenly in demand as 'one of the last Australians to leave Germany before the war'.

Then on New Year's Eve 1940 he set out to investigate Japanese activities in New Caledonia, recognising the French colony's strategic importance in the event of war with Japan. *Pacific Treasure Island* is the result of this trip. It was also Burchett's first book and he was obviously enjoying himself and his newly discovered writing talents, making the most of the exotic locations and colourful locals. The following chapter demonstrates this, but it also displays Burchett's acute sensitivity to geopolitical circumstances.

By the time this book was published, Burchett was on his way to Burma and China, and the start of his career as a war correspondent.

* * *

Mick Griffith is one of the best known mining characters in New Caledonia – and one of the best liked. Mick admits that he likes a drink or two – or more – but always hastens to tell you that when he's in the bush he's 'off the likker.' With his brother he came to New Caledonia in the early 1900's – as a timber-getter – helping to deplete the giant kauri forests which existed in the early days of the colony. When timber-getting began to be played out, Mick turned his attention to prospecting and mining, and found that one can have much more luxurious debauches from the results of a successful prospecting tour, than after years of toil as a timber-getter.

Thus when he returned to Sydney and Melbourne in 1939 after having sold his nickel mine to Krupps' representative he was able to go through £1,500 in six weeks with the greatest of pleasure. He borrowed his fare back to Noumea, and regarded his new situation quite philosophically. 'There's plenty more holes in the ground where a man can pick up a few more quid when he wants them,' said Mick, and promptly went bush again for a few weeks. The result of this trip caused a well-known Australian mining engineer to rush across to New Caledonia, and caused another even better-known industrial concern to send over their expert a few weeks later to check up on the report brought back by the first engineer.

When I met Mick he wasn't very sober, but he had such an open, likeable face that it was difficult not to take notice of what he said, even if his language was a little thick.

'So yer'n Australian journalist are yer, hic?' he asked.

'Well, I can show yer something that'll make yer ****** eyes pop right out of yer ****** head . . . We'll get a car, shove a bit of kai kai in a bag.

'Uve yer got any blankets?' he demanded suddenly. 'Well it don't matter, Priday and I'll get enough of 'ern.' (Mr. Priday, by the way, is Reuter's and United Press' correspondent in New Caledonia, and formerly well known in West Australian journalistic circles.)

'Yer don' mind sleepin' on the ground? Good. We'll get the ****** car to Plum, to the Forestière if we can, an' I'll ring the Jap so's he'll have the choot-choot motor ready for us to go up to the 23 kilometre.'

All these directions meant nothing to me, but as Priday nodded to me every now and again to agree, I made intelligent noises of assent. Without having the slightest idea of where we were going or what we were going to see, I agreed to be ready at 5 o'clock next morning for a three days' excursion – somewhere.

At 5 a.m. I was sitting on the edge of the bed waiting for a motor car to hoot, as arranged. At 6 a.m. I was still sitting there. At 6.15 I went down and had coffee, and commenced searching for Mick. Arrived at his hotel – everybody in New Caledonia who hasn't a home lives in a hotel – I found Priday vainly trying to remind Mick of the excursion he had promised for the three of us. My entrance clinched the discussion, and Mick jumped out of bed, apologising for his lapse of memory.

Blankets were rolled up into swags, Mick searched for and found his compass, while Priday went looking for a taxi. The next thing was the purchase of kai kai – which in any part of the Pacific signifies food. Priday, who had a bad cold, was in favour of taking along a bottle of rum, but Mick, to my surprise, was strongly opposed to this. He knew his limitations. Kai kai consisted of half a dozen long rolls of bread, 6 tins each of beef, pate (type of beef paste) and preserved fruit, with a couple of dozen small lemons with which to fight Priday's cold.

The 5 a.m. became 10.30 a.m. by the time our taxi rolled out of Noumea and turned south-eastwards towards our first destination – Plum, about 30 kilometres from Noumea. On the way we passed the St. Louis mission station, one of the earliest mission settlements in the island – and possessing 10,000 acres of the richest land within miles of Noumea. It was obtained by giving a few axes to tribal chiefs. Most of the colony's sugar used to be grown at St. Louis, but now there is only enough cultivated for the monks to distil the famous St. Louis rum, known by connoisseurs the world over. As we drove past, a new crop was flourishing on the flat level acres bordering the road – the monks' first attempt to grow rice in New Caledonia. Arrived at our Plum, we had to obtain permission from the gendarme before we could proceed. There had been an outbreak of the plague in a Catholic mission station at Touaourou, in the direction of our excursion, and a 'cordon sanitaire' had been placed around the entire district. As we were able to convince the gendarme that we weren't going within the prescribed distance of the plague spot, we were allowed to continue.

Mick and Priday explained to me then, that in normal circumstances we would have gone by boat to within a few miles of our destination, but the plague had interrupted the coastal steamer service, and as we had to reach the far side of the island we would have to go as far as possible by car and 'choot-choot motor,' and walk the rest. I was kept guessing as to the identity of 'choot-choot motor' until we arrived at 'La Forestière,' the site of a huge timber mill. My guides informed me that an Australian company had worked a kauri concession in this district and taken out millions of feet of some of the best timber in the world.

The place had something of the air of a ghost camp about it, with the engines, and lines of sideless trucks which had been used for bringing the timber down from the forests miles inland, all in perfect condition. The whole equipment was left just as it had been when the last log was handled. Tremendous transport difficulties would make the cost of dismantling and transferring the plant to Noumea heavier than importing a new one from Sydney. There were several neatly built houses but no sign of life, until we walked half a kilometre up the line and could see blue smoke curling up from one of the cottages.

Mick was hailed with a great shout, and a couple of Japanese who were at work in a nearby shed, repairing a boat's bottom, dropped their tools to come over and welcome Mick, and be presented to Priday and me. We dropped our packs on the ground alongside the railway line, and followed the Japanese up to the source of the blue smoke. Following our guides' example we slipped our boots off before we stepped on the spotlessly white, kauri floor of a tidy verandah. A couple of gravely smiling Javanese women came out. There were more introductions and we were invited into another spotlessly clean kauri-planked room.

Tablecloth and plates were laid, a tin of beef, loaf of bread and a litre of wine produced by the silent bare-footed Javanese. Anti-mosquito coils were lit, and while Mick, between mouthfuls of bread and beef, conversed with Japanese and Javanese alike in a vile mixture of French-Melanesian and Javanese, Priday and I concentrated on having a good meal and observing the cleanliness and tidiness of the bush establishment. Mick's French was enough to make any French scholar retch, but, as he said, it was based on utility rather than grammar, and Mick could certainly make himself understood anywhere on the island, whether he was amongst Javanese, Arabs, Chinese, natives or French. Of course his expressive hands played their part too.

The meal finished, we were introduced to the 'choot-choot motor' – a motor-bike engine geared to a small railway trolley. There was room for four passengers, one seated on the driver's seat, and three more on a long coffin-like narrow box mounted directly on the trolley floor. Our provisions were stacked in the box, a bag thrown over the top for upholstery and we were ready for our 23 kilometre journey. With a Javanese boy in the saddle and myself as cameraman installed on the front of the box we set out along the 24-inch gauge line, while Mick regaled us with stories of terrible accidents that had occurred along the line.

When the line was laid it seemed they had no curved rails, and the process of rounding the many hairpin bends en route was extremely painful, as we lurched round in a series of jumps as the wheels met the join in the straight rails. Mick explained that it was usually at these places that the accidents occurred. The 'choot-choot' sometimes didn't make the curve and went straight over, to land in the river a few hundred feet below us. While my legs were dangling down in front of the box, Mick remembered another accident that occurred to a native, who was sitting like me, when a truck load of ore swung round a corner, hit the 'choot-choot' head-on, and cut the native's legs off at the knees.

'You should have seen him as his legs went flying down into the creek,' he said enthusiastically. He relieved my feelings and incidentally Priday's too, by telling us that the line was out of use at the present time, so we weren't likely to encounter any traffic. Nevertheless I tucked my feet up and sat on them, as apparently the system of signalling wasn't very efficient and there seemed no way of telling if something was travelling in the opposite direction. The grade was uphill, so no record speeds could be attained, although I was mentally trying to work out how fast the contraption would travel when we were coming back with the weight of four men to give it impetus. For most of the journey the track skirted the Blue River, a wide rushing stream. With the river on our right, and steep barren-looking hills on our left, the track wound in and out, skirting deep gorges on crazy bridges – on which most of the sleepers had been gouged out by bushfires. The swaying of the bridge reminded Mick that sometimes sleepers get burnt, the pegs holding the rails in place get loose in their sockets, the line spreads and 'away goes the "choot-choot" over the bridge.'

The Javanese boy sat impassive at the controls, a cigarette drooping from the corner of his mouth, as we chugged up sidings, through great red-earthed cuttings, and past the poorest country

I had seen since arriving in New Caledonia. Practically the only vegetation was a few stunted – mainly dead – niaouli trees, and a poor type of ti-trees.

Just as the hills opened out into level country, and the seat seemed to have made common cause with my tail-bone, we sighted a small tin shed on our right. This marked the terminus of our 'choot-choot' ride. Mick arranged with the Javanese to pick us up a couple of days later, we helped him lift the 'choot-choot' round and point it homewards, then shouldered our swags – and the excursion had really begun.

Our first difficulty was the weight of our swags. With bedclothes and 12 or 15 pounds each of provisions they were heavy enough, and Mick's experience told him that by the time we had covered 10 or 15 kilometres they would be heavier still. We decided to leave a cache of food in the tin hut, and even if we went short en route, we would have a glorious 'beano' on the night and morning of our return to the terminus.

Mick took a compass reading, and we set off across the plain towards what I was convinced was Mick's gold mine. After about a kilometre of walking we had to strip off our trousers, and made across the coldest strip of water I have ever dipped feet into. Another compass reading by Mick, and within a few hundred yards of the river we struck a well-worn narrow trail. Except for the numerous trees along the banks of the river which we crossed and recrossed several times, the vegetation was mainly waist high reeds, with a lonesome giant kauri tree towering up in splendid isolation.

Mick relaxed his mysterious silence about our destination sufficiently to tell me that we were on the Plaine des Lacs (Plain of Lakes) to which in the old days many escaped convicts had fled, and were either recaptured or lost their way and died of starvation. After walking fairly solidly for an hour or more, the earth began to take on a more reddish tinge, vegetation became even sparser, and there was no living plant more than a few feet high.

Mick stopped us on a little hillock, where there had been a slight landslide and the subsoil had slipped down, uncovering bare rocks the colour of dried blood, with the same suggestion of red underneath. In a depression in the rocky bottom lay a pool of clear bluish water.

'There y'are,' said Mick. 'That's the beginning of the biggest ****** iron field in the world. See those rocks, they're dam' near pure iron. What you've been walking over's iron, only it's covered up with silt washed down from the mountains. But that's nothing. That's only the beginning of it.'

We trudged over a few more kilometres of the crumbly red soil, with Mick pointing out new outcrops of iron and signs that showed that iron existed.

'You see these dead trees,' and he snapped off a brittle grey tree that had grown up to five feet and died. 'Know why they can't grow? 'Cause their roots can't go down. They go down a couple of feet, then hit the iron floor and – k-r-a-a-a-k, finish. Some of 'em are lucky and find a crack in the iron. But that doesn't last long. They soon hit the solid stuff and that finishes 'em.

'Know why this place is called Plaine des Lacs?'

'I suppose because there's lots of lakes here,' I offered humbly.

'Course there's plenty of lakes here, but why? 'Cause the water can't get away. It just sits there on that iron bottom as safe as it if was in an iron bath tub. Iron – there's millions of tons of it. But you've seen nothing yet.'

That night we camped alongside a small lake. Firewood was no problem with all the stunted dead trees lying about. Mick produced a couple of onions from one of his pockets, and with a little manipulation with beef and fruit tins – we ate the fruit first to provide a billy – he dished up a first rate bully beef and onion stew. With a red coal fire to turn our feet towards we slept on the hard iron floor with a cool breeze on our faces, and the black sky stabbed with white stars above us.

Next morning we entered the iron field proper. For hours we trudged over solid iron, with hardly a score of stunted trees to the acre. Of grass or reeds there was not a sign. In some places the rusty-coloured iron floor was almost as smooth as if one was walking the decks of a battleship, in others it was broken up into boulders varying from the size of a cricket ball to huge pieces that must have contained many hundreds of tons . . .

The river seemed to cut a channel through the centre of the field. Along its banks were huge round boulders of iron, the river bottom was solid iron, and as far as one could see in either direction up and down the river was iron.

'Wherever a river cuts through it, she's like that,' Mick offered. 'That's the only indication we've got of her depth. There's millions and millions of tons of it here. The engineers that came here said it's the biggest thing of its kind in the world. They came here and camped on it. Both of them, and I brought 'em here. The first one came and camped out here for nine days with me. We tramped over the whole field, longways, crossways, every ways. When he had finished he said to me: "Mick, I've seen iron before, in many parts of the world. There's only one thing anywhere like this and that's in Mexico. But this beats it. This is the biggest show that I know of in the world. There's at least 250,000,000 tons in it."

'Well, he went back to Australia and a big crowd over there got interested in it, and they sends an engineer over here. Smart bloke he was too, but no fancy business about him. We come out here and camped just like we done this time. I tried to get out of him what he thought of it, but he kept saying, "Mick, you're a seller, but I'm a buyer. I'm not saying anything. I make my report when I get back to Melbourne." So after we had been out here for a few days, I said to him: "Well, the last engineer that was over this field says there's 250,000,000 tons of 55% ore here. What d'yer say to that?" An' he said: "Mick, I don't doubt the tonnage, but I do doubt yer percentage." So I said: "Well, that's easy proved. Yuh've only gottah take some back with you and prove that."'

Mick paused for a while, and wiped away the sweat after such a long statement.

'And what did the assay show?'

'She was what we thought, all right. ****, they had everything fixed to buy it. Never quibbled at the price or anything. All the papers were ready an' all. An' then that thing happened in France. France pulls out of the war, and the crowd in Melbourne is frightened that they might lose the field after they've shoved their money in. So the thing was called off.'

'And why doesn't someone here work it?'

'She's no good to them here. They've got no coal. Iron's only good when you've got coal. Now this's the way I had it figgered. There's boats comes every week from Newcastle bringing coal over to the Nickel works at Noumea. They go back to Aussie empty. Why not fill 'em up with iron ore, dump it straight at Newcastle where they've got the coal to turn her into steel, and bring another load of coal back here. There's more iron here than you've got in all Australian fields put together.

'Where does yer iron come from now? Well, I'll tell yer. It comes from Iron Knob in South Aussie. An' its further to take it from Iron Knob to Newcastle than it would be from here. An' she's lovely to get at from here. There's a railway line comes in from Prony Bay right to the start of the field. Prony Bay, why she's the best harbour in Caledonia. 20,000 tonners can come in there without any trouble'. . . .

Unfortunately we couldn't reach the far end of the field, where the valley widened out and entered the Grand Bay of Prony. This part of the island was taboo, and even had we got there, we might have been isolated there for a few weeks because of the plague. Over the other side of the mountains in front of us was Yate, where the waters of the Yate River had been harnessed to provide power for a large hydro-electric scheme. Mick had some interesting information about the Yate hydro-electric station.

'That's the ****** Nickel Company again. You know they built that plant to smelt their nickel there, and asked the governor if they could have a concession to use the Yate waterfalls to provide them with power for their plant. They was told they could have the concession an' it would cost them nothing, only they must agree to put in land lines across to Noumea, and provide the lighting for the town. They figgered that it'd only cost 60 centimes a unit (about 1 penny). Well, what did they do? After they got their plant up, they amalgamated with the Hauts Forneaux crowd that was running the old cobalt smelter at Noumea, and decided it was cheaper to smelt the nickel there.

'Well, the people were waiting for the electric light at Noumea, and the governor asks the Nickel Company when they're going to put their land lines across. The Nickel Co. just tells them to go to ****. The deal's off and they're not going to put in any lines. Then they offer to give Noumea electricity anyway, and bring out a bloke from Unelco in France, and he builds a power house. Lighting and power too, costs 3 francs (5 pence) now, and Yate's lying idle – never been used. Just keep an engineer there to maintain the plant in running order' . . .

Back at the terminus we collected the remainder of our food, and made camp for the night in the largest of a dozen thatched huts, which a few years previously had been the headquarters of the Anna Louise nickel mine. As our last day on the iron field had been a foodless one, we were able to enjoy the prodigious meal that Mick turned out of the remaining tins of food. Early next morning we heard the 'choot-choot' labouring up the sidings on its way to pick us up, and soon we were all aboard headed back to La Forestière, on the most reckless and the coldest trip of my life.

Light rain which was falling when we left, turned into a steady downpour, and in a few minutes our saturated shirts were flapping against our stomachs. None of us had coats on and with a spanking wind blowing through the wet cloth of the shirts they were turned into effective refrigerators. To make matters worse, the Javanese didn't seem to be worrying about trying to control the 'choot choot.' After we had negotiated the first half kilometre of level line he switched the engine off and 'let her rip.' Added to the icy prickling coldness was the deafening roar of the wind in our ears, and a sensation like sitting on top of a machine-gun as the trolley wheels hurtled over the joints in the rails. Every now and again there was a screaming rending sound as we lurched around a corner in about seven or eight distinct movements.

Mick roared a few words of encouragement in my ears. 'She's gotta stop when she gets to the bottom. She starts up hill again.' The Javanese sat there as impassive as Buddha, his cigarette, limp and wet, still hanging from his lips. Following protests from Priday and me, Mick shouted something into the Javanese's ear, and with a pitying look at me, the latter pointed to a lever, which he motioned me to pull. After Priday and I had used our united strength, leaning back against the lever, we succeeded in easing up the 60 or 70 mile an hour rush. For the rest of the trip we hung on to that lever mighty hard, giving it an extra pull when a bend or bridge came in sight.

Back at the headquarters, the bajous had breakfast prepared for us – and as a tribute to the cold of the morning, the wet of our bodies and our nationality, there was a huge pot of tea ready for us. From La Forestière our taxi was waiting to whisk us back to Noumea, where hot baths soon dissolved the red iron dust out of our bodies.

'Well, what did you think of her?' Mick asked a few hours later, under the verandah of the Hotel Central.

'It looks pretty good to me. If the stuff we've been walking over is really iron, why I never thought there was so much in the world.'

'She's iron all right. An' what's more she'd take nothing to work – start on an end where the river's cut a face in her. Bust up with a few sticks of dynamite an' yuh can load her into trucks as fast as they can shoot 'em along. They can take it out of there for hundreds of years an' yer wouldn't see where they'd been working. Why don't yuh tell 'em about it when you get back to Aussie? Tell 'em to send somebody over that knows iron. I'll show them just what I've shown you. Tell 'em if they don't get it someone else will. I have people nosing about here every few months after that lot. But I want to see Australia working it. It don't make sense to have this iron here, when you've got the coal just over the water in Newcastle. Marry the coal and iron an' you've got steel, and when you've got steel you've got railway lines, girders for your buildings, plates for your tanks, and sides for your ships. Tell 'em when yer get back that we've got the biggest thing in the world here, right at Australia's front door. I know they haven't got much iron over there. Why even the government expert reckoned yer didn't have more than 25 years' supply, an' that was a few years ago. Not that I take much notice of experts. You tell 'em to send somebody over and if they don't mind roughing it a bit, why I'll take 'em over and tramp 'em around that field for a ****** month if they want to. Let 'em stick down drills, an' see what she's really got, an' if I'm any judge she'll go down hundreds of feet out there in the middle of the field. For **** sake don't forget to tell 'em about it when you get back.'

I hope that Mick will consider that I've adequately presented his case in some half dozen newspaper articles and reports I've written about the Plaine des Lacs iron deposits. At least this chapter is something like a permanent record that I kept my promise to 'tell 'em something about it.'

[From Chapter 11 of *Pacific Treasure Island: New Caledonia* (David Mckay Company, Philadelphia, 4th edn, 1944), pp. 101–105.]

3

Who Is Wingate Anyway? [1944]

Burchett left Australia in August 1941 armed with a typewriter and a camera to travel the Burma Road into China and cover the Sino-Japanese war.

The morning after Pearl Harbor he interviewed Chou En-lai in Chungking. When he cabled his story to the Sydney *Daily Telegraph*, the reply was blunt – 'Uninterested in Chinese Communist pronouncements'. But London's *Daily Express* was interested, and Burchett thus became a war correspondent for one of the world's leading dailies.

In early 1943 he was in an Indian hospital recovering from wounds received when Japanese Zeros strafed the sampan in which he was travelling on the Mayu River in Burma. This was when he first heard of Major Orde Wingate. By then he had developed a strong distaste for the 'Colonel Blimps' and colonial types in the higher ranks of the British army. Wingate, on the other hand, was a maverick with a strong anti-colonial stance and a taste for guerrilla warfare.

They became friends and Burchett spent several weeks with him gathering material for his book *Wingate Adventure*. Wingate died in a plane crash before the book was published and Burchett was re-assigned to cover the war in the Pacific.

* * *

Who is Wingate, anyway? By what right is he entrusted to lead an army of men on such a desperate venture? What is his background?

If one hadn't seen him before, and came across him standing in the jungle, in a favourite pose, hands clasped together on the top of a long stick, head hunched forward and resting on his hands staring broodingly into space, one would take him for a scholar, a philosopher, an artist, a religious recluse, rather than a soldier. And one would not be far wrong. In any other age, he would have been.

When I first called on him at his hotel in Delhi, I found him sitting stark naked on his bed, eyes buried deep in a book. He hardly glanced up as I entered, and rather gruffly asked what I wanted of him.

I explained with some diffidence that I was writing a book about his Burma expedition and needed his assistance. He wasn't interested in me or my requirements, but seemed most excited about the book he was reading. He put it down every few minutes and scribbled something on the margins. Then Bernard Fergusson came in and the two of them started an animated discussion about this book, which turned out to be a critical commentary of Emily Bronte and her works, liberally annotated with Wingate's acid comments on the commentator. I got no further that night, except for a grudging permission to see him the following day.

Wingate dislikes any comparison between himself and Lawrence of Arabia. When I first broached the subject of his relationship to Lawrence, he said: 'People must have their heroes and their parallels. At the time I went to Abyssinia, of course, one only had to take off one's hat to an Ethiopian to be called "Lawrence of Abyssinia".'

Nevertheless, it's impossible seeing Wingate for the first time not to note certain obvious similarities to his distant but illustrious relative, Lawrence of Arabia. He has Lawrence's deep-set eyes, finely chiselled lips, and above all the same fierce hawk nose. He has a goodly crop of fine fairish hair, china blue eyes that are normally reposeful and slumbrous, but sometimes, when action is called for, a hood seems to be whisked back, his eyes flash and sparkle and bore straight through the object of their focus, while his face assumes a wolfish look. He is not tall and for all his life of soldiering inclines to stoop slightly. In repose he has a brooding, rather melancholy expression, and striding up and down his room with his head down between hunched shoulders, his hands clasped behind his back or rumpling up his hair, he looks as if he could easier wear the cap and gown of a mild university don than the uniform of the King's armies.

Bit by bit, during the course of a dozen or so interviews, I was able to piece together something of his life and background. I went to his hotel room morning after morning and the procedure never varied. I sat in a chair with my notebook, while he paced up and down the room, always naked, and usually rubbing his body meditatively with a rubber brush, replying to my questions. Often the work would be interrupted for hours on end while he gave a dissertation on the current political or military situation, or outlined his plans for the post-war world.

To my surprise, I discovered that his father was an Indian Army officer and he himself was born in India, in 1903, at the beautiful hill station of Naini Tal in United Provinces. He was taken back to England at the tender age of nine months and was reared and educated there. In 1920, when he was 17 years old, Charles Orde Wingate attended an Armistice Day lecture on the League of Nations delivered by Professor Gilbert Murry. He says he was much impressed by the idea of the League, but saw that it would only work if it had armed force in the shape of an International Police Force to implement its decisions. As they were not going to give the League any Army, he believed another war was inevitable, so he decided to become a professional soldier.

Accordingly, he entered the Royal Military Academy, and trained for a gunner at Woolwich, receiving his commission on 31 August 1923. The next few years he spent doing formalised training at Salisbury Plains, at the same time studying Arabic.

One of Wingate's uncles, Sir Reginald Wingate, had been Governor of the Sudan, and partly because his family had been interested in the Middle East, partly because he felt that the Middle East was going to play a great part in history during his lifetime, he entered the School for Oriental Studies in London, to perfect his knowledge of Arabic.

By 1927 he had acquitted himself nobly in the field of Oriental Studies, and he applied to the Language League for a bursary, which he received, and was given six months' Language Leave to allow him to visit the Arab countries of the Middle East. He bought a Raleigh all-steel bicycle, took a third class ticket from Harwich to the Hook of Holland, and cycled through Holland, Germany, Czechoslovakia, Austria, Yugoslavia, finishing up in Italy, where he sold his bike for the equivalent of five pounds sterling.

From Genoa he took a third class passage to Egypt, roamed around there for 10 days, then went down to the Sudan, where he stayed in the Nuba mountains and took a trip down the White Nile. During this time he mixed with the Arabs as much as possible, slept in their tents, travelled in their caravans, ate their food, drank their drinks and smoked their smokes. Although the purpose of his trip was to learn Arabic, he says he didn't learn much of the language, but did learn an awful lot about the Arabs, their habits, likes and dislikes, and most important of all, the way their minds worked.

His Language Leave was up, but he'd spent all his money. There wasn't even enough left to pay his fare back to England, and besides he still didn't know sufficient Arabic to take a first class interpretership.

He applied to General Huddlestone, at that time commanding the Sudan Defence Force, for a commission. The minimum age for the Sudan Defence Force was 25 years, and young Wingate 24, but as the name of Wingate was well known in the Sudan and he seemed the right type, Huddlestone waived technicalities and took him on as a 'Bimbashi' or Turkish Major, for a period of five years.

This should have completed his ruin. It takes a man of character to survive five years in a place like the Sudan and come out of it more or less normal. In the Sudan, even to a greater degree than in India, young officers have more than normal power and authority. They have wide administrative powers and are virtually answerable to nobody. They have an inflated sense of the importance of their physical well-being. They live on a far higher scale than they would do at home and drink three or four times their ordinary ration of whisky. Waited on hand and foot, with rarely enough to do to relieve the boredom of their existence, they are content to let the days roll by, and not only do they fail to develop, but any initiative or resource with which they may have started out quickly melts away.

Wingate broke away from the established order; he saw and seized on the possibilities and found plenty of outlet for his sense of adventure and initiative. He made the fullest use of his time in the Sudan. He learned the country and the people, studied the border area between the Sudan and Abyssinia, learned to use the theodolite and to march by compass, studied geology and anthropology, soaked up local lore, and made valuable contacts on both sides of the border.

His first military operation was along the Sudan–Abyssinian frontier against bands of smugglers and poachers. For the first time he engaged in long marches across waterless and trackless jungle with a large body of men, through completely unmapped areas, without guides or direction of any sort. This was a valuable preparation for the tasks that awaited him. And, most important of all, he learned to be a leader of men.

As a result of this and subsequent expeditions, he became conversant with the large tract of jungle that runs like a wedge right into the heart of Abyssinia, and which he made good use of in 1941. He mapped out trails and tracks used by elephant hunters and poachers, and got to know the border area better than any other white man. He studied the Abyssinians as formerly he had studied the Arabs, and formed a great attachment for them. When he could he slipped across the border and attended services in their little Coptic churches. Among his men, Wingate was given the title of 'His Worship the Judge' as a tribute to his learning.

After he finished his service with the Sudan Defence Force, Wingate led an expedition from Libya across the great Sand Sea looking for the 'Lost Tribes of Zerzera,' and then returned to England in 1933. Incidentally, it was during his trip back through the Mediterranean that he met the beautiful fifteen-year-old schoolgirl, who two years later dropped her Literature Course at Oxford University to marry him.

The next few years were uneventful. He joined the 9th Field Brigade on Salisbury Plains, where he spent a couple of years catching up with more modern theories of war. Then he got married. He was stationed for six months at Sheffield as Territorial Adjutant, and interested himself in social and economic problems of the workers there. It was the first time he had lived in an industrial area and come up against the problems of the working man. He went down coal mines, visited factories, and, as usual, came away with a better grasp of their difficulties after a few months than most social workers would in a similar number of years.

He was enraged at the weak-kneed attitude of the democracies towards the Italian attack on Abyssinia, and felt that the temper of the English people was far ahead of the will of the government at that time during the terrible period of appeasement. Town-workers who

12 months previously had been strongly pacifist and were slashing buttons off soldiers' tunics, by the end of 1935 were rolling along to enlist in the territorials, wanting to smash the armies of aggression before they had grown too strong.

In 1936, Wingate was sent to Palestine as an Intelligence Officer on General Wavell's Staff, attached to the 5th Divisional Headquarters at Haifa. He had a more or less quiet time there until the Arab revolt in 1938. Wingate had his own theories about that revolt and the way it should be settled, but his ideas were at variance with British policy at the time, and opposed to the idea of most British officers and the Military Police stationed in Palestine.

The Arab revolt was an ersatz production foisted on Palestine by the Axis, and more or less winked at by the British. Because our policy those days was one of fixed appeasement, that is, of quietening the howling jackals by throwing them any lamb they fancied, whether of Spanish, Jewish, Czech or Austrian origin, we allowed Axis money and Axis arms to pour into Palestine to be used against the people whom we had lawfully permitted to settle there.

Wingate believed that the Jewish colony in Palestine was the only bit of real strength in the whole of the Middle East at that time, and he was appalled to find that Jews had to hide their women and children behind bulletproof walls, while the menfolk patrolled their farms with antiquated rifles to protect their crops and livestock. The whole trouble could be settled overnight if the Jews were allowed to raise their own army, and most of the Arabs would have been pleased enough to have peace and order restored. The problem as Wingate saw it was a simple one. Exploit your friends to confound your enemies.

After a lot of trouble he was given permission to organise special light squadrons of British and Jewish soldiers, to form a mobile force that could be rushed wherever danger threatened. For the first time he had an opportunity to test his theories of dispersal groups. His special squads dashed round in fast motor transport. Wearing rubber-heeled shoes, they dropped off in twos and threes near their objectives, forming up at an agreed meeting place, and carried out their assault against a chieftain's hideout before the inhabitants had time to flee.

In Palestine today, five years later, Wingate's fabulous exploits still are the subject of countless anecdotes and discussions. In a few weeks he had squashed the Arab revolt in the area wherein he was allowed to operate. Speed, mobility, fadeouts, exploiting a friendly population for purposes of information, these were all tried out by Wingate for the first time in Palestine. Many of the General Staff officers, in accordance with the fashion of the day, had become anti-semitic, and Wingate's exploits were not looked upon favourably. To be accounted pro-Jewish was regarded as not very patriotic in those mixed-up times. The special squads were disbanded and, after waiting around with nothing to do, Wingate left for England again at five days' notice.

He arrived in England shortly after Munich. In November, just before the famous debate on Palestine in the House of Commons, a meeting was arranged between Churchill and Wingate. Churchill encouraged Wingate to talk and listened to his theories on Palestine with little comment. Wingate told him that the Jews in Palestine were hard-working and intelligent people, leading good lives, cultivating soil that hadn't been tilled for thousands of years, raising orchards where there had been desert; that they were entitled to our protection or at least to the right to defend themselves; that the whole Arab revolt was Axis-inspired and financed; 'give the Jews a free hand, let them have access to arms, and the Arab revolt would fade out like snow upon the desert's dusty face.'

The following day in the House of Commons, Churchill quoted the opinion of a 'very high military authority' that the Jews in Palestine were perfectly willing and able to handle the situation themselves, providing they were given the right to arm and train their own armies.

When war broke out, Wingate was Brigade-Major to a Light Anti-Aircraft Brigade stationed in south-east England, where he made a special study of defence of aerodromes and the employment of Bofors ack-ack guns. He was posted abroad just prior to the fall of France, but before he left came the evacuation of Dunkirk, and he was attached to headquarters of the Home Forces.

There he worked out a scheme for a special counter-penetration force to operate against an invading army. This was submitted to and approved by General Ironside, then C.I.C., but shortly afterwards Ironside was replaced and Wingate found himself out of a job.

From June till September 1940, Wingate was kicking his heels around London without a thing to do, apparently an unwanted man. His mind is too active to remain idle for long, and he filled in time by preparing a scheme for the reconquest of Libya, but thinking to cut through a lot of red tape, submitted it through Lord Lloyd direct to Anthony Eden. It aroused favourable comment, but nothing came of it.

Shortly afterwards, Wingate was ordered to the Middle East to take up a staff job at Wavell's Cairo Headquarters. He hoped at first that something had come of his Libyan scheme and was, in fact, negotiating for a job with Colonel Bagnold's Long Range Desert Patrol, when he was summoned for special duty in Abyssinia.

Although Wingate had a strong affection for the Abyssinians and abhorred the way they had been treated, he had no wish to get mixed up in any of the many peculiar schemes which were being considered for the conquest of Abyssinia. Cairo and Khartoum were thick with missions of various kinds, most of them backed by glorified camp followers who were looking for concessions and special areas to exploit as soon as the country was occupied. Haile Selassie was being ignored while financiers, concessionaires and speculators were falling over each other, drawing up blueprints for special areas for their investments.

The only people who didn't appear to have a say in what was going on were the Abyssinians.

Wingate discovered, however, that he was to be placed in charge of the whole Abyssinian revolt, with the title of Commander-in-Chief of the Patriot Armies under Emperor Haile Selassie. His first job was to fight all the other missions who were hanging around Cairo. One of them didn't want Haile Selassie to be allowed back to his country, and even had a Military Governor of Occupied Territories (Lt.-General Mitchell, former Governor of Uganda) ready to march in. Another wanted to carve Abyssinia up between Kenya Colony and the Sudan. A third had a brilliant notion of dividing the country by giving the Galla tribes their autonomy.

Poor little Haile Selassie, who had been driven from pillar to post and suddenly resurrected from a poverty-stricken existence to lead his armies back into Abyssinia, didn't know whether he stood on his head or his heels, surrounded as he was by a bunch of international sharks. Finally, the little Emperor, driven almost to desperation by racketeers and stock market strategists, was persuaded to play one last card.

'These militarists and bureaucrats really don't count, you know,' one of his advisers told him. 'You appeal over their heads to the people – the people of England, America and China. They hate the Axis just as you do. They are all on your side. They know the shabby deal you had last time. Appeal to the people of England, through their Parliament. Cable Churchill and state your case. He'll back you up.'

Haile Selassie followed that advice. He sent a cable to Churchill, and Churchill, man of integrity and vision, cabled back and settled the hash of the speculators and their bogus missions and assured Haile Selassie the democracies would see that his country was restored to him 'in toto.'

Without waiting for more complications, Haile Selassie jumped aboard the first available plane and flew into Abyssinia, where Wingate was already organising patriot armies.

Churchill, incidentally, had taken a personal interest in the Abyssinian revolt idea; it was one of his earliest 'babies' and he had despatched Anthony Eden to Cairo in November to investigate the reasons for such slow progress. It was as a result of Eden's investigations that Wingate was given the job.

Wingate approached the problem of revolt from a different angle to all his predecessors. He was critical of the orthodox idea of contacting Abyssinian leaders and offering them pots of money and plenty of arms and then telling them to go ahead and beat up the Italians. Courage, faith and self-respect were the qualities we had to inspire and exploit, he affirmed, and not cupidity. He wrote in a memo at the time as follows:

> First, we have to convince the Ethiopian, that contrary to his previous experience, these white men with whom he has to treat will give him a fair deal. He must see us first not fighting by his side, but in front of him. He must realise not only that we are brave soldiers, but devoted to the cause of liberties. Cease trying to stimulate revolt from without, but let's do something ourselves. Enter the country with small fighting groups. Example instead of precept is what we want.

Within a month of taking on the job, he'd established at Khartoum a Military School for training Ethiopian and regular staff officers, as well as British personnel. He went around among the Arab tribes, re-establishing contacts he'd made nearly fifteen years earlier. In eight weeks he had raked together 20,000 camels and 5,000 Arabs to look after them. He was in his element again. Organising, training, moulding a machine which he would soon be able to put to the test.

He went back to Cairo and submitted his proposals for the handling of the campaign. At a conference of Generals several of these brilliant exponents of textbook strategy almost had a haemorrhage when Wingate outlined his plan of campaign, the whole success of which depended on the loyalty of the local population to our, and therefore their own, cause. Wingate had little difficulty in disposing of staff criticisms, and in any case Wavell was prepared to back him. He was given a free hand.

The results of his campaign are now history. With about two thousand mixed Sudanese and Abyssinian regular soldiers, an average of 1,000 Abyssinian patriots and a handful of British officers, he chased nearly 40,000 Italian and Colonial forces through the Abyssinian jungle. By decoys and deception groups, by swift forced marches, ambushes, night attacks, above all by audacious strategy, Wingate won all along the line.

The final showdown came when the Italians concentrated 14,000 troops on the main road running between Debra Marcos and Addis Ababa. The roads ran along a broad valley which narrowed down to a panhandle at one end. Wingate decided to try and force the Italians to withdraw through this 1000-yard-wide panhandle. He had 2000 men with him. He sent his second-in-command with 100 regular soldiers and 400 Abyssinian patriots with plenty of ammunition and food for two days to take up positions on either side of the panhandle.

Wingate himself had 40 regulars with nearly 1500 patriots under Ras Kassa, who had rallied to his banner earlier in the campaign. He prepared plans for attack, drafted out at the same time terms for unconditional surrender, gave an old peasant a white flag and a handful of money, and told him to approach the Italian commander the minute he started to withdraw his troops. Then Wingate attacked with everything he had, and he had insisted on being provided with plenty of automatic weapons. After two days' fierce fighting, the Italians started withdrawing towards the panhandle. As soon as their foremost troops were within nice range, Wingate's second-in-command Thesiger poured in automatic fire. Meanwhile the old peasant was wandering round according to instructions waving his white flag and being passed on from one officer to another. By the beginning of the third day of the battle, on 23 May 1941, the surrender terms had reached the Italian commander, and had been accepted.

Wingate described to me the final act in his three-day show:

> When the great day came for us to receive the vanquished armies I felt more alarmed than at any time during the battle. Across a level plain, sloping towards a hidden valley, the Italian commander and his staff of 30 officers advanced on horseback. Behind them came 800 Fascisti, and then phalanx after phalanx of Colonial troops with their 250 Italian officers, guns, mortars, machine-guns and three million rounds of small arms ammunition. Altogether 14,000 men marched in order of battle, while to receive them stood 36 Sudanese. These formed five lanes through which the enemy poured, laying down his arms in heaps, to reform in units and pass on over the edge of the valley where they expected to find the great army that had beaten them.
>
> Instead they found myself with Ras Kassa [Abyssinian military leader who had been living in exile] and a few patriots; their faces were studies of baffled chagrin, but their arms already lay neatly piled up under guard of our Bren guns. Here indeed was a chance for the Abyssinians to pull off some of the atrocity stunts about which so much nonsense has been written. We marched these Italians with their beaten battalions back to the Addis Ababa road with one British officer and 30 Sudanese marching in front, myself with another 30 Sudanese marching behind. In between us were 14,000 unarmed Italians, troops who for weeks previously had been despoiling, looting and raping the very areas through which they now returned. I appealed to the patriots and through them to their local populations for Christian forbearance and they responded wholeheartedly. Every prisoner reached his destination unmolested.

In a few months Wingate with a force of about 3,000 men, 50 British officers and 40 British ranks, defeated 36,000 Italian and Colonial troops and 800 Italian officers. The Italians had 15 armoured cars, 22 field guns, 22 pack guns. They had 10 to 12 bombers and three to six fighter planes operating daily. Wingate had neither armoured cars nor artillery, and the only planes he had were a few old Junkers during the first few days of the campaign. Three thousand of the enemy were killed, 18,000 captured, the rest dispersed. Wingate wanted to follow the remnants down to Gondar, but it was decided to call a halt to the activities of the patriot armies, and the balance of the enemy were left for General Platt to deal with at Gondar.

Wingate entered Addis Ababa with Haile Selassie on what must have been the happiest hour of the Negus's life. His job done, Wingate took farewell of the overjoyed Emperor, flew back to Khartoum in June, relinquished his command, and flew on back to Cairo.

Wavell had been transferred from the Middle East Command by this time, and no one else seemed to have any job for Wingate. Inaction always chafed him. He became depressed and ill, and spent nearly two months in hospital, finally returning to London where he remained another three months, before he was sent out with General Alexander to see what could be done in the Far East.

In the Abyssinian campaign Wingate had evolved the column as a unit of convenient size and resilience for the new type of warfare which he pioneered. For the first time columns were used to strike deep into enemy territory, living off the country, harassing the enemy's communications, making night attacks on his strongholds and slipping away before he could strike back, exploiting a patriotic population's hate against its military overlords. Step by step, brick by brick, by his own accumulated experiences the idea of the practicability of long range penetration groups, composed of groups of self-supporting and self-propelling columns, took shape.

Wingate has often been described as an idealist, and his advocacy of the Jews' case in Palestine and Haile Selassie's case in Abyssinia have been cited to prove that he is motivated by ideals and emotions rather than by realistic policies. With all due respect to idealism and to Wingate, I don't think he can be called an idealist. He is actually an extreme realist, who sees further and more clearly than most of his colleagues. When he used the Jews to beat the Arabs, he had the necessary knowledge to know that that was the short cut to end the Arab revolt. A businessman is not an idealist because he subscribes to the adage that 'Honesty is the best policy.' He merely recognises that in the long run honesty pays the highest dividends. In Abyssinia, Wingate knew the quickest way to defeat the Italians was to gain the confidence of the local population, first by demonstrating that we were going to fight the Italians, secondly by assuring them that when the Italians were driven out the Abyssinians would be given a fair deal. He has likes and dislikes, sympathies and aversions like any other man, but he does not allow these to influence his judgments. He brings an open mind to bear on problems as they crop up and seeks only the most expedient means of solving them.

His attitude to instigating revolts is typical. He does not oppose on moral grounds bribing people and pouring in money and arms. He believes the method is wrong. It doesn't produce results. If buying and bribing people did produce the goods he would be the first to spend money like water.

He cites the story of a local baron who approached him just as things were starting in Abyssinia. This chieftain had been used to the racket of easy money and weapons from previous unsuccessful instigators of revolt. He asked Wingate for a lot of money and arms, but Wingate said, 'No! You're not a soldier. I'm the one that's going to do the fighting. What I want from you is food and information about the enemy. Don't forget he's my enemy as well as yours. Bring me food and information and you'll be well paid.'

The chieftain went away sorely disappointed. His old sales talk had failed to work. The white chiefs must be getting short of cash and arms.

Two days later, Wingate's men had a sharp brush with the enemy. Next morning the chieftain appeared agog for news. They'd really fought the Italians? Was it successful? How many had they killed? How many men had Wingate lost? Was he still keen as ever to fight the enemy?

When all these questions were answered to his satisfaction, not only did he forbear to ask for money, but he offered Wingate men and arms which he had hidden away in the jungle. From that time till the end of the campaign he was one of Wingate's most trusted lieutenants.

Wingate is a thinker and a fighter, with a mind nicely balanced between the theoretical and the practical. He has always been prepared to back his convictions by carrying out his theories himself. He is not the type to sit behind the lines, draw up his plans, and then send someone else in to see whether they work out or not. Because he approaches each problem with a fresh mind eager to ferret out and exploit its inherent strengths and weaknesses he must be regarded as unorthodox and therefore disturbing to colleagues who believe that one formula with slight variations to its component parts can be made to cure all diseases.

Wingate's peculiar talents are in demand only when other remedies have failed, and not much harm can be done the dying patient anyway. And that is why he was asked to try his hand during the latter stages of the Burma campaign. And that is how on 7 February 1943, he happened to be astride his charger at the head of his men, leading them along the track which led to Burma.

[Chapter 9 of *Wingate Adventure* (F.W. Cheshire, Melbourne, 1944), pp. 46–57.]

1: *Wilfred Burchett as war correspondent in 1943*

4

The Trial of Cardinal Mindszenty [1951]

After his World War II reporting, crowned by his Hiroshima scoop, Burchett returned to London. *Daily Express* editor Arthur Christiansen suggested he work in the editorial department of the paper, but Burchett wanted to avoid this at all costs. Eventually, the *Express* sent him on assignment in Berlin where he arrived 'late on a freezing New Year's Eve 1945'.

The gloom of post-war Berlin never quite lifted for him during the three years he reported from there. He wrote 'Was it so impossibly naïve to think in terms of a "new world" arising out of the ashes of World War II? It did not seem so at the time.'[1] But instead he observed a steady deterioration of relations between the Western powers and the Soviet Union, leading to a Cold War, if not World War III. As a witness to the devastation of Hiroshima, this appalled him.

In April 1949 Burchett moved his base to Budapest. He found his ideal of a 'new world' and 'more equitable social order' in the countries in the Soviet sphere of influence, the 'Peoples' Democracies' of Czechoslovakia, Hungary, Poland and Bulgaria – and, to some extent, in Tito's Yugoslavia. Here, anti-fascist popular fronts had taken over from fascist dictatorships, helped by the Red Army. Although material conditions were tough, he found a 'new spirit' among the workers, peasants and intellectuals who were enthusiastically rebuilding their war-devastated countries.

Peoples' Democracies, published in 1951, is an account of his travels in these countries and the political trials in Hungary and Bulgaria which he reported for the *Daily Express* and *The Times*. An optimistic assessment of the new socialist order emerging in Eastern Europe after the devastation of World War II, the gist of the book was that the young Peoples' Democracies were under permanent threat from the Anglo-American alliance, which was plotting to overthrow the new regimes to return to power the old capitalist and land-owning classes supported by the reactionary clergy. Tito played a devious role: his agents had infiltrated the ranks of the Communist parties in the Peoples' Republics to wrench them away from the Soviet bosom and back into the Anglo-American orbit. In other words, Burchett had swallowed the Stalinist line and happily parrots it in a book that, to this day, is used by his critics to present him as a Stalinist hack.

* * *

There had never been a trial in world history like that of Cardinal Mindszenty and Prince Paul Eszterhazy. The last Cardinal to face a court was Cardinal Wolseley [sic] in England in 1530. But that was a trial with all the pomp and ceremony that sixteenth century England could command. Powdered wigs and scarlet ruffles and maces, courtiers and dandies. And in the end a Cardinal sentenced to death.

Here in the People's Court in Marko Street in Budapest there was a minimum of ceremony and no trappings at all. Except for the uniformed guards only four people were not in civil dress and they were the Cardinal, his secretary, Dr. Zakar, Dr. Baranyai, Dr. Bela Ispanky. They all wore priestly dress and the Cardinal his ruby cardinal's ring. The courtroom itself was small and rather gloomy. The prisoners sat on a long bench opposite the panel of five judges, separated from each other by grey uniformed prison guards with purple bands round their caps.

First the Cardinal, morose, ill at ease, and glowering, but in a slightly obsequious way. Next to him, Dr. Baranyai, ruddy faced with twinkling eyes behind his glasses, looking like an irritable university professor. Prince Paul, tall, languid, fair moustache, and the long hooked nose and blue eyes which are the distinguishing marks of the Eszterhazy family. Completely self-possessed and in a way dignified. Zakar, well satisfied with himself, smiling and seemingly on good terms with the prison guards. The others were relatively unimportant except perhaps the sleek Bela Ispanky. Their roles were incidental to those of the chief accused. Toth, of the Catholic Action Society, had to listen to all the proceedings with a hearing aid.

Mindszenty and Eszterhazy represented the most powerful forces in Central Europe for centuries. After the Church, Eszterhazy was the greatest landowner in Hungary. The Church and the aristocracy were brought to bay before a People's Court. Sitting alongside the one professional judge, Vilmos Olti, were representatives of the political parties and trade unions, all in ordinary civilian clothes. Between the accused and their judges on the right sat the counsels for the defence. On the left was State Prosecutor Gyula Alapi, swarthy with close-cropped black hair and a sonorous accusing voice. Judge Olti, who directed the proceedings, is a youngish, pleasant-looking man, whose friendly manner inspires the accused with confidence, but who is liable at any moment to whip in a sharp question which will trip up the unwary if he has not been telling the truth.

The accused were all brought in together to be sworn in, then they left the room except the one to be interrogated. The Cardinal looked physically just as he did when I interviewed him four months previously, but there was a change. Some of the arrogance was missing. Correspondents were seated ten to twelve feet behind the accused, and it was particularly interesting for me to sum up in those first few minutes my impressions of the Cardinal compared to those of my visit – and I was the last correspondent to see him before he was arrested.

I was reminded of the bully who used to tease me at school, and the expression on his face when he was faced with his superior in weight and punch power in the school playground. An expression which reflected shame, defiance, fear and appeal for mercy all at the same time. And that was the expression on the Cardinal's face, as he stood and waited for the questions to start, his hands folded in front of him, leaning slightly forward as though obsequiously eager to catch every word the Judge spoke.

To understand Cardinal Mindszenty's behaviour in the Court, one must delve a little into his personal background and into the functions of a Cardinal in Hungary. For a thousand years a Cardinal held the next highest rank to a King. The Kings of Hungary, from the year 1000 when Stephen was crowned by Pope Sylvester, were always crowned by the Cardinal with the Holy Crown of St. Stephen. The Rev. Nicholas Boer, a great admirer and apologist of Cardinal Mindszenty, explained the position of a Hungarian Cardinal in his book, *Cardinal Mindszenty*.

The Primate is the Premier Prince of Hungary. He ranks immediately after the King as head of state. His office is the highest under the constitution. His rights were laid down in legislation dating back to St. Stephen and the eleventh century. He is the sole person entitled to crown a king and thereby is in immediate relationship with the Holy Crown of Hungary and the whole constitutional principle connected with it. The constitutional idea of the Holy Crown is a unique creation of Hungarian law, whose roots go back to the fourteenth century. It was fully developed by Stephen Verboczy in his famous *Tripartium*, written in the sixteenth century. In its essence the Principle of the Holy Crown of Hungary declares that in Hungary the source of all rights is the Holy Crown, which unites the whole country, people and soil in a mystical body. The Holy Crown consists of two parts, the head, i.e., the king, and the members. Up to 1848 only the nobility was included in the latter; since 1848 it is the whole nation. (The liberal revolution of 1848 under Louis Kossuth, which dealt the first heavy blow to feudalism in Hungary – and at the Hapsburg domination – was always severely condemned by Cardinal Mindszenty. – Author.)

The significance which Boer attaches to the Holy Crown is interesting in view of revelations during the trial. Neither Boer nor Mindszenty accepted the necessity for any changes in the role of a Hungarian Cardinal from the eleventh century onwards.

Mindszenty, or Joseph Pehm, which is his real name, was a Swabian of German origin. Until 1944 he was an ordinary priest and his parish was part of Prince Paul Eszterhazy's estates. Ten days after the setting up of the Szalasi fascist government, on 25 March 1944, Pehm was made Bishop of Veszprem, a quick promotion for a parish priest with no particular talents. He was nominated by the Papal Nuncio to Hungary, Msgr. Angelo Rotta.

After the end of the war Mindszenty posed as a hero of the resistance movement, because he was arrested by the Szalasi Fascists and interned for four months. When Mindszenty began to emerge as a leader of opposition to the government, he was immediately built up in the Western Press, as a martyr who had suffered for his faith under the Nazis. In fact, as Mindszenty later told the Court and as is proven by documents in the hands of the Hungarian government, Mindszenty was not arrested for political or religious reasons, but over a dispute concerning requisition of property.

'My arrest on 21 October 1944, was not for political reasons,' Mindszenty told the Court, 'but because Ferenc Schiberna, Lord Lieutenant for the County of Veszprem, had found 1,800 pairs of shirts and pants, close on 100,000 pengo's worth, hoarded in my palace, and because I had a disagreement with him over the requisitioning of accommodation. For this reason he interned me.'

Before the Russian troops liberated Mindszenty he wrote several letters proving his right-wing sympathies in order to try and secure his release, and pointing out that the Vatican had been the first to recognise the Szalasi regime.

In October 1945, Mindszenty was appointed Archbishop of Esztergom by the Pope, which carried with it the automatic title of Cardinal, Prince Primate of Hungary. For 25 years he had worked as a parish priest at Zalaegerszeg – and then within the space of eighteen months he rocketed from priest to bishop, from bishop to Cardinal. A meteoric rise to such heights was enough to make even a stronger character than Mindszenty dizzy with success. But the Cardinal saw even greater fame ahead. A Cardinal has the right to crown a King, and Mindszenty was an ardent admirer of the Hapsburgs all his life – a pronounced Monarchist, or Legitimist as supporters of the Hapsburgs are called in Hungary. From priest to bishop, bishop to Cardinal, with American help crowner of kings and emperors . . . and perhaps the next step to be called to Rome as Pope. Such dreams went like new wine to his head; his new-found American friends supported and encouraged his dreams. The Holy Crown of St. Stephen was in American hands; the Pretender to the Hapsburg throne, Otto, was living in America. The Americans would make war on Russia, Mindszenty's friends inside the country would open wide the gates to greet the 'liberating' American troops, Otto would come back, the Cardinal would set the Crown of St. Stephen on his head. Church and Crown would be united again, estates turned back to the Eszterhazys, Batthyanyis, Czirakys. Life would go back to the seventeenth, sixteenth, fourteenth centuries.

These dreams were rudely interrupted when officers of the Hungarian State Security Service called at the Primate's Palace one night and took the Cardinal away for investigation on charges of conspiracy against the Republic. This harsh reality was very difficult for the Cardinal to accept at first. He was aghast that the Hungarians would dare to arrest him, but certain that his American friends would soon rescue him. When that failed, he hoped that by admitting his guilt and expressing regret for those acts, clearly proven in the preliminary investigation by documents in the state prosecutor's hands, he could prevent the trial taking place.

Up to the last moment before the trial started it seems Mindszenty thought he would be released or rescued. It was only after he had completed his testimony that the prosecutor produced a letter which Mindszenty thought had been smuggled out of his room at the Marko Street Prison, to the U.S. Minister, Selden Chapin. It was obviously a great shock to Mindszenty when the letter was produced in court. It had been written ten days before the trial started.

'Mr. Minister, you must take action by Thursday,' wrote the Cardinal, 'and I request you to do so, for a death sentence is likely and the trial will be pointed against America. They want to prove that I was paid by America for secret information. Please send a car and a plane, there is no other way out. With warmest regards. Mindszenty, January 23.

'P.S. – Please instruct Koczak immediately to meet the bearer of this letter today to discuss every detail. Mindszenty.

'P.S. – Please promise the pilot 4,000 dollars in the interest of the cause. I shall refund it. Mindszenty.'

The first to be heard in the trial was Dr. Baranyai and the Cardinal's secretary, Dr. Andras Zakar. Although Baranyai pleaded not guilty, expert cross-examination by Judge Olti brought out a mass of damaging material which incriminated both Baranyai and the Cardinal. Baranyai was a lively personality who tried to deny every charge made against him, but he could not satisfactorily explain the documentary evidence. Some sections of the Western press, and especially the Catholic press, tried to present the trial as a fake, with the accused brought into court drugged and tortured, mumbling carefully rehearsed admissions of guilt, expressions of repentance and pleas for mercy. Baranyai and Mindszenty on the contrary made use of their priestly training to try and wriggle out of every charge against them. They did not know what documents were in the possession of the prosecutor and Mindszenty, of course, had no idea what Baranyai and Zakar had already revealed when he stood at the witness stand. Baranyai and Mindszenty were both rather indignant that the information they had given in the preliminary investigation would be repeated in the public court. They seemed to have regarded the investigator as a Father Confessor who would respect their confessions as confidential, as a good priest should. Baranyai was being questioned about a meeting with other Legitimists when they selected the new Royalist cabinet which should govern the country after the Americans had overthrown the Republic.

Judge Olti: Now let us speak of the first meeting at the Csekonics' apartment. What was the object of that meeting? What was discussed there? Was it mentioned that you were to make reports on Legitimists working in the different Ministries and pass them on to Sandor Cserto, who would hand them on to Jozsef Mindszenty?

Baranyai: This was not mentioned here.

Olti: But you yourself said so in your statement to the police during the investigation – here it is.

Baranyai: Are those the minutes of the investigation?

Olti: Yes. Is this your signature?

Baranyai: Yes.

Olti: Please look at the text also.

Baranyai: Well, if you please, this was not drafted by me.

Olti: But it is your statement which was taken down. The minutes which are kept by the clerks of the Court now are not drafted by you either.

Baranyai: I made this statement in the belief that only the minutes kept at the trial would be of importance.

Olti: Then you do not confirm what is written here?

Baranyai: No. I was late at the meeting because of official duties.

Dr. Baranyai then went on to discuss details of what happened at the meeting after he arrived, how responsibility for propaganda work was divided up among the various members of the Legitimist circle; of how each was allotted a certain number of counties in which to recruit new adherents, of how a shadow cabinet was drawn up with himself as Minister President.

Olti: Now in the spring of 1945 you prepared a plan in case the democratic State were overthrown here and a vacuum would have to be filled. Your plan named the persons who were to take over power and how they were to do it. Is that correct?

Baranyai: Please permit me to go back a little in time. The possibilities of solving the present world conditions, as everybody knows and sees that these conditions cannot last . . .

Olti: Now what exactly do you mean by this? That different forms of State are evolving?

Baranyai: I speak of world politics. I feel that the tension existing between East and West . . .

Olti: The international political tension will evidently be solved sooner or later.

Baranyai: Sooner or later. But it may well occur that the tension is solved by means of war. Well if this should happen through a war – this was our first supposition. Secondly, at the end of the hostilities the Western powers should come out victorious. The third supposition was that the Americans might take over here as military occupation authorities. The whole plan which figured in my confession and the documents were based on these suppositions only. The proclamation, the list of cabinet members, and the plan to found a party.

Olti: And do you think it right that high-ranking clerical personalities should speculate on war?

Baranyai: I beg your pardon . . .

Olti: And not only speculate but prepare for it?

Baranyai: No, I don't think it right at all.

Baranyai strenuously denied throughout, however, that he had actually helped to bring war about. He maintained he only made plans should the war start. He read to the Court a memorandum he had sent to Mindszenty.

When the great vacuum has come about (*sic*, the overthrow of the Hungarian Republic) the first most important and difficult problem will be the institution of a regime resting on an ethical basis. It would be a political impossibility to base ourselves on the ruins of defeated Bolshevism. Only one point of departure would carry in itself the possibility of evolution – the Prince Primate. The dignity of the Prince Primate is consecrated in this country by the traditions of almost a thousand years. According to ancient national laws the Prince Primate is the repository of the King's power in his absence. He seems to be the only acceptable and competent authority to appoint a new government, like the Metropolitan of Athens two years ago. He would have to appoint the new government at the beginning of the American occupation. The government appointed by him must naturally accept this decision without reservations, without manoeuvres, unconditionally and honestly. Here there are names . . . (and follows the list of the proposed cabinet).

This document, like so many others produced in Court, was contained in a tin cylinder buried by Dr. Zakar, on instructions from the Cardinal, in a cellar in the Cardinal's Palace at Esztergom. Zakar disclosed the hiding place to the police a few days after he was arrested.

Zakar filled in the details of Mindszenty's intrigues with Otto and Spellman in New York. He was taken to the United States and Canada as secretary and interpreter to the Cardinal. He was not present at the hour-long interview between Otto and Mindszenty, but was present at the interview with Cardinal Spellman where Mindszenty gave a detailed account of his meeting with Otto. With Zakar's statement on the court record, it was difficult for Mindszenty to deny his meeting with Otto or the details of his conversation with him, when he was later questioned on these points. Zakar gave also details about meetings between the Cardinal and the U.S. Minister to Hungary, Mr. Chapin, about reports prepared for the U.S. Legation, and collected, usually late at night, by the First Secretary, Mr. Koczak. Zakar himself prepared the reports which were compiled from data selected by himself and material handed him directly by the Cardinal.

An amusing sidelight was presented by Zakar when he described Cardinal Mindszenty bartering a car with the Vatican Radio Station for space on the air for Hungarian language broadcasts. The car was one of three bought by Mindszenty during his trip to the United States.

Olti: Tell me please, why did Jozsef Mindszenty give a car to the Vatican Radio Station? After all, there were the dollars. There were many dollars; why did you leave this car there?

Zakar: Well, partly in order to . . . to bring home the dollars.

Olti: But you did not bring them home and the car was left behind also.

Zakar: On the other hand, and this was the main point, because the director of the Vatican Radio named this concretely as something they needed.

Olti: Yes. And what did the Vatican Radio give in return.

Zakar: This was not, so to speak, a formal deal. But the Prince Primate declared that there are news broadcasts in every tongue and why not in Hungarian. The director said there is not enough coal in Rome and not enough money either, and not enough cars to bring over the individual speakers on schedule for the programme.

Olti: And this is what it was needed for?

Zakar: So the Prince Primate thought it best that he donate a car.

Olti: So he left it there. And what happened after this?

Zakar: Then they started Hungarian news broadcasts.

Zakar concluded his evidence by relating the numerous black-marketing activities of the Cardinal in bringing dollars into the country without declaring them, and selling them at high rates on the black market.

As noted earlier the Cardinal thought he could avoid being brought to trial by a repentant statement addressed to the Minister of Justice a few days before the trial was due to start.

'Dear Sir,' he wrote, 'I beg the Minister of Justice to consider this announcement, or request. For some time publicly and repeatedly, there had been raised against me the complaint that I stand in the way of an agreement between State and Church, and that my attitude is hostile to the present order of the State. As for the former, it is a fact that I always emphasised the prerequisites. Now I want to contribute to an improvement in the general situation. Before the trial which is soon to open, I voluntarily admit that I have committed the acts I am charged with according to the penal code of the State. In the future I shall always judge the external and internal affairs of the State on the basis of the full sovereignty of the Hungarian Republic.

'After this admission and declaration, the trial regarding my person does not seem to be absolutely necessary. Therefore, not because of my person, but considering my position, I ask that my case be exempted from the trial on February 3. Such a decision more than anything else would facilitate a solution, even more than the wisest judgement of the court.

'After 35 days of constant meditation, I also declare that apart from other reasons, it may have been due to my attitude as described above, that reconciliation has been delayed; and also that I consider the establishment of true peace between the State and the Church necessary, as long as it has not been made. I too, would take part in the realisation of the reconciliation, according to the teachings of laws of the Church, were there not complaints against me just in this respect. But in order that I should not be an obstacle to reconciliation and that all efforts should be concentrated on avoiding the usual material obstacles, I declare hereby, of my own accord, without any compulsion, that I am ready to withdraw for a time from exercising my office.

'If the wisdom of the Bench of Bishops considers it best to make peace, I do not wish to stand in the way at all. Even at the Apostolic Holy See, which has the last word in the matter, I would not oppose the materialisation of the cause of peace. I make this statement in the knowledge that a true state of peace can be only to the good of both the State and the Church and without it the life of the country is threatened by discord and decay.

'Please accept my sincere respect.

'Jozsef Mindszenty, Cardinal.'

The court decided, however, after a short recess, that the Cardinal would stand trial with the rest of the accused. Mindszenty had played his last card and failed! He tried to make the best of a bad job in court, however, by evasions and half replies, by an amazingly poor memory when it served his purpose. Asked whether he pleaded guilty or not guilty, he answered, in low, measured tones:

> To the extent that I did commit a considerable part of the activities charged to me in the indictment, or as I indicated in my letter to the Minister of Justice, which you kindly read out this morning, substantially, to that extent I feel guilty. What I have done, I do not wish to try to place in a favourable light. Of course this does not mean that I accept the conclusion of the indictment. For example with regard to the offences mentioned in Section A, I do not deny one or another part of it, but I do not subscribe to the conclusion that I might have been involved in the planning of the overthrow of the democratic State and the Republic, even less as the indictment states, that I might have played the leading role . . .

The small courtroom was packed, with relatives of the accused, correspondents and the ordinary public, workers, peasants, petty government officials, a cross section of the Hungarian population. Most of them were Catholics who a few weeks previously had regarded the Cardinal as their supreme spiritual leader. His moral stature was gradually destroyed before their eyes, as he disclosed himself to be a clumsy intriguer who would not hesitate to plunge Hungary into a war and destroy everything that had been accomplished since 1945. Stripped of his scarlet and privileges, standing before the People's Court he appeared as a common criminal, a shifty parish priest caught out in anti-social crimes, trying to deny proven facts, shifting the blame on to others where he could. He was put to shame in his conduct in court by the more dignified Prince Eszterhazy and the fiery Dr. Baranyai who at least admitted openly much that they had done, and spoke up in support of their own reactionary convictions. Mindszenty showed himself to be an enemy of the people in every one of his dealings, but in an oily speech at the end of the trial claimed he was never an enemy of the Hungarian workers or peasants. At the time when Hungary was struggling against unprecedented inflation, when the State needed every ounce of foreign currency it could lay hands on, Cardinal Mindszenty was trading with dollars on the black market . . .

Mindszenty was questioned for five hours by Judge Olti. He was repeatedly asked if he was tired, if he would like a break, but always answered that he felt fit. There were, however, two half-hour intervals during the session.

During those five hours, Judge Olti established for the court record from Mindszenty's own lips that the Cardinal conspired for the overthrow of the Hungarian Republic with American help; that he openly demanded armed intervention; that he tried to ensure Hungary's defeat in the event of war by sending out espionage reports on questions of military, political and economic importance; that he plotted for the restoration of all estates up to 2,000 acres to their former owners; to re-establish Fascist officials in office and drive out all Jews of public life; that on Cardinal Spellman's initiative, and without the knowledge or approval of the Hungarian government or Hungarian Catholics, he gave a written declaration appointing Otto Hapsburg the leader of all Hungarian Catholics in the event of Mindszenty himself being removed from office; that by secret correspondence with the U.S. Minister and U.S. Army authorities, he prevented the return of the historic Holy Crown to Hungary; that he had dealt extensively on the black market with currency speculation.

Many of these conclusions the Cardinal denied, but the facts and documents produced, the Cardinal's own testimony and that of his fellow-accused made it apparent to every observer in the Court that these conclusions were established.

[From Chapter 6 of *People's Democracies* (World Unity Publications, 1951), pp. 101–119.]

5

Liberty in Eastern Europe [1951]

Burchett's coverage of show trials such as that of Cardinal Mindszenty was certainly something he later regretted. But *People's Democracies* was written at a time when the propaganda war on both sides of the Iron Curtain was increasingly shrill. It falls into the category of simplistic partisan Cold War literature, but it remains of interest as an example of such writing from someone on the spot, a journalist observing the emergence of a new 'socialist' world that was closer to his ideals than, say, the old British Empire. The following short conclusion is a summary of what he, like many others on the Left, saw as a whole new value system being writ large in the countries of Eastern Europe.

He was not alone in subsequently discovering that those ideals were betrayed and subverted by regimes such as those he praises in this book. There were, however, exceptions to these betrayals. Tito, for example, was soon reinstated in his pantheon of heroes when Yugoslavia joined the Non-Aligned Movement, which Burchett wholeheartedly supported till the end of his life. But by the time the book came out, Burchett had parted company with Fleet Street and moved on to write about China and later report from Korea.

* * *

Bulgaria and Hungary about which I have written most in this book are countries which are virtually excommunicated by the Western world. They have been denied membership to the United Nations. Their crimes are that they have defended their independence, have resolutely brought to trial those who plotted and intrigued against them – even British and Americans, as Mr. Sanders and Mr. Vogeler found to their sorrow when they became involved in espionage against the Hungarian State.

For this they are ostracised by the Western nations. Bloody coups and counter-coups could be permitted in other countries, in South America or in Syria, in countries where America and Britain had much closer interests than in Bulgaria or Hungary. But suppression of coups could not be tolerated in the People's Democracies. The Anglo-American official conception of Democracy in the Balkans, seemed to be on the Greek pattern with overflowing prisons and firing squads executing the country's best citizens at the rate of ten or twelve daily. The truth of the matter is that any country which can guarantee safety for British and American investments, no matter what the colour of its regime, is acceptable to Whitehall and the White House, whether it be a personal dictatorship in Santo Domingo, clerical Fascist in Spain, semi Fascist in South Africa, or a gangster regime in a South American republic.

The corrupt regimes of Eastern Europe before the war, the periodic massacre of a few thousand Communists, the complete suppression of civil and political liberties, were never the subject of official criticism from England and America. If the dictator were a Horthy, a Tsankoff or Filov, a King Boris or King Carol, with their feet well planted on the neck of the people, there were no protests about denial of liberties. If it were a Dimitrov, a Rakosi, a Pauker flung into jail for years without trial, there was no flutter of excitement in the Foreign Office or State Department.

The difference is that today the people, an alliance of workers, peasants and intellectuals, are in charge in these countries, they are building the new life that their poets have written about for centuries. There is no place in this new life for foreign trusts or for foreign influence which can be used against the interests of the people. The money-changers have been driven out and given something of a scourging into the bargain. One after another, the reserves of British and American capitalism have been marched into the front line against these governments and one after another they have been shot down. Their last trump card, Marshal Tito (probably played unwillingly because he was at best cutting their losses), failed as miserably as did the local opposition and the Church, and the traitors in the Party ranks. Bitter disappointment and tragic blunders in the past have forced men like Rakosi and Dimitrov to build on a sure foundation this time and to maintain that eternal vigilance which is the price of liberty.

Liberty itself is a relative term. There is a suppression of liberties in Bulgaria and Hungary. When one type of regime has been violently destroyed and another has taken its place it would be courting suicide for the new government to grant full rights to the supporters of the regime it has supplanted. The French revolutionaries adopted the great human slogans of 'liberty, equality and fraternity,' the slogan of the bourgeois revolution, glowing words that kindled hope in the hearts of Europe's masses struggling to free themselves from the shackles of feudalism. The slogan blazed across Europe like a forest fire sweeping away feudal privileges and inspiring revolutions in a dozen states. But the French revolutionaries certainly had no intention to grant 'liberty, equality and fraternity' to the Royalists. They quite properly chopped their heads off and prevented as many as possible from leaving the country to plot a counter-revolution with British and German help . . .

The whole of Bulgaria's working population get free medical and dental attention, their children free education and the possibility for higher university education. There are three times as many university students as under King Boris, and most of them children of workers and peasants . . .

Try and tell the artists who receive monthly advances for their uncompleted work, to whom the government has given studios, for whom the finest villas and castles in the country have been thrown open to work in, that their liberties have been taken away from them. Try and tell the Hungarian factory workers who have been selected for their capabilities and are being trained for posts in the foreign office that their liberties have been suppressed. Visit workers in their rest homes in the mountains or on the coast all over the People's Democracies, former villas of the landowners and industrialists, and ask them where are their liberties. Ask the coal miners of Pernik (now Dimitrovo) where Georgi Dimitrov grew up and organised the first great strike in 1906, if they have been robbed of their liberties. They will tell you that liberty in the days between the wars meant to work on an average of two or three days a week only, to live in miserable hovels miles away from Dimitrovo, to see their families starve, to be shot down if they tried to organise. Liberty in 1950 meant a full working week, wages equal to twice that of a Cabinet minister for underground workers, the finest education for their children, new apartments into which they were being moved at the rate of 20 families weekly throughout the year in the city itself, for which they paid no rent, no gas or electric light bills; four weeks' paid holiday every year, constant free medical attention.

I spoke to one miner who had been a university student at the time of the 1923 revolt. He was suspected of being a sympathiser and expelled. In the end he drifted to the mines as an underground worker. He had worked there ever since and was still working. 'My sons now have the chance which I was denied,' he said. 'One has just graduated in Slav studies from Sofia University, the other will graduate next year in Law' . . .

Ask the hundreds of thousands of youths who turn out each summer to work on the great construction projects, on roads, dams and railways in the People's Democracies, what restrictions there are on their liberties. They are joined by thousands of youths from all over Western Europe, England and the New World each year, who work with them for a spell to go back to tell of the new life, but not of suppression of liberties. The truth is that each of these youths can look forward to a full and creative life. He will be trained according to his abilities at the expense of the State and he can be sure of a job awaiting him when the studies are over. The job will not depend on his social background, not on the colour of his tie, not on his accent, but on his qualifications. Liberty is a relative term with different values as it moves East into the People's Democracies. Under English liberty who could think of a career in the British Foreign Office without the correct tie, accents and contacts? The son of a Welsh miner, a Scottish shepherd, a Cockney taxi-driver? . . .

There are suppressions of liberty in the Western sense of the word, but nothing which can offset the undreamed of liberties which have been brought to 90 per cent of the people by the People's Democracies. If you want an affirmative answer to your question, join the landowners and former Horthy officials in the Vaci Street cafes in Budapest. Their liberties have been suppressed. They cannot leave the country; their estates have been taken away from them; they have been dismissed from their jobs; in short they are oppressed. Better still go to the country and talk to the kulaks in Hungary or Bulgaria. They are the ones who are really finding life hard today. Their liberties are disappearing. Landowners, bankers and officials probably have some hobbies or are at least adaptable in idling the time away and are not bound to stay in one place. The kulak, the wealthy peasant, is a man with no spiritual resources, no interest in life but adding another few decares of land to his holding, a few more cows to his herd, a little more money in the bank (or more likely in a hole under the fireplace). The only pleasures he knows are adding to his property, eating himself full and drinking himself stupid. Avaricious and gross, he is traditionally the most merciless employer, a would-be large landowner with none of the saving social graces. And today, bluntly expressed, he has no future, and the present is hard. If he read books, he would know that he had no future, even if he read the newspapers he would know it. But each individual kulak thinks he is cunning enough to trick the government by hoarding his grain, hiding his machinery, slaughtering his livestock illegally, salting his money away, leasing his ground to straw men, and other devices tried and condemned as useless as far back as the time of the Soviet revolution. But each one in each district in each country goes through the same motions and slowly but surely he comes to a bad end . . .

If one adds the kulaks, the large landowners, dispossessed industrialists and dismissed Fascist officials together, one would have a figure well under 10 per cent of the population who really suffer from a restriction of their liberties. They are much more articulate however than the 90 per cent, so their voices are heard more abroad. The restrictions on their liberties will increase in direct proportion to the war preparations made by the Western powers and to the Western efforts to develop espionage and sabotage networks in the People's Democracies. The leaders of this 10 per cent would imperil the historic extension of liberties to the 90 per cent. The injustice to the overwhelming mass of the people in Hungary and Bulgaria has lasted for centuries, the injustices to the former privileged 10 per cent will endure at most for a generation.

Over a period of four and a quarter years, from the end of World War II, I have been constantly travelling into the countries of Eastern Europe. For the first three and a quarter years, I was based in Berlin but travelled to Poland, Czechoslovakia, Eastern Germany, Greece, Yugoslavia, Hungary and Bulgaria. For the past year I have been based in Budapest, dividing my time between Hungary and Bulgaria, with an occasional trip to Yugoslavia. I have been forced to the startling conclusion that while in Eastern Europe, with the exception of Greece and Yugoslavia, the mass of the population has been granted an extension of basic liberties on a generous and ever-expanding scale, the opposite is the case in Western Europe. The mass of the people there are faced with a constant shrinkage of their basic liberties, which surely include the right to work and to human happiness, the right to lead a creative life, to care for their young and be cared for in their old age.

What liberties have two million unemployed in Italy and two and a half million unemployed in Western Germany? Does it help a starving Ruhr worker that a director of his factory has the liberty to get a passport and travel to the United States? What does a landless peasant in Italy care if the absentee landlords have the right to passports to the gaming casinos of Monte Carlo, while he starves or is shot down for daring to seize the unused land?

Liberty is a relative term! Let Mr. Bevin and Mr. Acheson be sure what they are talking about.

Over a great part of the earth's surface today, millions of people are beginning to understand the difference of liberty in its Eastern and Western concepts. The Korean people understand what the Western world means by liberty as their towns and villages are destroyed, thousands of men, women and children are executed for their political sympathies. The miserable peasants of China who received land from the Communists understand it and so does the crowded population of Shanghai bombed almost daily by American planes with American trained pilots. The partisans fighting in the Grammos mountains in Greece understood it when they were burned to death by fire bombs, dropped from American planes, often enough with American observers aboard. The Vietnamese understand it as they are shot down with American weapons wielded by German S.S. troops on orders from the Republic which invented the slogan 'Liberty, Equality and Fraternity!' The Malayans and Indonesians understand well enough what the British and Dutch mean when they speak of liberty. It is a word to shudder at. Even Chief Seretse Khama of the Bamangwato tribe in Bechuanaland understood what liberty in the British sense meant when he exercised his personal liberty to marry a white woman and was hounded out of his country for it by a British Socialist government.

Even the British government is beginning to find out the American understanding of the word, as pressure is constantly increased by the groups behind the Marshall Plan for Britain to buy American oil, American food, and dozens of other items for which she has no need.

Liberty which is paraded in the West as a holy grail to keep the masses quiet, descends on their necks as a rubber truncheon when they organise to demand their real liberties, their basic rights to work, to land, to a secure future. There are hundreds of millions of people in the world today who have decided that liberty is something to do with everyday life and work. They are not interested in a liberty of the press to promote religious and racial hatreds; not interested in a liberty for publishers to flood bookstalls with pornographic literature; not interested in the liberty of scientists to devote their best brains to inventing hydrogen bombs or other means of destroying the world; not interested even in the theoretical liberty of the ballot box to decide between two groups of political parties both bent on maintaining the privileges of one tiny group of people over the great majority of the population.

If the same advance is made in the next twenty years as has been made in the past five years in bringing real liberties to the workers and peasants of the People's Democracies, and if the Western powers give up their morbid plans to destroy the People's Democracies by force of arms and the hydrogen bomb, the whole population will be enjoying liberties of a quality not yet dreamed of in the Western world.

[From Chapter 16 of *People's Democracies* (World Unity Publications, 1951), pp. 277–287.]

6

The Microbe War [1953]

In September 1950 Burchett left Europe and briefly returned to Australia to campaign against the atom bomb and the ban on the Australian Communist Party. Then, on 4 February 1951, he crossed into Communist China: 'My intentions were to stay in China for a few months and gather material for a book about what was going on in Chairman Mao's China . . . In fact, things turned out quite differently. Among other things I was not to see Australia again for almost twenty years.'[1]

The reason he would not see his country for almost twenty years was Korea.

As he was ready to go home with enough material for a book, the left-wing French paper *Ce Soir*, edited by Louis Aragon, asked him to cover the ceasefire negotiations in Korea. He set out for Kaesong intending to stay for just three weeks.

Burchett's writings on Korea merit special scrutiny because they earned him the label 'traitor' in the country of his birth, Australia. He was accused of fabricating the germ warfare story detailed in this chapter, and of brainwashing American and Australian POWs and torturing them to extract confessions.

In February 1952 the Korean Foreign Minister accused the US of waging bacteriological warfare against North Korea. Wilfred Burchett investigated the claims and came to the conclusion that the US had indeed conducted experiments in bacteriological weapons delivery. He stood by his story till his death in 1983. The US has always denied germ warfare allegations. An International Scientific Commission was set up to investigate the claims. It was headed by Professor Joseph Needham of Cambridge University and concluded that North Korea and China had indeed been the objective of bacteriological weapons. To this day the matter is still contested.

* * *

When the Korean Foreign Minister announced in February 1952 that the Americans were dropping plague and cholera-infected insects from the air in North Korea, my mind went back to a press conference in Chungking in the autumn of 1941. The Kuomintang spokesman was Dr. Tsiang Ting-fu of the Chinese Foreign Office. He charged that Japanese planes had dropped sacks of old rags containing plague-infected fleas in Changteh, Kiangsi province. Competent experts (including bacteriologists who later fought against U.S. germ warfare in Korea) had made careful investigations, so Dr. Tsiang assured us, and confirmed that the bundles of rags had been dropped by Japanese planes, that they contained plague-infected fleas, and that a plague epidemic had broken out. Most pressmen filed stories at the time on the basis of Tsiang Ting-fu's statement. We knew also that confidential reports on the subject had been circulated by the Kuomintang government to ten western embassies in Peking.

Confirmation of Dr. Tsiang's charges came later when the Soviet government placed on trial, at Khabarovsk, in December 1949, the chief of the Japanese Kwantung Army and leading Japanese germ warfare experts. The accused described how germ warfare was waged against China and the huge-scale preparations for germ warfare against the Soviet Union. They gave details of the actual case at Changteh referred to by Dr. Tsiang.

The chief Japanese germ warfare expert, General Shiro Ishii, was not available for trial at Khabarovsk. He was being sheltered by General MacArthur in Tokyo. MacArthur refused Soviet requests for his extradition and took it upon himself to deny that the Japanese had ever used germ warfare or contemplated using it. It was impossible not to connect up this chain of events as soon as the charges were made that U.S. forces were dropping germ-infected insects on North Korea, the more so as Reuter had reported that General Shiro Ishii had arrived in South Korea at the end of December 1951.

A little more research provided some more interesting links. The American Embassy had received a report on Japanese germ warfare methods in the autumn of 1941. Within a few months germ warfare research had started in the United States. Confirmation of this was contained in the report submitted to the U.S. Secretary of War, Patterson, on 4 January 1946 by George Merck, former Chairman of the Biological Warfare Committee of the U.S. Army Chemical Warfare Service. The report was made public at the time, but quickly withdrawn as its horrifying revelations were too much for the public stomach. But for those interested a summary of the report and other details of American and British bacterial warfare preparations was published in *Keesing's Contemporary Archives* for 2–9 February 1946.

'Mr. Merck's report,' cites *Keesing's*, 'stated that systematic study of germ warfare started in the U.S.A. towards the end of 1941.'

There was any amount of evidence from American sources that intensive research was continuing right up till the moment the Korean Foreign Minister made his accusations. Typical of these was the remark made by Brig.-Gen. William Creasey, Chief of the Research and Development Branch of the U.S. Army Chemical Warfare Service. He was reported in the U.S. press as saying as late as 25 January 1952, that 'germs, gas and radioactive materials' might prove to be the 'cheapest weapons' for conquering an enemy, and he added gleefully 'without destruction of his economy' – heartwarming words for the Wall Street camp-followers. There was also Mr. Truman's curious remark at the end of August 1951, just after the American Air Force had bombed Kaesong and broken off the talks – just before Dulles was whipping the Allies into shape to sign the Japanese Peace Treaty.

'We have fantastic weapons,' reported Mr. Truman, 'and ready for use now.' To what was Mr. Truman referring? Certainly not the atom bomb.

With all these facts there was evidence enough for any journalist to start delving a little further. We were four foreign correspondents in Kaesong. Alan Winnington of the London *Daily Worker*, Tibor Merai of *Szabad Nep* (Budapest), Lucian Pracki of *Zolnierz Wolnosci* (Warsaw), and myself. As journalists we felt we had to be convinced by our own eyes and ears and not by secondhand reports. For several months, we took it in turns to leave Kaesong and carry out independent investigations. We were only laymen, but at least experienced reporters used to interviewing people and evaluating their evidence.

We soon realised the difficulty of the work. Reports came in of raids, but by the time we got to the spot, there was nothing to be found except strips of burned earth. Insects could not be held until journalists and photographers arrived. They had to be dealt with swiftly, while they were still dazed from their sudden descent. And the methods being used were designed to leave no trace of material evidence.

One of the first cases which Winnington and I investigated was one in which Chinese Volunteers had seen three F.51-type planes dropping insects at a point about 30 miles east of Kaesong and 10 miles north of the battle-line. 'They circled low,' said our C.P.V. informant, 'and it looked as if brownish smoke was coming from their tails. After they had gone, we found clusters of flies and fleas on the snow-covered hillsides. In one place there were over 1,000 fleas in a square metre of snow.' We questioned Chen Chih-ping, head of the local insect-reconnaissance unit, and he confirmed the account and said that tests at battalion headquarters showed that the fleas were infected with bubonic plague. We interviewed other volunteers and Ku Tse-san, an old Korean peasant, and the stories were all roughly the same. Ku said he had lived in the area for 63 years and had never seen fleas in the open before, and that flies never appeared until the end of March (it was then February 12). 'How could there be flies and fleas while there is still snow on the ground?' he asked.

The nearest that Winnington and I came to being on the spot of a germ attack during the first few weeks was at the little village of Chuk Dong, only six miles south-west of Kaesong. In this case, as it was close to Kaesong and the incident was fairly promptly reported, we were on the spot within 24 hours. All there was to see, however, was a long strip of ground on which straw had been burned, round clumps of straw on the fields adjacent to the strip with pin-head size remains of insects on the edge of the ashes. Again, we had to rely on eyewitnesses, but we were able to question Chinese Volunteers and Korean schoolchildren independently. Because of language difficulties (there is no relation between the Korean and Chinese languages) the Volunteers had not been able to speak to the children.

Chuk Dong is a village of two tiny hamlets, separated by a hump-backed hill. At about 11 a.m. on March 9, a group of Volunteers had seen a plane flying so low they thought it must have been hit by anti-aircraft fire. It disappeared behind the hump-backed hill. A patrol was sent to the other hamlet and found along a strip of land about 200 yards long and 20 wide, in a direction corresponding to the flight of the plane, hundreds of clumps of flies and mosquitoes, swirling around on the ground in such a density that 'if you put your foot down,' as the patrol leader expressed it, 'you would kill a hundred.' A patrol had been along the same path at 8.30 a.m., and there were no insects there then. Sentries were posted and the rest returned to report to Company headquarters. Within 80 minutes of the insects being discovered, Volunteers were on the spot with petrol. By the time they arrived the mosquitoes were hovering about a yard above ground but the flies were still swirling around. Samples were taken and then the Volunteers – helped by the children – gathered straw and laid it over the entire area, including on some insect clusters which had fallen off the main strip. They poured petrol over the straw and set the lot alight.

When we asked if anybody had seen a container drop, the Volunteers said they had not, and they could not speak with the children or peasants who would be the only ones to know. Through an interpreter we spoke to the peasants and children. They had all seen the plane, but immediately dived into the air-raid shelters and did not come out until the sound of the plane had faded away. Later they had seen the Volunteers gathering straw and went over to see what was happening. Then they too saw the insects – and they described them just as the Volunteers had done. They then helped spreading out straw. One child took us over to where a swarm of mosquitoes had flown off and settled on the warm, white wall of a cottage. The children had twisted some straw up into torches and jabbed them into the mosquitoes. We could see the smoke marks on the wall and the stubs of the improvised torches. There were patches of snow on the ground and a stream nearby was frozen over – most unusual climatic conditions for mosquitoes.

Merai and Pracki came back from the rear with similar stories. They had not had the 'good fortune' of being in a germ raid, but were on the scene shortly after numerous raids.

It is necessary to stress that bubonic plague has never been known in the recorded history of Korea. The only case of a cholera epidemic for 60 years was in 1946 and directly traceable to the fact that an American vessel had dumped ashore at Pusan the bodies of two men who had died of the disease. The epidemic which followed did not spread to North Korea. Cholera and plague follow definite patterns. Plague is carried by rats and humans and naturally spreads along communication routes. Cholera usually branches out in every direction from its focal point. But in North Korea in early 1952 isolated cases of plague and cholera cropped up in places widely separated and not connected. There was no other explanation for this phenomenon – even if there were not the evidence of American air-dropping – than that the diseases were being artificially spread. And the laboratory tests showed that the bacteria were artificially cultivated, with different strengths and characteristics from the natural varieties.

After Winnington returned to Kaesong I left for the P.O.W. camps – and there had my closest experience of an insect raid. After lunch on June 6 I had planned to drive from Camp 5, 45 miles to Camp 1, but I was delayed for about an hour by an air alert. I then had to cross an arm of the Yalu, with my jeep aboard a ferry. About halfway across, I noticed that schoolchildren aboard were excited about something in the water, and the two ferrymen too were gazing fixedly at the water. Thinking it must be a school of fish, I got out of the jeep and saw the water was covered with a patch of insects on an area of about 200 by 50 yards. While we watched they began clambering on to the ferry, shaking their wings and trying to fly. There were two types, both of them winged. One an inch long with trailing abdomen and pincer-like jaws which moved horizontally, the other a smaller one, something like a very slim house fly. The two old ferrymen were obviously puzzled and on subsequent investigation said they had never seen such insects either on the water or any other place before.

Later in the day, reports came from two other points – that insects had been dropped from American planes. In one case the insects had landed in the middle of P.O.W. Camp 2, in the other a container was seen to drop into the Yalu not far from Camp 3, and boatmen had found many insects in the water. Early next morning reports came from Camp 3 itself, that the beach was covered for a distance of about 50 yards with winged insects swarming ashore. In Camps 2 and 3 prisoners of war helped destroy the insects and signed statements as to what they had seen. The times of the droppings, the sighting of the container and the air alert at Camp 5 all tallied within a few minutes. The air distance between Camp 2 and 3 is about 50 miles, with Camp 5 in between. The whole area is part of what are known as the Finger Lakes, formed by the damming of the Yalu, and providing the water supply for that area of North Korea.

I interviewed many prisoners in both camps who testified to having taken part in dealing with the insects. The raid had taken place in the South Korean section of Camp 2 and I spoke with a medical orderly who supervised the activities of his squad in sweeping the insects into heaps and burning them. Samples had been preserved and they were identical with the larger type which I had seen. As the raid took place just after lunch, the P.O.W.s had been enjoying their post-luncheon two hour rest period, and none had seen anything drop. But schoolchildren in a school, actually within the prisoners of war compound – they shared the same basketball court – had actually seen containers coming down as planes passed overhead. They described them as 'shining globes as big as two baseballs.' (From the report of the International Commission of Scientists, it is obvious that what the children saw was what was named the 'egg-shell' bomb, made of calcareous material, porous enough to allow insects to breathe and which shatters into a thousand fragments on impact and would pass unnoticed by anyone looking for containers.)

My main interest in the camps was to interview American airmen. The testimony of those who admitted to taking part in germ warfare has already been published. I talked to all of these airmen at length and on several occasions. I am convinced that the statements they made are accurate and were made of their own free will.

Many people are puzzled as to why these airmen spoke out and told everything they knew, even to naming other of their comrades who had also taken part. The short answer is that they are men who know they are taking part in an unjust war. (It must be remembered too, that there are many more airmen prisoners of war who have undoubtedly also taken part in germ warfare but who have not yet spoken out.)

A good example of a man who felt he was in an unjust war is Lt. Paul Kniss of the U.S. Air Force, serial No. A01909070, of 1103

Southwest Military Drive, San Antonio, Texas. It so happened that I was the first person to speak to Kniss when he arrived at the P.O.W. camp, a few days after he was shot down. I was collecting material for an article on the morale of U.S. airmen at the time, and I did not raise the question of germ warfare with him. I was too fascinated with his story of the grumblings in his squadron when Van Fleet's son was shot down and every pilot had to turn out and search for the missing Van Fleet jun. And every plane in Kniss's squadron was shot up. Two crashed on the way home, others landed back full of bullet holes and wounded pilots. 'Nobody came looking for me when I got shot down,' he said wryly, 'but then I'm not a general's son.' Kniss, in fact, was the son of an agricultural labourer, himself an unskilled odd-jobs man before he joined the armed forces. He talks in the simple, straightforward way of a worker, and is an honest-looking man who has known misery and poverty.

I was surprised shortly after this interview to hear that Kniss had immediately admitted that he had taken part in germ warfare and had given a vast amount of factual information which tied in with everything already known, including specific details given by another member of Kniss's own squadron, Lieutenant O'Neal. I talked with Kniss again and asked him why he had decided to speak out.

'Well,' he said, in his serious way of talking, 'the last thing before I left the States, I and the five other pilots travelling with me had a lecture at Camp Stoneman, our processing centre, about germ warfare. It was given by a Captain Holleman. The main thing about it was that we might hear rumours that America was waging germ warfare, but this was just North Korean propaganda and we must deny it wherever we heard it. Then he went on to say that other nations might use it, so America was prepared, and he told us how we would retaliate, the different ways of waging germ warfare by using artillery, planes or secret agents to infiltrate behind the lines.

'That was fine. I was pleased he'd scotched a rumour, because I'd seen a paragraph in the paper that the North Koreans said we were dropping germ bombs. Then we came to K. 46, that's the 18th Fighter-Bomber Group base. The day after we arrived, we were sent for by the Group Intelligence Officer, Captain McLaughlin.

He took us into his office, locked the door, and after telling us that what he was going to say was top secret, and not even to be discussed among ourselves, he told us the 18th Group had been carrying out germ warfare since the beginning of the year and that all other Groups were doing the same. Then he went on to tell us how it was being done.' Kniss then went into the sort of details which have already been published, describing the types of bombs and bacteria McLaughlin said were being used, and other information.

'And at the end of the talk,' continued Kniss, 'he produced a statement for each of us to sign promising not to discuss the subject of the lecture with anyone, under penalty of being prosecuted under the Articles of War. McLaughlin said he'd keep the statement in his office and use it against us at a court-martial, if we broke security.'

That is the moment when the U.S. Armed Forces lost a faithful officer. It was the beginning of Kniss's disillusionment in his government, in the military hierarchy and in his immediate military superiors. 'It knocked me,' he said, 'coming right on top of the lecture at Stoneman. For the first time I began to wonder who was right and who was wrong in this war, if they'd lie like that to us and to the people at home.' He went on to relate his gradual disgust at the type of missions the pilots were flying. He had been trained as a fighter-pilot but his missions in Korea were mainly dropping napalm or high explosive on peaceful villages. 'And the way they put it in the communiques,' he said disgustedly. 'A village of mud huts that we'd blown sky high or burned out with napalm was so many "military barracks." Raids in which towns were blindly plastered with high explosive were against "specific military targets." And on top of all this, the germ missions. All this, we were being told, was done to liberate the North Koreans. I never could figger out how it happened you had to wipe people out so you could liberate them and teach them democracy.' And he concluded by saying, 'As far as germ warfare was concerned, I'd made up my mind that if I was ever shot down, I'd tell everything I knew about it as soon as anyone asked me. I'm ashamed to have had any part in it and I'm sure the American people would be ashamed if they knew it was going on.' And Kniss told the whole story as soon as he was questioned.

Other captured airmen helped fill in details. Lt. Floyd O'Neal's testimony was particularly interesting because having been trained as a scientist, he absorbed much more of the preparatory germ warfare lectures than the others. He was able to present a vivid and horrifying picture of American scientists poring over their microscopes and test-tubes, turning back the record of medical science to the Middle Ages when the Black Death and cholera ravaged the populations of Europe. He described in detail how these perverted men worked to develop more virulent types of bacteria than those naturally spread, of how they were developing bacteria – and insects to carry them – which would flourish in cold, sub-zero climates where diseases were formerly unknown.

One of the inhibiting factors which kept O'Neal silent for a time was, as he expressed it to me, 'because I was ashamed for the outside world to know of the degradation of American science. But I soon realised it was more important that the world should know the truth so that this black sheep of science could be halted and banned before these madmen in the laboratories destroy civilisation itself.'

One thing common to these airmen was that immediately they decided to speak out, they developed a fervour to let the people of the whole world, but especially the American people, know what was going on. They felt they only had to speak out and the news would be flashed throughout every newspaper in the United States and the American people would take action. It was difficult for them to imagine that such a stupendous piece of news would be suppressed, that American journalists in South Korea, either were prevented or deliberately refrained from going to the various airbases to check whether such persons as Captain McLaughlin existed or to get comments from officers named as having briefed pilots on germ warfare, or pilots named as having attended such briefings or as having taken part in germ missions. These airmen who spoke out were dumbfounded to learn of the shameful conspiracy of silence.

An extraordinary document published in the Report of the International Scientific Commission is a photostat copy of an article on germ warfare, published in the Japanese newspaper *Mainichi*, on Sunday, 26 January 1952. It is typical of the infamous conspiracy of silence on germ warfare, that no Western pressmen ever cabled a copy of this article abroad. It is signed by a Sakaki Ryohei, who describes himself as ex-commandant of the Prevention Epidemic Corps of Japan's elite Kwantung Army.

It starts by describing a night conference in October 1936, when the decision was reached by the Japanese High Command to start large-scale production for germ warfare. Preliminary research had been good. A plan had been submitted to the top military authorities and at this conference the go-ahead signal was given.

For a country like Japan, extremely poor in raw materials, germ warfare is the most appropriate arm. With a few square metres of laboratory and some test tubes, one can easily produce a weapon capable of decimating tens of thousands of people.

Sakaki Ryohei goes into precise details of the Japanese development of germ warfare and states that it was decided that bubonic plague was one of the most favourable diseases to be employed. He names the officer in charge of breeding rats, the officer in charge of raising fleas and explains how it was possible to increase the virulence of plague bacteria by one-third by passing it first through the bodies of rats. He gives instructions for the loading of bacteria and insects into containers and stresses how important it was to pump a sufficient supply of oxygen into the containers to keep them alive. The article is illustrated and photostats of the illustrations are contained in the Report. The infamous 'Ishii' porcelain bacterial bomb is shown, named after MacArthur's war criminal protege.

A few of these bombs were recovered intact from the germ warfare factories the Japanese maintained in Manchuria – and which they blew up when the Kwantung Army surrendered. More interesting even than the Ishii bomb is that *Mainichi* carries an illustration of the almost exact counterpart of the four-compartment leaflet bomb, which was the favourite container used by the Americans in Korea and North-East China. The *Mainichi* illustration actually shows a three-compartment bomb, split lengthwise (as is the American one), with a parachute attached and a rat leaping out of one of the compartments. It describes a self-destroying reinforced paper container – also similar to ones used by the Americans – dropped by parachute which ignites after it has deposited its cargo of rodents, destroying both container and parachute.

This article was published after germ warfare had started in Korea, but before the Korean authorities knew it had started. It is the perfect answer – from the criminals themselves – to

MacArthur's claims on behalf of the Japanese militarists, that the latter never employed germ warfare. The only possible explanation for the article is that it was intended to tell the Japanese people that Japan still had a weapon suitable for her status in the world, capable of winning wars.

Why did germ warfare carried out against a completely unsuspecting Korean and Chinese people fail? The Korean and Chinese people were not quite unsuspecting and certainly not unprepared. In fact germ warfare caught both North Korea and China in the middle of vast sanitation campaigns which had been started several years earlier and were conducted on an intensified scale each year. The North Koreans even had some prior experience of germ warfare. One of the tasks of the secret agents of Rhee Military Intelligence, in the first part of 1950, was to infect water and food supplies in the North with bacteria.

When the Americans retreated from North Korea in December 1950, the North Korean Ministry of Public Health announced that they had infected four cities with smallpox – another disease previously unknown in Korea. Epidemics broke out in Pyongyang, Chongjin, Kuwon and Yongdok, in each case six or seven days after American troops withdrew. The incubation period for smallpox is ten days and the bacteria must have been spread a few days before withdrawal. The bacteria were found to be of artificial culture – and in this case less virulent than the natural variety. The four cities are widely separated, but the epidemics broke out simultaneously and no other centres were affected. The cities were not connected by the retreat route, that is to say troops withdrawing from Chongjin, did not pass through Pyongyang, Yongdok or Kuwon and vice-versa, so the epidemic – even if started naturally – could not have been transmitted by the troops. And in any case there were no outbreaks in intermediate towns or villages.

A highly suspicious circumstance in connection with this is that in March 1951, American press agencies reported that a special bacteriological research ship was anchored in Wonsan Harbour, where a medical team headed by Brigadier-General Crawford Sams, chief of the U.S. Army's 'Public Health and Welfare Section' (the Japanese also used high-sounding names like 'Anti-Epidemic Organisation' to camouflage their germ warfare organisations) carried out medical tests on prisoners picked up from the North Korean main-land. Sams later told the American press that he 'knew there would be epidemics after we withdrew' from North Korea. American correspondents who wished to go on the Sams' expedition were refused permission and there was a great hue-and-cry at Tokyo headquarters to discover how correspondents got wind of the mission. It was given the highest security classification used by the U.S. Army – hardly necessary if Sams were going on a 'humanitarian' mission to try and halt epidemics in Korea.

In the smallpox epidemic, 3,523 people were infected of whom 358 died, mostly babies under 12 months. Due to the American occupation babies born in that area had not been vaccinated – American humanitarianism could not be stretched that far.

Primarily the Americans failed in germ warfare because they were fighting against an entire people led by real People's governments. It was impossible for American fascist-military mentality to understand what this meant or to evaluate the changes which had occurred under the People's governments. There was not even any way of the American authorities knowing what had happened. The State Department had blown its brains out and anyone who dared suggest that important reforms had taken place was hounded out of public service as a 'Red.' American military intelligence relied for information on Kuomintang landlords and reactionary missionaries whose only interest was in bolstering the idea that the entire Chinese people were sighing and panting for American 'liberation.' The American militarists fell into the same error as did Hitler by relying on reports from White Russian emigres that the entire Soviet people were awaiting the Nazi liberators with bouquets. There was no one to inform the American militarists that People's China had carried out the greatest and most successful anti-epidemic campaign that any nation had carried out in history – in a little over two years, completely eradicating epidemic diseases which had been endemic for generations. Hundreds of millions of people were inoculated every year. Plague, cholera, smallpox, the recurrent scourges of Asian peoples, were completely eliminated. And from the application of inoculations on a scale never before known, the Chinese, with the aid of the most advanced science of the Soviet Union, had accumulated rich experience to be placed at the disposal of the Korean people in their hour of need.

At a time when medical teams were plodding on foot through snow to that typhus-ridden mountain village in South Korea, virtually the entire population of North Korea, including troops at the front and Chinese Volunteers, had been inoculated against cholera, plague, typhus, the typhoid group and against every type of disease which it was known the Americans were disseminating. Literally tons of serum were given first priority of transport from China. By the end of March every person had been inoculated.

Every military unit, every town and village had its insect reconnaissance and sanitation squads. Reports on germ and insect droppings had first priority on all civilian and military communication channels. All-out war was declared on rodents, flies, mosquitoes, spiders and other disease carriers. The entire country – and later when the Americans extended their operations the same applied to north-east China – was mobilised to fight germ warfare. The governments could count on the people, the people had complete faith in the authorities. There was no panic, as the Americans had counted on to spread the epidemics. If a case of plague was reported, the house was isolated but the people stayed on to fight the rats and fleas instead of spreading them in all directions by flight. The people were mobilised and the finest scientists of Korea and China were mobilised also. First-class modern laboratories were set up in caves hewn out of the mountains. Among the 16 Chinese bacteriologists who played a leading part in the fight were four Research Fellows from the Department of Bacteriology, Harvard, three from New York State University, two from the London National Research Institute, and others from the Rockefeller Institute, Paris. All of them held science degrees from Western universities and their names are internationally known in their respective fields. The two medical scientists in charge of anti-epidemic work in Korea were both decorated by the American Government for their work on the Anti-Typhus Commission in Burma in 1946. (They returned their decorations after the Americans launched germ warfare in Korea.)

After insect droppings one could see literally thousands of people with improvised gloves and masks, tweezers of two sticks used like chop-sticks, slowly moving over the field, picking up insects and dropping them into buckets to be burned in heaps. They were the 'first-aid' teams. Later would come truckloads of figures, cloaked in white except for where their trousers were tucked into black, knee-high rubber boots, equipped with anti-insect sprays.

Every house was equipped with D.D.T. sprays and fly-swatters. Rat-holes in the ground and in walls were blocked up, even holes in trees which might have provided breeding places for mosquitoes were filled in with a kind of cement. Every propaganda medium, from newspapers and films to the primitive wall newspapers in the tiniest hamlet with their crude drawings of flies and insects, rallied the people to fight against the microbe war. Sanitation squads went from home to home, from office to office to ensure that anti-germ warfare measures were being rigorously applied. It was impossible to enter marketplaces, ride on buses or trains unless one could provide an up-to-date inoculation certificate. Regular checkpoints were set up on every road in Korea, where certificates were produced, the traveller and vehicle sprayed with D.D.T., and the vehicle had to roll over a D.D.T.-soaked matting bed to ensure the tyres were also disinfected. Trains coming from Korea or the North-east were emptied of passengers at certain points, certificates produced, passengers and train sprayed. Goods trains were shunted into special tunnels where an ingenious system of pipes with holes in them quickly and effectively sprayed cargo and freight cars.

In government offices – even in Peking – cadres were given a certain quota of flies and mosquitoes to be destroyed each day – and they had to produce the results in paper envelopes for inspection. As a result visitors to Peking in the spring and summer of 1952 were amazed to find it a city without flies or mosquitoes. And the same in every village and town in China and Korea. Garbage piles – some of which had been added to for centuries – were moved and the strictest control of all refuse enforced. In some cases where cats and dogs were known to have picked up infected rodents dropped from planes the entire cat and dog population of villages and towns were destroyed.

Only in countries where government and people are entirely one could such measures be taken. Such mass organisation and mass discipline are outside the comprehension of American militarists and so their monstrous scheme failed. They did succeed in killing innocent Korean and Chinese men, women and children, but they did not succeed in their main plan of starting vast epidemics to weaken the Korean–Chinese will to resist their aggression.

One point which has puzzled many people is why did the Americans follow the 'old-fashioned' Japanese methods instead of using the highly-publicised push-button methods of aerosol, bacteria suspended in air and disseminated in clouds of mist from high-flying aircraft. Reams of newspaper articles had been written in the United States boasting of the perfection of such methods.

According to the opinion of competent Western scientists who investigated germ warfare, there are many technical objections to the use of aerosol. In the first place, if it were as terribly effective as the publicists claim it would not have been possible to keep the matter secret and American prestige was dependent on it being kept secret. Second, for spreading most diseases it is ineffective. It is fine for the armchair strategists to sit back and look at administrative charts showing how many pounds of plague and cholera bacteria is necessary to infect a given number of square miles and to wipe out a given number of people. But in practice it is a different matter.

(The world can be thankful for the infantile faith of American militarists in their administrative charts.)

Bacteria are extraordinarily sensitive things. Plague bacteria die within a few minutes of exposure to sunlight. For most diseases spread by bacteria or rickettsia (plague, cholera, typhus, the typhoid group, etc.), spraying in aerosol would be a waste of time. Unless the mist happened to settle on its intended victims immediately, and unless conditions of temperature and humidity were just right, the bacteria would be useless. Certain types of sub-microscopic viruses and toxins could be employed, but in Korea adequate protection could not be given to American troops for virus and toxic diseases for which no antidotes have yet been developed. Aerosol mists are at the mercy of every wind which blows – and they could easily blow back to South Korea or even Japan. (The Americans did try spraying bacteria suspended in jelly, but this was done from low-flying aircraft, with no possibility of dispersal beyond the area sprayed.) Bacteria-carrying insects are a much more effective medium – and complete protection could be given to American troops, as every type of disease employed had its known antidote – and American troops, as we know from the P.O.W.s, were given inoculations against every disease employed.

Plague-carrying fleas can infect from human to rodent host and back again for an indefinite number of generations. They are not dependent on temperature or humidity – especially the acclimatised ones bred by American scientists. Anthrax-infected tarantulas dropped by the Americans live to a ripe old age of several years, including two years without food or drink, and even naturally bred can withstand light frosts. For years they are capable of biting animals or humans and infecting them with anthrax. A type of fowl-mite known to spread encephalitis transmits the disease through its eggs for endless generations. Humans can be secondarily infected by eating the poultry.

By using artificial means of producing bacteria, normally harmless insects can be turned into deadly disease carriers. By spreading out a typhoid culture medium on glass slabs and letting millions of midges wade about in it, the normally harmless midge is converted into a deadly typhoid carrier. Flies and any other insect inhabiting human dwellings can be used in the same way. The same thing with the ptinid beetle, normally a harmless creature living in granaries or any place where food is stored – converted by American scientists into an anthrax carrier. Its life span is up to five years.

For the conditions and circumstances in North Korea, the Japanese type of germ warfare was the only one that could have been used. And there is ample evidence that at least one branch of American germ warfare research was based on adaptation and improvements of Japanese experience. That is not to say that under other circumstances the Americans would hesitate to use aerosol. There is good reason to believe that they did carry out an experimental aerosol spraying of encephalitis over Mukden, but at the time the International Commission of Scientists made their investigation the evidence was not conclusive. They noted the suspicious circumstances, however, in the Annex of their Report.

That the Americans failed in their initial attempt to use germ warfare in Korea and North-East China should not lead to any complacency or relaxation of the fight to have germ warfare banned. The conditions in Korea were peculiar ones with American troops exposed to dangers if the aerosol method was used and America

2: *With Allied pressmen at Panmunjom, Korea, 1952. From left to right: Norman McSwan – Reuters; unnamed INS correspondent; Wilfred Burchett; unnamed AP correspondent. [Courtesy Norman McSwan]*

fearful of world public opinion. The American germ warfare experts have boasted that they have isolated the very essence of bacteria, the botulins – a few ounces of which, they claim, could wipe out the world's population. Whether this is so or not, we do know that America's 'best' scientists – to their everlasting shame – are working day and night to produce ever more virulent types of bacteria, viruses and toxins and to develop more effective methods than those used so far. Doubtless they are doing their best to rectify the failure of the Korean experiment.

Humanity can only be safe from this scourge when America and Japan, the only two world powers who refused to ratify the 1925 Geneva Protocols outlawing germ warfare, are brought into line with the rest of the civilised world by banning germ warfare. The death factories of the U.S. Army Special Projects division at Aberdeen, Maryland, and Camp Detrick must be put out of operation and American scientists return to the honorable road of using their talents to preserve life rather than destroy it.

[Chapter 17 of *This Monstrous War* (Joseph Waters, Melbourne, 1953), pp. 306–326.]

7

Koje Unscreened [1953]

The prisoner of war issue was a major stumbling block during the ceasefire talks in Korea, each side accusing the other of atrocities, presenting lists and counter-lists of prisoners and trying to score propaganda points. Wilfred Burchett set out to investigate the veracity of each side's claims and thus, for instance, established that the highest-ranking US POW in Korea, General William Dean, who had been reported dead, was indeed alive and well. He also contrasted the generally good conditions he had observed in North Korean and Chinese-run POW camps with the reportedly appalling conditions and brutality in Allied prisoner of war camps, though in writing about this he indulged in some hyperbolic language he would later regret using.

Koje Island was South Korea's most populous prison camp and became notorious as the scene of riots between Communist and non-Communist POWs over the issue of forced repatriation or 'screening'. Their actions were brutally suppressed by their American captors, and the story of that suppression is covered here by Burchett with his colleague Alan Winnington. They wrote two books together, *Koje Unscreened* and *Plain Perfidy* (see Chapter 8). The contents were based largely on interviews with prisoners who had escaped from Koje Island, and on other eyewitness accounts, rather than Burchett's usual 'on the spot' reporting.

* * *

. . . The order for ruthless and energetic action must be given at the slightest indication of insubordination, especially in the case of Communist fanatics. Insubordination, active or passive resistance, must be broken immediately by force of arms (bayonets, butts and firearms). . . Prisoners of war attempting to escape are to be fired on without previous challenge. . . The use of arms against prisoners of war is as a rule legal . . .

No these are not the words of Ridgway, Mark Clark, Van Fleet or Boatner. Except for the change of one word, this was a quotation used by Judge John J. Parker, a US member of the Nuremburg tribunal, which helped to send to the gallows Keitel, Kaltenbrunner and Jodl. Instead of the word 'Bolshevist' in the original, we have substituted the word 'Communist,' to bring it into line with dozens of similar statements made by 'UN' commanders in Korea. It was an order issued on 8 September 1941, for the treatment of Soviet prisoners, by General Reinecke, head of the prisoners of war department of the Nazi High Command. The order was approved by the above named generals and became key evidence in sending them to the gallows.

Orders such as this were recognised as war crimes under international law in 1945–6 and punished as such. Since then the Charter of the International Tribunal of Nuremburg has been accepted as part of international law. And since that Tribunal sat, the Geneva Convention has been adopted, after discussions lasting more than four years.

The officers responsible for the massacres of Korean and Chinese prisoners and for the policies that led to those massacres are not less guilty than Keitel, Kaltenbrunner and Jodl. Under international law, and under United States law, the American government is bound to bring these men to judgment.

But in fact the slaughters and the orders for them did not arise from the aberrations of American generals. They were geared to a specific schedule of political manoeuvres and also fitted exactly into the general policy of making 'Asians fight Asians.'

By the time the Americans broke off the talks, they had publicly announced that the prisoners had been divided into two groups – the 'anti-Communists' said to be refusing to be repatriated and the 'diehard Communists,' as all prisoners were called who insisted on going home. But even after that forcible segregation and its results on world opinion, the Americans were still not content to let matters rest.

Two distinct pressures were still exerted on the prisoners with unrelenting ferocity. The 'diehard Communists' were still being 'screened' and 're-screened' in further efforts to force their 'conversion'. Identical pressure was being applied to the others to force them to take one more 'final' step – to join the armed forces of the 'UN' (Syngman Rhee's army) and of Chiang Kai-shek. This pressure was violently increased after the disastrous American manpower losses in the October–November 1952 offensive on the Kumhua front.

'Voluntary repatriation' had achieved its political aim of wrecking the truce talks and the war could go on. But more cannon fodder was needed and the best part of a potential ten divisions existed among the prisoners of war.

During October, the Americans announced that the remaining 11,000 of the former 38,000 'reclassified civilians' would be handed over to Rhee for 'release,' which meant for press-ganging into the Rhee army. This again displays American disregard for arithmetic. They never admitted holding 44,000 but at one time said 7,000 of the 38,000 wanted to be repatriated. They now said the entire 38,000 were to be handed over to Rhee.

From the sort of excuses given for the continued killings and woundings of prisoners during October, there can be no doubt that the prisoners were still being 'screened' and were still not coming up with the right answers. UP reported from Koje on October 13 that seven prisoners were wounded while they 'were being moved from one compound to another.' On the following day four prisoners in one compound were wounded because 'they protested against the removal of one of their companions for questioning' and 15 were wounded in another compound for protesting against the removal of four of their comrades 'for questioning.' A week later another nine were wounded at Pusan on the mainland because they refused to form work details due to their comrades having been taken away 'in a routine transfer' (it should be noted that using typical press-gang tactics, one way the Americans tried to 'capture' prisoners for 'screening' was to grab work details while they were outside the compound). Finally by killing and wounding 75 prisoners on Koje because, as the 'UN' Communique said, 'prisoners started drilling in their compound,' the Americans capped what their own figures show was the bloodiest month of all.

The shocking total of prisoners killed and wounded during October was 506, according to American figures – an average of 16 every day. All through November and December, the shootings went on, and it was notable that during this period there were several incidents on Pongam Island where the attention of the executioners seemed to be directed to the 'civilian internees.' Syngman Rhee appeared to be having difficulty in persuading the last 11,000 to be 'released' to join his army. The 'UN' Command decided to discipline these reluctant prisoners on Pongam in an effort to speed up the recruiting campaign.

American troops killed 87 and wounded 115 Korean prisoners on December 14, in the bloodiest massacre they had yet admitted. Once more the excuse was that the prisoners had staged a mass escape attempt, about which the 'UN' Command had been forewarned but had taken no action to prevent. Once more the troops that did the shooting were inside the stockades and there were no prisoners outside the compounds. No correspondents were on the spot but from the reports they wrote later from Pongam it is perfectly clear that the 'mass escape' excuse was as false in this case as it was in the case of Cheju.

In explaining the 'mass escape attempt,' the propaganda service of the US State Department, USIS, on December 15, quoted the 'UN' Command as saying that the prisoners 'organised drills and demonstrations in each of the six compounds on Pongam in defiance of lawful orders. The Communists then moved according to plan, the Command said, to the top of a high terrace where they hurled a shower of stones at ascending US troops.'

Was this high terrace a point from which prisoners could leap in a mass escape attempt? It appears not. Just as it is clear, even from the USIS report, that the prisoners, far from trying to escape, retreated into the compound in front of the advancing troops and answered rifle fire with stones.

For an eyewitness account of this 'mass escape' attempt, UP correspondent Fred Painton on October 16, quoted the island commander in charge of the blood-letting, Lieutenant Colonel Miller. 'They were standing in rows four ranks deep with their arms linked,' Miller said, according to Painton's report. 'They were singing and swaying back and forth. After our first volley, the wounded were held upright and kept on singing. Ones that were down were pulled up by the arms ... when my men tried to remove the dead and wounded after the battle, the prisoners lay on the ground with locked arms. Our men had to force them apart.' As on Cheju Island, it seemed that the prisoners adopted curious procedure for a mass escape.

Painton's report goes on '. . . he (Miller) said the prisoners made a "tremendous noise" by singing prohibited Communist songs, cheering and chanting slogans. Miller, an expert on tactical problems, said the terrain was the reason the prisoners got such an edge over their captors that bullets became necessary. The slope where the prisoners have their compounds and barracks rose upward at a 30-degree angle. It is terraced to allow construction of barracks and other installations. Miller said "It was a tactical situation in their favour. They were perched 15 feet higher than my troops *with their backs against the barracks' walls . . .*"'

And there we have it. Faced with troops advancing and firing on them, the prisoners retreated until they could retreat no longer. With their backs to the barracks' walls, they linked arms and sang until the bullets cut them down, just as the victims of the Nazi gas chambers linked arms and sang until the gas choked off their voices.

'The Communists stood straight up,' Miller said, 'and made no attempt to dodge the bullets fired from light machine-guns, shot guns, carbines and rifles at less than 30 yards. Some tried to fight hand-to-hand with the UN guards.'

What a picture of the depraved mentality of the American military mind is given by this brief description! Miller had no idea that the picture he was drawing was of the courage and proud dignity of the prisoners faced with such Hitlerite barbarity.

The Pongam massacre took place because the Americans were meeting resistance to their plan of turning over the remaining 11,000 'civilian internees' to be impressed into the Rhee army. According to American reports, this was the second large-scale butchery of 'civilian internees'. But the reports of the ICRC show that this was by no means the whole story. Tucked away discreetly in their French language bulletins, which never seem to find their way into the press, the ICRC reported that four days after the prisoner lists were exchanged on 18 December 1951, almost 800 of these 'reclassified civilians' were beaten up, six were killed and 41 wounded by rifle fire for protesting against being classified as 'South

Korean civilians'. They demanded their right to prisoner of war treatment as loyal members of the Korean People's Army.

The spokesman for the prisoners repeated these demands after the incident when a representative of the ICRC went to investigate. He reported that the incident was caused by 'the application of political coercion' on the question of repatriation. How did it happen?

The inmates of the compound had been lumped together as 'non-Communist South Korean civilians'. They protested so strongly against this that the Camp Commandant told the ICRC representative that 'half the prisoners had changed their minds after signing a declaration'. In order to 'screen' them – or force them to change their minds back again – the Commandant sent in a team of Rhee guards to interrogate them. The prisoners objected and the guards withdrew. They returned with 95 'anti-Communist' prisoners, according to the Commandant (according to the authors' information they were members of Syngman Rhee's fascist Anti-Communist Youth League), who tried to enforce the 'screening.' They started by taking away 17 'agitators' whom they regarded as the prisoners' leaders, to security headquarters, and they arrested many others. They separated the other prisoners and one group was taken to a special building where they were mercilessly beaten with clubs and then forced to squat on the ground all night with their hands clasped behind their necks. The rest were forced to stretch out in their tents, face down to the icy ground, and remain there all night, with guards patrolling to beat them if they moved.

Next morning they were lined up and orders were given to start 'screening'. When the prisoners still refused, the ROK guards opened fire, killing six on the spot and wounding 41.

During his visit in mid-January, the ICRC delegate was assured by the Camp Commandant that after this shooting, Compound 62 was regarded as an entirely 'Communist' compound and that known 'Communists' from other compounds would be concentrated there.

What shines through every line of this report was that in this compound, as in all others, a prisoner who demanded repatriation was at once branded as a 'diehard Communist,' with all the brutal treatment that entailed. But even after officially acknowledging that all the inmates of this compound wanted to be repatriated, the Americans were again trying, within a month, to coerce these prisoners by individual 'screening' and in the dead of night, to 'change their minds'. For it was in this same Compound 62 that the American 'Wolfhounds' attacked on February 18, killing 85 and wounding 129.

That is the story according to the ICRC. But there are far more revealing reports available from some of these 'civilian internees' who, after being press-ganged into the ROK army and sent to the front, managed to cross the lines back to the Korean People's Army. One of these was Kim Sung Tae, from Compound 64, POW serial number 94990. Kim had joined the KPA after Seoul fell in July 1950 and was captured by the Americans after the Inchon landing.

'Our life was nothing but misery and torture from the first days of our capture,' Kim said. 'We were beaten, starved, tortured and made to work like slaves. We were treated worse than beasts. But we managed to keep our flag flying in the compound and we swore revenge. We kept our flag flying until June 1951, and then the Americans demanded that we pull it down and run up the flag of Syngman Rhee. Nobody could be found willing to do such a thing. There were 7,000 prisoners in our compound and they were all loyal to the KPA and the Fatherland. So the Americans sent in tanks and troops with rifles and grenades and again demanded that we haul down our flag. We refused so they opened fire on us. Fifteen of our comrades were killed and I was among the 20 wounded.

'After they had torn our flag to pieces, they put up the Rhee flag and then our real misery began. We were forced to attend meetings, sing Rhee songs and recite stupid, disloyal verses and slogans. We were beaten on the soles of our feet with steel and bamboo rods for not singing or shouting loud enough.

'At the end of the year (after discussions had started on the prisoner issue at Panmunjom – Authors) we were told that the quickest way to go home was to sign a petition in our own blood asking for "voluntary repatriation". Otherwise they said we would all be kept there. We were told that anyone who wanted to go North could go if they signed the petition. But we were suspicious of this and very few signed. And the more they tried to force us the more suspicious we got,' said Kim Sung Tae, a bronzed, stocky

Korean lad with suffering bitten into every line of his honest young face.

Then in February they massacred the comrades in Compound 62 near ours and told us that we would get the same if we didn't cooperate. Eight days after the shooting, the Commandant of our compound, Lieutenant Colonel Lim San Cho of the ROK army, came to us and said that all who wanted to go North could do so. Everyone shouted that they wanted to go, but nothing happened. In April he came again and told us the same thing. This time he said that those who wanted to go North should start moving out of the gates, but the guards were waiting there and when the first ones stepped through, the guards rushed at them, lashing out with their clubs and rifle butts.

Everybody stopped for a moment. The gates were slammed shut and Colonel Lim shouted that everyone had made his choice and those who had stayed in the compound had decided to stay in South Korea. Those who had got out were dragged off and loaded into trucks. We never saw them again.

In July 1952, the Americans started 'releasing' the first 27,000 of the 'civilian internees'. They were handled in 17 batches and Kim Sung Tae was in the sixteenth batch (he had been in hospital because of injuries originally received in the incident over the flags. In hospital he and 200 others were automatically enrolled in the 'Comrades Association for Exterminating Communists' and were forced to take an oath to join the Rhee army and fight 'the Communists').

'My home was near Seoul,' Kim continued, 'and with the rest of those in my batch who lived in that part, we were taken by train to Seoul and escorted to the police station to register. An officer there read out the copy of the oath I had been made to take in the hospital and said I could return to my home only if I promised to carry it out.'

Kim Sung Tae returned to his village and the day after he arrived, a local policeman called and told him that he must register immediately as a second-class reservist. The policeman called every day until this was done.

'As soon as I was registered, he kept coming back and telling me I had two choices. I could enlist for the front or for the Labour Corps,' Kim said, adding that he chose the Labour Corps as the lesser of two evils. He soon found that the 'Labour Corps' was a camouflage name for HID, a hush-hush outfit of American military intelligence. Within less than a month after leaving Koje, Kim Sung Tae was already at the front, after very brief training for intelligence work.

A very similar story was told by Cha Kun Su, formerly of Compound 65, POW serial number 16584. In his case an American lieutenant colonel and an American priest had taken part in the almost daily harangues, urging the compound inmates to change sides. When he was 'released,' he was ordered to report for military service or he would be regarded as a deserter and liable to be shot. On the day he went to Seoul for physical examination, there were more than 1,000 prisoners from Compound 65 going through the process.

Many former inmates of the 'civilian internee' compounds have told almost monotonously similar stories, although they were released, press-ganged and captured at different times. They confirm everything known about these compounds from American and ICRC sources. There is only one distinction – the prisoners are able to tell what happens after they are handed over to Syngman Rhee. From their evidence it is clear that the prisoners were given the choice of being mown down in the compounds or being sent to the front.

The same batch of ICRC reports which carry the details of the brutality meted out to the 'civilian internees' reveals many other massacres and incidents reported neither by the US Command nor in the press. In particular it mentions the killing and wounding of 125 Koreans, including women, for celebrating their National Day, 15 August 1951. It confirms charges that American NCOs entered women's compounds committing rape, and other indignities such as – on the pretext of searching for stolen property – forcing women prisoners to strip nude. (Corporal Jollymore, the Canadian former guard on Koje, described instances in which American guards committed rape in the women's compound on Koje. He also states that the women prisoners were in general reserved for officers, but other ranks 'with influence' could also take part.)

As for the responsibility for all these crimes, the ICRC is obliged to state that '*these incidents were the result of serious prejudice on the part of the detaining authority.*'

Having regard to the known bias of the ICRC in favour of Americans, that must be considered about as grave a denunciation as the Committee could make, and certainly graver than any it made against the Nazis.

[Chapter 11 of Wilfred Burchett and Alan Winnington, *Koje Unscreened* ('Published by the Authors', Peking, 1953), pp. 129–140.]

8

The Ball-Point Pen Murders [1954]

Alan Winnington was a British journalist who became a reporter for the *Daily Worker* in the 1940s. On travelling to the Far East in 1948, his reports, like Burchett's, became indispensable for anyone who wished to know what was genuinely happening in Asia. Most notably, he was with the victorious Chinese Communist Party leadership as the People's Liberation Army entered Beijing in 1949. On meeting Burchett, the two men became the only two Western journalists reporting from Korea from the Northern side. In an extraordinary parallel with Burchett's experience with the Australian government, in 1954 the renewal of his British passport was refused. Like Burchett, he was said to be a traitor, and accused of interrogation and torture of Allied POWs, and endured abuse for reporting that germ warfare had been used against the Communists. After Korea, Winnington spent some time in Peking, then made his base in East Berlin where he settled in 1960.

Plain Perfidy describes some horrific cases of torture, mutilation and murder of North Korean and Chinese prisoners at the hand of ROK (Republic of Korea) and Kuomintang (Taiwan) agents, supervised by US Psychological Warfare experts. Both this book and *Koje Unscreened* were dismissed as 'Communist' propaganda in some circles during the Cold War, but these abuses have since been corroborated by other published accounts, and now seem disturbingly plausible. On the other hand, evidence of atrocities against Allied POWs is much scarcer; conditions for Allied prisoners were harsh early in the war, but improved once the Chinese became involved.

* * *

It was very awkward for the American Air Force. For three years they had publicised their incessant bombing of the single road from north to south under the charming title of 'Operation Strangle' and now they had to face the possibility that the American and other prisoners would travel down that road and provide living proof that the air interdiction programme was indeed a 'fizzle.'

It was very awkward for the Psychological Warfare Section. Letters to their homes, which the Army authorities had been so unmannered as to open and read, showed that the vast majority of American and British prisoners had nothing but good words to say about their captors.

It was equally awkward for Eisenhower's backroom advisers. The Korean–Chinese offers to exchange prisoners and agree to have the prisoner issue decided by neutrals had sent a wave of joy round the world and made many more millions of people aware that the Korean and Chinese desire for peace was genuine and that peace was being prevented by Washington stubbornness.

Immediately it became plain that the sick and wounded prisoner exchange agreement would be signed, the US Air Force developed a frantic all-out air offensive to try to make the north-south road impassable. Night after night aircraft were sent to attack towns and villages along the route, with special concentration on the bridges. Fighter-bombers flew along the route by day, bombing and rocketing bridges from low levels. Noting this strange increase of activity, a correspondent of the French Press Agency asked the reason in Tokyo, and wrote on 9 April 1953, two days before the agreement was signed: 'Observers here today considered that continuous bombing operations by the UN over North Korea were intended to deal a heavy blow to Communist lines of communication before a possible armistice was signed. The number of sorties flown by UN planes yesterday was one-third larger than the average daily.'

While the American, British and other prisoners were collecting at Pyoktong and having a series of hilarious farewell parties with their colleagues and Chinese guards, Okinawa-based Superforts were ranging the night skies pouring down hundreds of tons of bombs to delay their arrival at Kaesong beyond the deadline and thus conceal their 'Strangle' fiasco. As they bade farewell to their friends, the returning 'UN' prisoners swore to do all in their power to make Eisenhower keep his promise to end the Korean War and get the other prisoners back. They said goodbye with genuine sorrow at leaving so many friends, and set out in lorries, loaded with provisions, fruit, beer and cigarettes, for the trip to Kaesong.

As they left, US reconnaissance planes swept the skies looking for the red-flagged convoy, but after a two-day search were still admitting failure to locate it. This was another Air Force fizzle, and as usual 'Operation Strangle' fizzled. The non-Korean prisoners arrived in Kaesong three hours ahead of schedule, having been spotted by American aircraft only at lunchtime on the last day. All down the road, prisoners remarked on the recent bomb craters dotting the rice paddies around bridges.

On April 12, the day following the signing of the agreement, the Defence Department began a campaign to destroy in advance anything the prisoners might say about their excellent treatment as captives. In admitting that 29,000 POW letters had been opened and 'virtually all' contained some statements reflecting well on the Korean and Chinese authorities, the Defence chiefs disclosed the real feelings of the American prisoners and their own fear. An inner-office message to the chief of the UP Tokyo bureau said: 'The Army doesn't want them spreading Communism at home, but is well aware of the demand to get the boys home regardless of it.' Here is already disclosed American intention to detain their own POWs who might not say what Washington wanted.

Behind a Press ballyhoo about 'Freedom Gate' through which the prisoners would step, 'Freedom Village' where they would be processed, and 'Freedom Airlift' which would fly them home, barbed wire cages were got ready and the Army prepared a 're-orientation' course and special planes to fly the prisoners to jails camouflaged as 'mental hospitals.' There was much sinister talk of mental sickness and psychiatric treatment, 'brain-washing' and 'counter-brain-washing', all the catchpenny phrases of the Psychological Warfare Division. This was a grotesque fraud to convince the public that the prisoners were mentally sick and to keep any prisoner who spoke well of the Koreans and Chinese out of sight until he could be 're-oriented.' It was clear that atrocity stories would be required by the Army as the price for a prisoner's return to his family. The puppets of South Korea, unhampered by public opinion as were the US Defence chiefs, announced that all the returning South Korean sick and wounded would be isolated in concentration camps for at least six months.

When the first American and British prisoners stepped out of the Korean ambulances in the crisp April sunshine, there were signs that the American propaganda machine was not geared for all possible situations. Perhaps the Americans believed their own propaganda and expected to receive a similar collection of mutilated ghosts to those they were delivering in the North. In that case, the Press could be left to itself to wring the Stateside heartstrings. But instead, the non-Korean and Rhee soldiers, warmly clad in quilted clothes, stepped jauntily out, sunburned, ruddy, happy and laughing, shaking hands with their Chinese escorts, as fat and healthy a group of sick and wounded as could be imagined. Although the Korean–Chinese side had made the rule that any person with even a minor leg disability had to have a stretcher, there were few stretcher cases.

Waving and cheering happily to the pressmen, they stepped through the 'Freedom Gate' into a tent, from which they emerged a few minutes later, silent and thoughtful, like men who had suddenly been brought face to face with a reality they did not expect. In that tent they had their first briefing as pawns of the American psychological warfare experts.

Surprised, but like the prisoners not yet 'oriented,' the correspondents at first wrote factual accounts of what they had seen. Even with all the 'processing' to eliminate prisoners classified as too 'mentally ill' to meet the Press, the Army could not find prisoners willing at short notice to tell flat lies.

Associated Press reported interviews with selected prisoners that day, and said: 'American soldiers returning from the Communist prison camps told a story today of generally good treatment.' AP reported that prisoner Kenyon Wagner, praising his medical treatment, said he had been given 'the whole works.' According to AP, another prisoner, Corporal Theodore Jackson, spoke highly of the treatment. 'To my idea,' he said, 'they did fair, about the best they could do, I think, with the medicines they had.' AP was told by Pfc William R. Brock, Jr., that there was no barbed wire round their camps, they were issued with a quilt and blanket for each man, and that their houses had floor heating. He had never seen a prisoner ill-treated.

The returnees told of the complete religious freedom they had in the camps for all types of religious creed. Football matches were held all the time, with prizes given by the camp authorities. The prisoners had their own barbers and were shaved every day. UP reported on the first day that a British prisoner, Arthur Hunt, said that there was a daily sick call and all prisoners were inoculated against various diseases. Albert Hawkins, a British prisoner, told UP that when he left the camp the authorities had returned all his personal belongings to him. 'He said his feet have been "slightly numb" for about six months, and the Chinese have been feeding him vitamin pills,' the UP reporter wrote.

This was coming out too much like 'Communist propaganda.' It might even raise hopes of peace if allowed to continue. Something had to be done to stop it, and something was done. United Press Tokyo office received an urgent inner-office message from New York:

NEED ONLY LIMITED COVERAGE ON RETURNING POWs EXCEPT FOR TALES OF ATROCITIES AND SENSATIONS PAYETTE.

For newsmen covering the world's biggest story of the day, such a cable meant only one thing – at all costs get atrocity stories. The order was obeyed. Atrocities, that was the thing! On one hand, any prisoner who refused to join the atrocity campaign was clearly a 'Red.' On the other, an atrocity campaign was just what was needed to divert public feeling away from peace.

Once United Press had started the atrocity campaign, the 'rat race' was on. From that moment it was nothing but a scramble for the bloodiest, most incredible, tear-jerking, headline-catching lie that could be thought up and put into a prisoner's mouth. Behind it, the infamous Counter-Intelligence Corps (CIC) pulled the strings. The returning prisoners were rushed to an interrogation centre masquerading under the title of 121st Evacuation Hospital. According to 'UN' pressmen, a 'cloak of secrecy' was flung round the camp and all phone calls referred to the CIC. From inside this atrocity factory, the CIC allowed fantastic inventions to leak out, unimaginatively based on crimes committed by 'UN' troops in Korea. From there, too, a few prisoners were allowed out to meet the Press, where under batteries of Klieg lights and popping flashguns they nervously answered 'Yes' or 'No' to loaded questions hurled at them by scores of rabid press-wolves who sought mainly names and addresses to lend a faint air of authenticity to already-written sensations. Real journalists, of whom there were few enough at

Panmunjom then, told the authors they were horrified at the way in which the American pressmen would build an entire fabrication on a single mumbled word given in answer to a series of loaded questions. Not all American pressmen were willing to lend themselves to this palpable warmongering. State Department officials complained to Columbia Broadcasting System that their man in Panmunjom was not entering into the spirit of the atrocity campaign. The CBS correspondent concerned told his office that he was simply reporting what he saw and heard.

Writing of the 'rat race' in 'Freedom Village,' Munsan, *Time* magazine's correspondent said: 'Somehow a headline-hunting competition for "atrocity" stories had started. Most of the voluminous file of atrocity stories last week was highly exaggerated, and the total impression was entirely false. Under Press interrogation at Munsan, prisoners talked of cruelty only when pressed by leading, insistent questions. Most of the prisoners said they had not seen their comrades murdered or subjected to deliberate cruelty. And when successive prisoners talked of deaths in the prison camps, some newsmen piled statistic on to statistic of "atrocity deaths" without checking how much they overlapped.'

Blandly cynical, *Time* puts it down to a 'headline-hunting competition' that began 'somehow.' But everyone in Panmunjom knew how it began. It was no coincidence that USIS, voice of the US State Department, and UP led the field in peddling these fabrications. Here was a dreadful example of press and radio manipulation by a militarist junta in Washington to destroy the atmosphere of the truce talks and head off the prospects of peace.

Medieval horrors based on strip-cartoon culture and supposedly committed against American prisoners poured from the swift-moving ball-point pens of more than one hundred scurrying US pressmen. Thousands were journalistically killed and mutilated as each scrambled for the next edition's 'splash.' Although the British Press failed to give a true picture of the exchange, on the whole it refrained from scavenging for atrocities. Indeed, it would have been hard for them to do so because it was already known that only a few more than a thousand British prisoners had been declared missing in Korea and that just below a thousand were listed as prisoners, in good health. The US Command however made it a practice to inflate their missing figures by including in them thousands of names of GIs they knew to be dead in action. This at once allowed them to minimise their figures of killed-in-action for propaganda purposes and also provided room for atrocity inventions.

One American prisoner who knew the whole story talked to the authors a few hours before he was handed over. His story was typical, but we select it because Captain M. Green, of Lawton, Oklahoma, one of the few officers among the sick and wounded, was captured only three weeks after the war began and went through all the experiences of prisoner-of-war life. He was then forty-two, old enough to judge for himself. Captain Green, captured near Taejon, was marched north in two stages of three nights each to Seoul (some American prisoners who marched by day had been picked off by US fighter planes). He ate rice and fish, exactly the same as his captors, and once during the six nights a pig was killed for the group, which consisted of eighty men.

'We got three meals a day,' said Captain Green. 'Sometimes the planes were very active and we got two or even three meals in one. We were hungry enough, but we couldn't eat three meals in one. We didn't want to take it all. But the Korean sergeant made us. He had his orders, I suppose. Three meals was so much rice and fish and so we had to have it.' From Seoul he went by train to Pyongyang and later also by train to Manpo. 'We rested by day, well away from the railway tracks, and the only thing that scared us was being strafed by our own aircraft. One badly wounded man died and we left behind a few dysentery cases with drugs and guards. Fellows got dysentery because they would not keep discipline. The Koreans provided boiled water all along the route, but some fellows would drink from the paddy fields.' There were times when the food was rough, said Green, but they always ate as well as or better than their guards. 'If different or better food wasn't there, we couldn't have it. But it was enough to live on and conditions kept improving. In my opinion there was no difference between treatment in Korean and Chinese camps. They gave us what they could, and conditions improved throughout.' Green also praised the medical treatment, the excellent sports facilities in the camps and the general care taken of prisoners' health and morale.

This sort of story available from any of the returning Americans would have painted the real picture and set at rest the worried hearts of parents whose sons still remained in the POW camps. But

Washington policy was that all prisoners, their own and others, were so much political capital. From their own returning men, in whom they had never shown any previous interest, they wanted only 'atrocities and sensations' to whip up pro-war hysteria among a public long jaded by phoney 'anti-Red' horrors.

For those prisoners, the great majority, who refused to lend their names to 'atrocities or sensations,' or who spoke well of the generous treatment of the Korean and Chinese authorities, there was the reality of 'Freedom' Gate, Village and Airlift – a 'cloak of secrecy' and a secret flight to the dreaded army mental home at Valley Forge. 'Not all of the prisoners came home to banners and trumpets,' wrote *Newsweek*. 'One US-bound plane from Tokyo travelled in nearly complete secrecy. Its passenger list was confidential . . . The reason: some of the passengers, after "limited" screening in Tokyo, had been tentatively listed as "victims of Communist propaganda" – brainwashing . . . They would be given psychiatric and medical treatment at the Valley Forge Army Hospital in Pennsylvania.' The patients were 'burned up' and so were the hospital staff, *Newsweek* recorded, and stated the men were met with armed guards at the airfield. Among them was Private Carl Kirchhausen, the first prisoner to be handed over in Panmunjom, and ballyhooed as the first to reach 'Freedom.' What sort of 'Freedom' was also defined by Associated Press in a cable from Bill Barnard. 'In a sense they are still "captives",' he wrote, but were 'in fair condition . . . they are held incommunicable in US Army hospitals.' Barnard noted that they were being interviewed 'intensively' by intelligence men and even denied a 24 hours' pass.

In an unusually revealing phrase, *Time* said: 'For every man and tired US soldier who walked or hobbled or was stretcher-borne along the quick road home last week, there were stories to tell . . . The price of a ticket *along the quick road home* was simply a story, atrocity or sensation.' [Emphasis added by WB.]

Reasons for this deceitful atrocity campaign were not hard to find. For six months the Americans had tried to drag their allies into a hotter war in Korea and into committing acts of war against China. The pretext was 'humanitarian tenderness' toward Korean and Chinese prisoners. In the end, the Koreans and Chinese had brought them back to the conference table by means of their sincere offer to exchange sick and wounded prisoners. In the exchange they had shown where real humanitarianism lay. Coupled with this, the extreme reasonableness of Chou En-lai's offer to reopen negotiations to solve the overall prisoner issue brought warm welcomes from every major capital of the world except Washington. Time was needed to reshape American policy and find new stumbling blocks. The atrocity campaign was whipped up out of nothing to provide an excuse for holding off the resumption of talks which Harrison had broken off six months earlier.

While General Mark Clark in Tokyo gained time by asking for 'clarification' of issues that needed settlement at the conference table, Washington set loose a torrent of anti-truce propaganda. 'Wary,' 'alert,' 'keep our powder dry' occurred in hundreds of news messages. Eisenhower's administration tried to muddy the waters by considering 'the possibility of a future settlement of the Korean War that would move the North–South Korean boundary some 80 miles north of the 38th Parallel.' Republican Senate leader Taft followed up by saying that a truce at the battle-line (which had been already agreed) would not 'really contribute to the peace of the world . . .' Van Fleet said that 'only a crushing military victory by the UN could bring a lasting peace in Korea.'

Nobody listened. And nobody listened to the atrocity tales except a handful of cave-dwelling Senators who crept out of their holes to demand an investigation, found no one listening and crept back. It became apparent that, for the moment, the jig was up. In London, Paris and Tokyo, correspondents were persistently asking why the Americans refused to respond to the great effort which the Koreans and Chinese had made to reopen the talks. 'The 80 Press correspondents who had rushed . . . from Tokyo, Hong Kong and even the US to attend the resumed armistice talks are increasingly mystified as to why the head of the UN delegation has not yet answered his Communist colleagues' letter on the subject,' wrote AFP's Max Olivier on April 14.

At length Harrison answered, in a snarling note trying to set such conditions for the resumption as would doom the talks to failure.

[Chapter 2 of Wilfred Burchett and Alan Winnington, *Plain Perfidy* (Britain–China Friendship Association, London, 1954), pp. 18–24.]

South of the 17th Parallel [1955]

At the 1954 Geneva Conference, Vietnam was temporarily partitioned along the 17th parallel. North of the 17th parallel was the Democratic Republic of Vietnam, proclaimed in August 1945 by the Communist Ho Chi Minh. In the South, the ultra-Catholic Ngo Dinh Diem, backed by the US, had replaced France's proxy ruler, Emperor Bao Dai. Following the Geneva Agreements, internationally supervised elections were scheduled for July 1956 to unite the country and elect a new government. In 1955, Burchett moved his base to Hanoi to observe developments north of the provisional military demarcation line in Vietnam and the implementation of the Geneva Accords.

In the Introduction to his book, Burchett states that *North of the 17th Parallel*:

> deals with the achievements of reconstruction, the legacy of colonialism, the problem of moving the people's administration from the jungle to take over the cities and industrial centres, the immediate and long-range perspectives for economic progress. Application of the Geneva agreements and the activities of the International Control Commission are analysed and the situation south of the 17th parallel dealt with briefly. The book describes the drama of land reform, the sweeping changes in the lives of the peasantry and the new deal for the minority people.
>
> It is especially directed against the professional line-freezers: those Western politicians and diplomats who during the past ten years have concentrated their energies on creating situations favourable to drawing lines across other people's territories and then freezing them into semi-permanent political boundaries. The book exposes the myth, so popular in certain circles, that the drawing of a line to separate the combatants acted as a magic wand to create two different Vietnams, two different peoples. It is shown that for the Vietnam people, there is only one Vietnam just as there is only one China, one Korea and one Germany.

* * *

Saigon at the end of 1954 was a seething cauldron in which hissed and bubbled a witches' brew of rival French and American imperialisms spiced with feudal warlordism and fascist despotism. The vapours from this simmering brew obscured to a certain extent what was really going on in this capital of 'free' Vietnam, as the American psychological warfare experts hastened to call South Vietnam after Ngo Dinh Diem was installed as supreme dictator.

It was a city of gangsters and assassins, of shots, knife thrusts and the strangler's cord in the dark: a city where people spoke in whispers and disappeared without leaving a trace. A mortally wounded French imperialism struggled feebly here for breath, while hovering vulture-like overhead, American imperialism waited the chance to kill and pick clean the bones.

Fifty paces from the city's most luxurious hotel, Vietnam families lived in shelves on the waterfront piers, packed in like bolts of cloth with not enough headroom to sit upright and just enough frontage for two adults and a child to huddle together with water lapping over the floorboards at high tide.

In the main street linking Saigon with its twin Cholon, a taxi-rank and refreshment stalls outside, was what French troops called the 'meat-market', a brothel for the use of the Expeditionary Corps where between two and three hundred girls stood around, jammed into an enclosed courtyard to be inspected by the customers. African non-coms seated at the doorway handed out prophylactic kits as the soldiers trooped in (a 'superior' mirror-lined establishment with two hundred girls had just been completed for the anticipated influx of American personnel).

Luxury limousines and military trucks raced cheek by jowl down the main streets, killing daily on the average slightly more than one Saigon citizen and knocking down another twenty-three, of whom between three and four were gravely injured. The French seemed conscious that the sands were running out and it was necessary to do everything in frantic haste.

Gaudy neon signs invited one to drink and dance from midnight to dawn, and the most expensive bars and restaurants had grenade-proof grilles. Beautifully lit and decorated shopfronts in Rue Catinat and Boulevard Gallieni displayed luxury articles from

Paris, mountains of imported foods and wines, silks, nylons, radios, refrigerators – but little which had any relation to Vietnamese needs or purchasing power.

'Free' Vietnam, as one found by the blank columns in the first newspaper one picked up on arrival at Saigon, was heavily censored, and even publishing the strictly censored news and articles did not prevent papers being suppressed by the government at the rate of two or three monthly. A few minutes after I arrived at Saigon airfield aboard an International Commission plane in mid-November 1954, black-painted bombers were roaring off the field and after them paratroop-carrying transports. South of the 17th parallel, people were still being killed in battle four months after the ceasefire agreements were signed . . .

The streets were full of beggars. The Municipal Theatre opposite the Continental Hotel – Saigon's second-best – was filthy and crammed with Catholic unfortunates from the North, who had believed the fables of excommunication and certain death from atom bombs if they remained in the North, and of lush rice-fields and buffalo, fishing boats and nets awaiting them in the South. Instead they found filth, hostility and beggary, an invitation to stand in the 'meat market' for the young and pretty women, and for the men, if they were young and strong, the choice between a rifle and uniform in Diem's army or a slave job in the rubber plantations – beggary and starvation for the rest.

If one sat at a boulevard cafe for ten minutes, a score of young beggars or street hawkers clustered around, mutely holding out their hands or placing their pitiful wares on the table. They passed in an interminable procession. It was one of the latter who clandestinely sold me, at double the normal price, a copy of *Time* magazine. Why clandestinely? Because there was a portrait of Ho Chi Minh on the cover. Despite the slanderous, illiterate rigmarole about President Ho inside, the issue was banned by Ngo Dinh Diem. All copies except a few already sold were seized from the news stands until the scandal of suppressing *Time*, major propaganda organ of Diem's real masters, was so great that the US ambassador intervened to have the ban lifted. All copies were then sold out in a few hours. Few regular European customers got any, but for days following the lifting of the ban one saw Vietnamese in Saigon streets with

President Ho's portrait under their arms – protected by the magic word 'Time'.

General Lawton Collins had arrived in Saigon as special United States ambassador. Designated by the American press as General 'Lightnin' Joe' Collins, he was a special ambassador because he had the 'special' task of transforming 'free' Vietnam into an American military base and making it safe for American investments. His predecessor Donald Heath (previously declared persona non grata in Bulgaria for his flagrant interference in that country's internal affairs), had been withdrawn from Saigon because he had recommended the removal from office of Ngo Dinh Diem, regarded by Heath as incompetent to implement American plans.

Collins held a press conference two weeks after his arrival in which he somewhat brutally informed the foreign and Vietnam press, that Diem was the one and only figure in South Vietnam's political life that Collins and the American government was prepared to support, and that despite French objections (and the Geneva Agreements), the USA was going to take over the training and equipping of the South Vietnam army. There were some remarkable features about this conference. 'Lightnin' Joe' Collins spoke as the assured master in his own house. Although the majority of journalists present were Vietnamese, the conference was conducted in English with no translation.

A Vietnamese correspondent who put two variations of the question as to whether the USA would be prepared to support a government that was nationalist, anti-Communist but not headed by Diem, was rudely silenced: 'Now you've had enough to say, young fella'. When the General was asked what he thought of Vietnam, he put his thumbs together and said, 'Waal, I've always had the greatest admiration for the Vietnam people and their culture. Now . . . er, . . . take the ruins of Angkor Wat for instance – one of the great monuments of civilisation . . .' 'Lightnin' Joe' of course was getting the rooms of his house mixed up in confusing South Vietnam with another object of US interference – Cambodia.

Collins' forthright announcement that the American Stars and Stripes were going to replace the French Tricouleur [sic] in South Vietnam greatly inspired American investors. During the month that followed his press conference, carpetbaggers arrived with every plane. Businesses and real estate began to change hands at a rapid rate. The sellers were French, the buyers Americans. The latter paid two years' rent on flats and houses and never questioned the figure – their piastres were all obtained on the black market.

The Collins' plan which inspired so much confidence in American investors, was to implant Diem solidly as an American puppet on the basis of what was known as the Philippines' experience. Diem was not a popular figure – that everybody knew, including the personnel of the American Embassy. It was not necessary that he be popular, only that he be a dictator, capable of implementing US policies. And if he were shaky as a dictator, then by God, the USA and General Collins would make him solid, unshakeable and irremovable. General 'Lightnin' Joe' Collins after a lightning-quick look at the situation evolved his plan. He had arrived with pre-fabricated ideas, formed by newspaper reports from politically illiterate American journalists and agents of the American military and political intelligence apparatus. The latter were scared to reveal anything resembling the truth, in case they should later become targets for McCarthy and other 'un-American activities' committees. The example of witch hunts against colleagues who ten years previously had sent reasonably objective reports on the situation in Kuomintang China was still too fresh in the minds of US State Department personnel to permit any real home-truths being reported back to Washington from Vietnam or anywhere else. So, for General Collins, it was a military problem of 'cleaning up the Reds the way we did in the Philippines,' and building solid props and stout wires for the chosen puppet, Ngo Dinh Diem.

South Vietnam should be made really 'free' by cleaning it up, province by province from south to north, from all 'Vietminh' elements. As the 'Vietminh' were cleaned out, a new pro-Diem administration would be installed. A certain amount of land would be divided up, some schools, shops and cinemas built, enough to keep the people quiet. And in case the people did not like this, portions of Diem's new Collins-created military repressive machinery would be left behind in each province to maintain 'order.' By the time the country was cleaned up to the 17th parallel, with American nylon stockings, soaps, powdered eggs, comic strips and technicolour films keeping the people quiet, nobody would dream of wanting unification with the North. And if they were so stupid as still to want it, then by God, the machinery would be there to stop them. American efficiency would take over from French muddling and make the colony a paying proposition. With such a stable base and the United States training and equipping the new army, the US psychological warfare department softening up the North with radio broadcasts and hosts of infiltrated agents, 'free' Vietnam would soon be in a position to clean up the North as well. No need for any elections to unify the country. It should be unified in a way guaranteeing 'democracy, Christianity and individual freedom'.

If an adviser dared mention possible difficulties with other elements apart from the 'Vietminh' – the armed religious-political sects, for instance – Collins had an answer to that also. There are three sects. Give Diem a fourth, a Catholic super-sect with an armed force bigger than all the rest put together, trained and equipped by the US. Purge the army of all pro-French elements, and create a new pro-American machine. Diem is a Catholic in a Buddhist country hostile to Catholicism. Bring the Catholics down from the North by every possible means and put them into a Diem-American uniform. Kick the French and the pro-French out of military and administrative positions. Be a little rough with them. Make an example of a few and frighten the rest. If – and it is unlikely – anyone whispered that 'cleaning up' the Vietminh was a violation of the 'no reprisals' clause of the Geneva Agreement, Collins undoubtedly replied 'To hell with the Geneva Agreement. That's not our affair. We never signed it. Diem never signed it. What have we got to worry about?'

It was another of those diabolical plans, like the Hoa My concentration camp, that must have looked clear and feasible to the machine-like mind of the former US army chief of staff, General Lawton Collins, whose studies of Vietnamese history had not gone beyond the Angkor Wat ruins in Cambodia. But it did not work. Collins found it was not so easy to slip from feudalism to a streamlined fascism in one step, especially after an important proportion of the population had some experience of democracy in the resistance areas. A machine could be created. Repression could be – and was – intensified. Assassination committees started work. But Collins kept tripping over bits of machinery created by previous imperialist adventurers in Vietnam. There were the religious-political sects armed by the French against the Thais, by the Japanese against the French, by the French against the resistance. There were sect leaders who in return for the support of one side or the other had been armed and given virtually autonomous regions where they ruled supreme, collected head-taxes from the population under their control, transit taxes from anyone who passed through their domains and customs taxes on goods that entered and left their areas. Diem's authority – despite Collins' plan – could not be exercised in these areas, without major military operations. And Collins' orders to purge the army resulted in the multiplication of minor warlords in the form of officers, who rather than await the assassin's knife or the purge order, broke away with units up to battalion size and carved out small fiefs for themselves, defying Diem's attempts to liquidate them.

On top of all this, over three million of South Vietnam's population, one third of the total, had been used to the democratic administration of the resistance areas. Two million of them had been in a solidly liberated area ever since the August 1945 uprising. Diem could assassinate or remove the chairman of a village or district council, but the people demanded elections for a replacement. At first Diem agreed but his candidates were always defeated. After that elections were suppressed and Diem nominated replacements, but real authority remained with those trusted by the people during the resistance days.

Within two months of his arrival, Collins was already throwing up his hands in despair. Despite the knocking together of a Diem military machine, despite the anti-guerilla 'experts' imported from the Philippines, including a sinister Colonel Lansdale of the US psychological warfare department, the real problem of making Diem's authority function and Diem and America acceptable to the people of South Vietnam remained unsolved. By the end of December 1954, Collins was in despair. American investors were having second thoughts and the tempo of their purchases had dropped considerably. Members of the multitudinous American diplomatic, military, psychological warfare, economic and propaganda agencies in Saigon were blaming the French for their difficulties, the

French were chuckling and saying openly: 'You were going to show us how to run the show. Now look at the mess you're in.' Collins returned to Washington and recommended the removal of Diem. But this was just what the powerful pro-Cardinal Spellmann clique in the State Department were determined to oppose at all costs. Diem must stay, and Collins was sent back again with orders to ensure the puppet's stability (Collins' renewed insistence three months later that the task was impossible, and Diem must be replaced, led instead to Collins being sacked like his predecessor, Donald Heath).

American experiments in grafting a streamlined fascist dictatorship on to the shaky feudal structure of South Vietnam were paid for by the blood of thousands of former resistance workers in South Vietnam. In Saigon-Cholon in May 1955 hundreds of innocent civilians, including women and children, were indiscriminately slaughtered as Franco-American rivalry broke out in armed clashes between the American trained and equipped troops of Diem and the French supported troops of the Binh Xuyen sect. The Americans were determined to enforce Diem's effective dictatorship, at least over Saigon-Cholon. Hundreds more were slaughtered as Collins' policy of reprisals against former members of the resistance forces was applied. One of the first cases of this sort to be brought to the notice of the International Commission after the arrival of Collins was an incident at Binh Thanh, on the Mekong River in Long Xuyen province. A Commission team arrived there on 8 December 1954. They had been notified that a short time previously seventy-four villagers had been arrested on the pretext that they had supported the resistance. Twenty-four of them were said to have been executed, after which their bodies had been burned and the ashes thrown into the Mekong River.

Lodged by the French in a motorboat anchored offshore in the Mekong River, it was very difficult for the Commission team to make contact with the population. The village was full of Diem troops, with machine-gun posts mounted at every crossroads, guns pointing towards the houses. With the team constantly surrounded by Diem's soldiers it was not surprising that most villagers were afraid to answer any questions. But by the end of the first day's activities, seven had come forward and confirmed that there had been mass arrests and executions. They stated also that people had been threatened with death if they testified before the Commission.

Next morning the bodies of two of the seven witnesses were found, including an old woman who had been beheaded and disembowelled. The others, it was found, had been arrested, including a mother with two children who had approached the commission about the arrest of her husband. A boy of 17 had also been detained because he was found with a letter addressed to the Commission in his pocket.

While the team members aboard the motorboat were discussing what to do next, a canoe paddled by three men appeared out of the mists. The occupants asked if their security could be guaranteed if they came alongside. A French liaison officer gave the assurance, and the three men said they had come on behalf of some other villagers who wanted to approach the Commission but were afraid of reprisals. Assurances were given and the three men disappeared again into the mists. An hour later a flotilla of no less than ninety-five small sampans bore down the river with almost five hundred peasants aboard. They had been hiding in the rice-fields for over a week because of the massacres in Binh Thanh village and were frightened to return as long as it was in the hands of Diem's troops. They confirmed with minute details the story of the arrests, massacres and disposal of the bodies.

All the Commission's inspection team could do in such cases was to make notes and an eventual report to the chief delegates, with a subsequent note from the latter to the French High Command. The Binh Thanh incident was typical of many others investigated and verified by teams of the International Commission in the South . . .

One could occasionally find a reflection of the endless massacres and assassinations even in the heavily censored Saigon press. Thus *Tien Chuong* [*The Bell*] in its issue of 13 December 1954, commented:

This atmosphere of insecurity must be done away with. The cannon of war are silenced. In theory the people should be able to enjoy the blessings of peace and security. But in the countryside tragic incidents occur very often . . . in the course of which the peasants must always pay with their lives and belongings. The number of such incidents reported in the papers does not at all correspond to the real truth. Because many of the events take place far from Saigon, they often go unreported. In the city itself, the same insecurity reigns. Armed hold-ups, blackmail and cases of rape are reported daily and are becoming more and more frequent. This must cease . . .

And *Tin Moi* [*New Information*] on the same day, commenting on the fact that tens of thousands of peasants had fled from the countryside to the comparative calm of Saigon during the war, and still could find no security in their villages, wrote:

It is urgent to help the return of our peasants to the countryside so they can get back to the land and step up food production. After nine years of bitter war, during which they came to seek a more peaceful life in the cities, our peasants are now happy to return to their ricefields. Unfortunately the first hopes and enthusiasms of many of them have been dashed to the ground. They have found it very difficult to restart their life in the villages. There are thousands of unexpected difficulties which they cannot overcome alone. They need to have their personal security assured, a little capital to help them at least buy a few implements, some seed, a buffalo, something to eat until the first harvest is reaped. Above all they need security permitting them to live and work in peace . . .

Instead of the incidents and massacres ceasing, as *Tien Chuong* and *Tin Moi* demanded, they increased, and it was the newspapers that criticised events which soon had to cease publication. Up to the end of July 1955 – that is the first twelve months of peace – according to incomplete figures forwarded by Vo Nguyen Giap to the International Commission, there had been over three thousand cases of reprisals against former resistance supporters in South Vietnam, resulting in over six thousand killed, wounded and missing and more than twenty-five thousand arrested. Added to these dreadful figures are an estimated seven thousand killed and twice that number wounded in the three months starting May 1955, when Diem's 'National' army attacked the Binh Xuyen sect and subsequently the Hoa Hao forces of Tran Van Soai and Ba Cut.

Reprisals, massacres, assassinations, a civil war designed to eliminate minor dictators and establish Diem as the sole, supreme dictator – this was one side of the face of 'free' Vietnam, as it emerged under American tutelage and the Collins' plan. The other side was the total suppression of anything remotely resembling the democratic liberties provided for under Article 14c of the Geneva Agreements. Any activity in opposition to the government, in support of the Geneva Agreements, was regarded as treason. Political parties in opposition to Diem were banned and their leaders assassinated or arrested. This included even leaders of parties like the reactionary Dai Viet (Greater Vietnam Party), which by early 1955 was forced into armed opposition to Diem. Newspapers operated under a drastic censorship and publishing only censored material was no guarantee against having the paper closed down for two or three months or permanently without any reason. All the committee members of the Saigon-Cholon Peace Movement, formed to struggle for implementation of the Geneva Agreements and which included Saigon's best known intellectuals, were arrested. Amongst the main proofs of their 'treasonable' activities was their publication of the statutes and rules of the Movement and the text of the Geneva Agreements. Due to strong pressure of public opinion, the fact that every magistrate but one in Saigon refused to try the accused, and International Commission interest in the case, the members were never brought to trial – but were exiled from Saigon in forced residence.

Likewise arrested were members of a committee coordinating over two hundred organisations in Saigon-Cholon including religious bodies, trade unions, professional and sports associations, women's and youth organisations, almost every organised body in the twin cities, set up to aid the victims of the fighting between Diem's forces and the Binh Xuyen in May 1955. Over two thousand Saigon-Cholon homes had been destroyed and forty thousand people made homeless. The committee organised volunteer Sunday working parties in which tens of thousands of people took part, clearing away debris and helping rebuild the homes. But such 'subversive' social activities could not be tolerated. It was disbanded by Diem police action and its leading members arrested.

Special press regulations were issued in February 1955 warning against the use of the words 'democracy, independence and liberty.'

The performance of folk songs and dances was banned on the grounds that they were 'Vietminh' inspired. Listening to Radio Hanoi was also forbidden. An item published by the official South Vietnam news agency on 24 August 1955 illustrates the quality of 'freedom' in 'free Vietnam.'

'For some time', reported a Vietnam Presse bulletin, 'the police have been on the track of a Vietminh propaganda organisation in favour of elections in 1956. Their method was to try and persuade people to listen in to Radio Hanoi and to arrange special meetings amongst "friends" for this purpose . . . After lengthy enquiries, the agents were recently surprised in a bar at one of their secret meetings. The owner was taken to the police station and the closing of the establishment immediately ordered.' It is one of hundreds of such examples proving that advocating unity or adherence to the Geneva Agreements was a punishable crime in 'free' Vietnam.

Democracy and freedom in their most elemental forms were trampled underfoot. And there was no one to turn to for relief. Those who presented petitions to the International Commission for the release of relatives wrongfully arrested were themselves arrested or simply disappeared. In scores of cases they were assassinated. The Diem police arrested people at the very gates of the International Commission's Saigon Secretariat, at 141 Rue de Champagne. A former Minister of Justice, a wealthy lawyer, was arrested and interrogated on three separate occasions solely because his car had once been seen outside the Saigon Secretariat.

All this was done in the name of preserving liberty and democracy in 'free' Vietnam. In an age when the US psychological warfare department and other organs have all but killed noble words like democracy, liberty and freedom, it was still a shock to many people that 'free' Vietnam, the regime south of the 17th parallel, could be commended openly by the US State Department for refusing to discuss elections with the government of the DRVN because the latter was 'totalitarian' and there was no 'freedom or democracy' in the North. True 'freedom' existed only in the South. In fact, the form of the regime of Ngo Dinh Diem is that of the most rigid, personal, totalitarian dictatorship that exists anywhere in the world today. American arms, dollars and 'know-how' are being employed to the maximum to give it the content of a modern, streamlined fascist State. In 'free' Vietnam there are not even any of the trappings and camouflage of democracy with which American imperialism decorated its puppet Syngman Rhee regime in South Korea. The Americans it is true put pressure on Diem to hold at least some sort of elections, to set up a National Assembly and create a facade of legality for his regime. With their experience of faking elections in South Korea and other places, the American advisers assured Diem he would have nothing to fear. Diem promised to do this and several times announced the date by which elections in the South would take place. But he is afraid to take the risk, even with the modern organs of repression now put in his hands by the Americans. After setting a date for February, then August and finally for December 1955, in the end he told the Americans that it was impossible. The danger of defeat was too great.

The only elected government and the only National Assembly in all of Vietnam is the National Assembly of the DRVN, the government headed by President and Prime Minister Ho Chi Minh . . .

It only remains to add one last quote from the *Time* correspondents' story – and with *Time's* connections with the State Department and the upper crust of the Republican party, no journalist was better qualified to describe the intimate Diem–American relations at Saigon. The article illustrates who are the real masters in 'free' Vietnam, who the real instigators of the massacres and agonies of the South Vietnamese people. Describing Diem as he faced a typical crisis (it was the period when Collins was convinced of the incompetence of Diem, but pro-Cardinal Spellmann zealots in the various American missions at Saigon, including General O'Daniel, in charge of training and equipping Diem's troops, were urging the puppet premier to liquidate his opponents by armed action) the Saigon *Time* correspondent reported: 'An odd procession passed in and out of the palace doors for hours on end to deal with the crisis – three of the man's brothers, one in the cloth of a Roman Catholic Bishop, his beautiful politics-minded sister-in-law; US diplomats and US military officers in mufti, eye-rubbing ministers of state summoned from their sleep for emergency consultations . . . Through US influence he finally won . . . US aid and advice gradually began to take hold . . .' The article might well have been headed 'Profile of a Puppet'.

This then is the man presented by the Americans themselves as the champion of 'Free' Vietnam. With a final piece of advice, the *Time* article urges Diem to steer clear of general elections as 'neither mathematically nor politically is "free" Vietnam remotely ready for the contest . . .'

Small wonder that this foreign-imposed despot dictator was universally hated and despised in the South, that all eyes and ears were turned towards the North, and that people counted the days till elections should be held to unify the country as stipulated under the Geneva Agreements.

My last contact in the South, where the government of 'free' Vietnam had withdrawn my facilities to cable stories critical of the regime and had refused to grant me further visas to report the activities of the International Commission, was with a certain Mr Hoang Van Co, director of 'Vietnam Presse', the official news agency and as such, chief mouthpiece of the Diem regime. Like all other informed people, including American officials in Saigon, he did not bother to deny that ninety per cent of people in the South looked towards the government of President Ho Chi Minh for their salvation. 'This is because people in the South don't know Communism as yet', he explained. 'They still have their illusions about it. It is our duty to protect them from the harsh realities'. His formula for 'protecting' the people, of course, was to refuse to allow them to decide for themselves by free elections what sort of government they wanted.

And how did he see developments if there were no elections? Did he believe a people that had fought so heroically for nine years would sit with bowed heads and folded arms because a foreign-imposed despot said their country was to remain divided?

'We'll fight to the last against elections but the Vietminh will probably take over anyway,' replied this astounding cynic who was typical of the collaborators Diem had gathered around him, 'and as for me – when that happens I'll be well away in Paris or New York.'

How would the 'Vietminh' take over? 'Infiltration,' he said, adding darkly, 'They are here already. They are everywhere. Take my office. I can trust no one. Everything of importance I have to do personally. If I continue the way I'm working now, in another six months I'll have tuberculosis.' When I pointed out that in the North many cadres, by their sacrifices during the resistance war, were in fact stricken with tuberculosis, he shrugged his shoulders and said, 'Not for me.'

I asked him why 'Vietnam Presse' distributed so many supplementary articles taken from the world press, attacking the Soviet Union.

'The Americans insist that we attack Communism', he replied. 'USIS (United States Information Service) sends us many articles attacking the Vietminh and China but we can't even distribute them. No one would publish them. But BIS (British Information Service) is cleverer. They know the Soviet Union is much further away and they send us articles attacking the Soviet Union which we can distribute. Even then most editors won't publish them but at least this keeps the Americans happy because they see our agency does its best to fight the Communists.'

When I expressed skepticism that with all the machinery in their hands they were not able to assure the publication of anti-Vietminh articles he said 'Editors fear physical liquidation.' This was of course nonsense, but I found that the circulation of newspapers which attacked the government of President Ho quickly fell away to nothing and the only way of maintaining a high circulation in Saigon was to find some way, no matter how camouflaged, of attacking Diem and his regime. This was usually done by exposing the corruption and the shocking conditions under which the majority of the population was living. Thus *Buoi Sang* [*Morning*] wrote in its issue of 26 August 1955:

> It needs volumes to describe how the poor are living in this city, with the sky as their mosquito net and the ground as their sleeping mat. They litter the pavements, huddle under the arches of the bridges and in nooks and crannies of the market places. They are people who have toiled all their lives but are homeless and have neither anything to eat nor anything to wear ... Able-bodied persons have become beggars, many young girls find no other outlet but prostitution.

Anh Sang [*Light*] takes up the same theme with a despatch on 30 August 1955:

3: *President Ho Chi Minh, Hanoi, 1966*

The weather is already sweltering, the stench of filth unbearable. There is one smell in particular, stinking and rancid. Shrunken children, their bodies covered with dirt and filth, sweat streaming down their temples, are raking away with their fingers at rubbish heaps, plunging in their hands. Occasionally they pull out a broken bottle or a twisted can. Young women brush the dirt off old bread-crusts or tuck sticky condensed milk tins into bags hanging from their hips. The sun beats down, hotter and hotter. The flies swarm in the clouds . . .

It was impossible during two visits I paid to Saigon to find any-one, even in the upper ranks of those paid by Diem and the Americans to popularise the regime, who had any faith in the dictator or the regime they served. Among the broadest sections of the population on the other hand, one found a unanimous desire to end the dictatorship and unify the country by democratic means. One found also among the ordinary people a rather touching faith that the great powers who had negotiated the Geneva Agreements would ensure fulfilment of the provisions for unification by free, general elections. It was this belief that enabled them to endure with stoicism and discipline, the terrors of the American-imposed Diem dictatorship.

[From Chapter 13 of *North of the 17th Parallel* ('Published by the Author', Hanoi, 1955), pp. 283–309.]

10

Front-line Village [1959]

At the 1954 Geneva conference to end the conflicts in Korea and Indochina the world suddenly discovered that Indochina was in fact three distinct countries inhabited by people of different races and cultures, each with its own individual language and writing. Though Burchett wrote much more about Vietnam, he produced two books about Cambodia and Laos, *Mekong Upstream* and *The Second Indochina War*. The former, written in 1957, combines Burchett's eye for the exotic with his political insights.

His Introduction states that 'the main purpose of this book is to introduce Cambodia and Laos, their people and their leaders, to those who, like the author, only recently discovered them, but who sympathise entirely with their aspirations to build up a new life in peace and free from outside interference or threats of interference. The book is the fruit of three visits to Cambodia and Laos, during which the author was an eyewitness to the vigorous way in which the peoples of these countries – each in their own way – resisted the attempts to reshackle them with the fetters of colonialism.'

* * *

By the time we had reached the outskirts of the village, women were seated at their weaving frames under the houses or at their spinning wheels on the platforms which project from all Lao Lum homes. The track climbed steeply. Where the terraced fields ended abruptly in a wall of undergrowth, sliced only by the foaming stream, we were already hundreds of feet above the valley floor. Soon the valley was entirely blotted out and there was left only a shallow green tunnel through the jungle, occasionally opening out into magnificent natural gothic archways. Lined with noble pillars of iron woods, oil trees and other jungle giants, they were laced together with broad-leaved creepers.

It was a day similar to many others. Often we managed in a dawn-to-dusk march to clamber up and down only one of the ridges which separated the valleys. Sometimes we managed two or even three. On this day, as our guide had planned, by half an hour before sunset we had slithered down from the jungle on an abrupt rocky path into a broad valley. Our destination for the night lay ahead of us – a bamboo and thatch village, houses high up on piles and surrounded by banana and areca palms. The stream which had been a leaping, foaming fury a few hours before now lay in placid, sunfilled pools into which naked children were jumping and splashing. A few score paces upstream, fishermen were standing on rocks intently regarding the water and now and again throwing a weighted net and leaping in after it to secure the fish. On platforms flooded with sunlight at the end of the thatched homes, women were twirling their spinning wheels and in the last moments of the day, their men sat with them, contentedly puffing at bubble pipes. As our convoy crossed the swaying bamboo bridges spanning the stream and bringing us among their houses, the men and women abandoned their pipes and spinning wheels to gather around and welcome us . . .

When I asked about living conditions, the villagers were silent; but after a pause, they nudged one of their number into speaking. He was Pham Sik, a small, round-headed man with deep furrows across his forehead and a back bent with hard work. He looked much older than his thirty years.

'Before I tell you about our life now,' he said, 'I will tell you how it was before.'

In this part of the country, each village had *a nai ban* (chief). Under him were two *thao khoun*. One of the *thao khoun* neither paid taxes nor did he go on corvee. The other paid taxes but did not go on corvee. They were nominated by the *tasseng* (sub-district chief who was appointed by the French). The *nai ban* had three times as much land as the rest of us. The *thao khoun* had twice as much. We had to work the land for the *nai ban*. He did nothing except collect taxes and bring us in for corvee. We paid 120 piastres (then about twenty-five shillings) for every member of the family as head tax, 70 piastres for the paddy-field, 30 for the jungle patch, 5 piastres for each alcohol jar and 3 for each of the children who did not drink.

Any time the *nai ban* wanted to give a feast, he would impose a levy of 40 or 50 piastres. We had to sell our pigs and buffalo and the cloth our women wove to pay the taxes. But worst of all was the corvee.

He paused to take a turn at the bubble pipe. Our fire had burned down to a glow of red ashes. The portable brewery still functioned and the rice beer seemed to lose none of its flavour or strength even after a dozen or so horns of water had been emptied into the malt. Night had well settled in. There was an occasional grunt from buffalo and pigs stalled under the house, a whinny from our ponies, a shriek from a nightbird or harsh cough of some wild animal in the surrounding jungle, but otherwise complete calm.

I asked how many days corvee they had to give in a year. Faces grew bitter at the question. Pham Sik said:

They took us whenever they wanted. They would take us for ten or fifteen days. We would come home again and after four or five days be rounded up again. You never knew when or for how long. No matter what you were doing, you had to drop it, pack up some food and go. We were paid nothing and had to provide our own food.

When we had to go as porter coolies, they marched us from before dawn till after dark with hardly a stop. The French were always on horseback, and they changed their guards at the different posts. They marched us with guns at our backs. Plenty died on the road. Even in the rainy seasons, if they were going to fight the Pathet Lao, they made us carry their food and equipment. Once when the French were attacking Muong Sai we came to a river too high and the current too strong for any but the strongest to cross. We refused. They shot six of us on the spot and forced the rest to cross. The youngest and weakest were swept away and drowned. How many days?

He turned to the villagers and there was an animated discussion between the men. He summed up their opinions:

'From the time the French came back, it was at least a hundred days a year.' (This explained why labour power was so precious, especially the labour of women who were generally exempt from corvee.)

'This was in addition to what we had to do for the *nai ban* and *tasseng*,' Pham Sik continued. 'The *tasseng* could force people to work for him for nothing for all their lives and take as many as he wanted to work his fields or reap the harvest. He took our women whenever he pleased. We were slaves and draught animals.'

As for life now, this was another matter. 'First of all, the system of *tassengs, nai bans* and *thao khoun* is finished. Instead we have a committee elected by all the villagers. Corvee is finished. We pay a single tax based on our actual production.'

There was a long discussion at this point to establish just what they did pay. The tax varied according to the quality of the rice-field and the area. There were three categories. The first paid six, the second five, the third paid three kilograms of rice for every kilogram of seed sown. (A kilogram is a good two pounds.) This applied only to the valley rice-fields. Pham Sik for instance had twelve kilograms of first quality rice-fields – that is an area on which he sowed twelve kilograms of seed. He had reaped just short of one thousand kilograms of which he must pay seventy-two kilograms in taxes. First quality land yielded eighty fold for every kilogram of seed sown. As for the jungle patches, nothing was paid if they harvested less than sixty baskets of rice, but if they sowed over twenty kilograms of seed, they paid twice that amount in tax.

'This is very reasonable,' Pham Sik said in his serious, deliberate way. 'Before, the more we produced, the more we were plundered. Now we have good reason to produce more. We have become human beings again. We have something to live and work for. All pay their taxes willingly and often give up more than they need, because they know it goes to the army and the cadres who brought us our new life. The same with labour. The corvee system is gone for ever, but we know the needs at the front. 'The imperialists and feudalists are attacking us. They want to put the *tassengs* and *nai bans* back in power. Some of us fight at the front, others who stay in the rear give fifteen days labour a year to the administration. These are things we have discussed among ourselves and agreed on. Many volunteer to give more days on transport and other work. Nowadays we provide the first two days' food ourselves and the administration looks after the rest. It's regulated how many hours a day we march and how many pounds we carry. If a team decides to march more, it can, but no one may increase the loads' . . .

When I asked for other changes, a young woman in the background spoke up: 'We never had schools before.' Blushing furiously, she was then pushed forward to the square of smouldering ashes around which the men were sitting. Little more than a girl, her sturdy bare feet showing from under the embroidered skirts that are the pride of Laotian women, she was the village schoolteacher.

'We never had any schools at all before,' she said. 'But I went to an Itsala cadres' school. Now we have a little school and I teach twelve children to read and write so they will later be able to go to a sub-district school. It will open before the rainy season.'

Pham Sik interrupted to say: 'She teaches at night, too. All our village is now divided up into ten mutual-aid teams. The same teams that work the land together in the daytime study together at night and she keeps an eye on them all. She's a very clever girl.'

Covered with still deeper blushes the schoolteacher wriggled her way to the back of the crowd again.

Public health? The local health officer was away having a three weeks' course learning how to give injections. 'We haven't got very much yet,' Pham Sik said apologetically, 'but we had nothing but sorcerers before. Now we have a little dispensary. The health officer collects roots, herbs and leaves from the forest and makes medicines from them. If anyone is badly ill, he can send to the district office for a nurse. He gives us talks about the importance of cleanliness and that we can drink cold water in the village but if we move anywhere else we should boil water before drinking it. People can get advice and treatment free from the health officer. Before you had to give a chicken or a pig to the sorcerer according to the sickness. He would burn some paper or make some coloured smoke and no one got any better from it.'

It was already quite late. Ours was the only house showing as much as a pinpoint of light. The visitors began to glide out like shadows to be swallowed up by the jet black night. One stocky, middle-aged man with his head wrapped in a scarf turned before he left to say:

'We have a new life now. It's what our fathers and grandfathers dreamed about. But if we don't defend this village and the others, if we don't organise our defences and hold these provinces in the north, everything we have built up will be destroyed. We'll have the *tassengs* and *nai bans* on our necks again.'

He was the head of the local self-defence corps. Mention of the *nai bans* prompted me to ask what had happened to the *nai ban* and *thao khoun* of the village.

'They are still here,' the sturdy guerrilla replied. 'But they behave themselves now. They still have their land. But they work it themselves like everyone else. If they need extra labour, they have to pay for it,' he added with evident satisfaction.

The last of the guests left at that; more bamboo was piled on the fire; mosquito nets were lowered and we turned in for what was left of the night with the stertorous breathing and frequent belchings of the buffalo as a lullaby. It seemed after a wearying day that we had scarcely closed our eyes when we could hear what sounded very much like mortar fire and as my eyes opened there were suspicious looking flashes between the slits in the bamboo. Investigation showed that the noise came from a dozen women of a mutual-aid team, six standing on each side of a long wooden trough pounding at rice with long wooden clubs. The flashes were from bamboo torches in the hands of sleepy-eyed, yawning children watching their mothers. It was only 4 a.m. and work had started especially early that morning because the whole village was going to the sub-district centre to elect a new committee.

The village was typical and so was the evening discussion, as I learned during the weeks I spent travelling in the Pathet Lao areas.

In the front line, I found a battalion almost entirely composed of Lao Thenh guarding two of Katay's battalions treed on six mountain peaks. A sturdy lad with cheeks of burnished copper, who was squatting in a clump of bamboo cleaning a machine-gun when we met him, replied that it was much too cold, when asked how he felt. Nheua Noi was only sixteen years old and had been a guerrilla for two years. Only recently he had been transferred to the regular forces. He was a Lao Thenh from the Komadome country and joined the guerrillas in late 1953 because 'Six French and sixty other troops came and burned down our village. They killed all the buffalo and pigs. My father was beaten up and my brothers arrested. We had an old hunting rifle that the French never found, so I took it and joined the guerrillas.'

4: *Wilfred Burchett visiting the Laos front in Sam Neua province*

A few days before our arrival, his squad of four, well entrenched on a mountainside, had held up an enemy company which was probing around and trying to join up with another holding a neighbouring hill.

'A platoon came first,' he said, 'and we opened up with machine-gun fire. Several were killed and the rest rushed back. From both hills, they poured mortar fire for over an hour on where they thought we were. But we had moved up closer to them. Another platoon came swinging down the track and we took them completely by surprise. They must have thought we were wiped out or at least had moved further away. They pulled back very quickly after we opened up with the machine-gun.

'The area was shelled again for a couple of hours. But we had moved again and changed our tactics too. We split up into four different positions, further away this time. Three of us divided up all the hand grenades and I took the machine-gun to the rear. They attacked with two platoons. This time they moved very cautiously until they had passed our first two positions, probing into the jungle each side of the track. Then they became more confident and marched straight ahead. We allowed their forward elements to pass and then we hurled our grenades as fast as we could throw them right in the midst of the enemy lines. I opened up on the forward elements and swung my machine-gun back and forth along the track, sending bursts into their forward and following elements. They thought they were surrounded by a big force and pulled back again.

'They shelled the whole area very heavily – but shells don't do much in this sort of country,' and he waved his hand to the clumps of giant bamboo and its almost impenetrable cover of tightly interlaced trees and creepers. 'Towards evening,' continued this bright young hunter–tactician, 'they attacked with their full company. And then they were really surrounded, because our company had moved up in the meantime. They lost heavily and haven't tried anything since. They have no morale,' he concluded. 'They don't want to fight and whenever they get a chance they come over to us.'

As to how he felt far from his native province, he repeated, 'We find it very cold here after the south. But it must be colder still on the mountaintops. The main thing is that ever since I've been here, apart from the cold, I've felt as if I were in my native village. The people treat us just like their own sons. If we don't hang on and defend our bases here,' and he pointed round to the sombre encircling mountains, which extended in every direction as far as the eye could see, 'then we can never return to our own villages.'

Many of the troops from the south felt the cold: they contracted malaria and bronchial disturbances. In November–December 1955, the period of Katay's greatest efforts to wipe them out, they went cold and hungry for days on end. But they never complained. They knew why they were fighting. And the people throughout all the regions administered by the Pathet Lao knew why they were fighting. On the mountain summits, Katay's troops did not know why they were fighting. They had been told they were being sent to deal with 'invaders' from Viet Nam or China. But they found they were being called on to kill their own brothers and tribespeople.

As the press-gangs scoured the royal provinces for new recruits, young men in the south fled to the mountains. There were demonstrations in Vientiane demanding an end to the civil war and as a first step, negotiations to end it. The defeat of Katay's November–December operations perhaps could be concealed for a time but not for ever. Vientiane hospitals were full of armless and legless victims of the policies Katay was carrying out on behalf of the Americans. And buried in the jungles of distant mountaintops cursing Katay as they went into battle, cursing him as they died, were many more. Katay tried to disperse the wounded as far as possible in the provinces and during the campaign for the December 1955 elections, he presented his defeat as a great 'victory'.

As he controlled the electoral machinery, Katay's party won a majority of seats. It was noteworthy that in Vientiane, where voting and counting procedures were fairly well controlled, the party headed by Thao Bong Souvannavong (who had been the victim of the frame-up in the assassination of Kouvoravong) came out well on top. He had campaigned on the basis of real negotiations with the Pathet Lao to end the civil war. Soon after the elections were over, the real state of affairs at the front became known. Also certain economic scandals in which Katay was involved.

Some people began computing the number of peaks in Sam Neua and Phong Saly in relation to the number of battalions it was possible to raise. Two thirds of the Laotian Army were already engaged and had got nowhere. Katay tried to push Laos into SEATO and made an unsuccessful attempt to get SEATO intervention against the Pathet Lao. But France had no more interest in having Americans take over in Laos than had the British of their taking over in Malaya. Katay's appeal was rejected.

Upon the initiative of Thao Bong Souvannavong, a group of National Salvation was formed inside the National Assembly, pledged to end the war against the Pathet Lao and to base Laotian foreign policy on the five principles of coexistence. Some members of Katay's own party joined this group and when he tried to form a Cabinet, he could not get sufficient support. There was a prolonged government crisis at the very time when Sihanouk's stubborn defence of Cambodian neutrality and rejection of SEATO was attracting world – and Laotian – attention.

Katay tried a second time to form a Cabinet and failed. The Crown Prince wanted Thao Bong Souvannavong to form a government and his name was put forward – but the U.S. Ambassador said he would not be acceptable as Prime Minister. Eventually after almost three months of crisis, Souvanna Phouma succeeded in forming a government. He pledged himself to settle the dispute with the Pathet Lao by diplomatic means, to pursue a policy of neutrality and to base his foreign policy on the five principles of coexistence.

Katay and Dulles and everything they stood for had been defeated in one more round of U.S. efforts to put the chains back around the necks of Asian peoples. The U.S. Government had spent 50,000,000 dollars a year on smashing the Pathet Lao forces. But they reckoned without the people, without the Lao Lum, the Lao Thenh and Lao Kung warriors defending their own mountains and villages, or fighting for the right to go back to their own villages with full citizen rights as promised by the Geneva agreements.

With their superior technique of planes and parachutes, Katay and Dulles overlooked the volunteer porters toiling up and down endless steep slopes to feed munitions and rice to their warrior sons and brothers. They could not imagine the peasants in the rear villages planting extra pounds of seed in their paddy-fields and jungle patches to send food to their compatriots at the front. Nor could they imagine the unity of front and rear, unity of racial groups, the hospitable reception that those of the north accorded to those that had come from the deep south.

The fall of Katay was a sign that a settlement with the Pathet Lao could not be achieved by military means. There could be no liquidation of the Pathet Lao forces and there could be no military occupation of the two northern provinces.

[From Chapter 19 of *Mekong Upstream: A Visit to Laos and Cambodia* (Seven Seas Publishers, Berlin, 1959), pp. 254–269.]

11

Welcome Home [1961]

At the 20th Congress of the Communist Party of the Soviet Union Khruschev denounced Stalin, thus beginning an era of greater openness and tolerance within the Soviet Union and of 'détente' with the West. Burchett moved to Moscow in the spring of 1957 as Moscow correspondent for the left-wing New York weekly *The National Guardian* and was soon recruited by the *Daily Express* – and later the *Sunday Express* and the *Financial Times*.

Burchett was more interested in the conquests of space and virgin lands in the furthest corners of the Soviet Union than in 'Kremlinology', and he produced three books on these 'pioneering' topics.

Cosmonaut Yuri Gagarin: First Man in Space, written with Anthony Purdy, was described by the publishers as 'the first Western evaluation of man's greatest exploit and of Russia's amazing achievements in the exploration of space', and it became an immediate bestseller, except in the US where it was banned as 'Soviet propaganda'.

* * *

At midday on 14 April 1961, an *Ilyushin-18* plane, escorted by seven *MiG* fighters, swept over Vnukovo Airport and on to circle low over Moscow. The Man from Space was about to arrive. Half an hour earlier a similar plane had brought Khruschev from an interrupted Black Sea holiday at Sochi. The airport was decorated with flags and bunting and slogans hailing Yuri Gagarin, Conqueror of the Cosmos. Party and government officials, marshals and generals, leading scientists and engineers who had built the spaceship, ambassadors and the world press, delegates from factories and offices were gathered in a huge, expectant crowd as the silvery plane touched down and taxied up to the end of a long red carpet.

As the single uniformed figure stepped out and tripped nimbly down the gangway, a wave of applause rolled across the expanse of tarmac. A band struck up an old Soviet Air Force song: 'Fly Higher and Higher and Higher.' Journalists scribbled furiously in their notebooks, TV and cine-film cameramen zoomed in with their longest lenses to get the world's first glimpse of the world's first space traveller.

Yuri Gagarin, deceptively tall at first sight in his long military greatcoat, strode down that eighty yards of red carpet to the beginning of an ordeal that must, at moments, have made him pine for the silence and blissful state of cosmic weightlessness he had known so shortly before.

At the other end of the carpet, the distance closing rapidly, was Nikita Khruschev, a chuckling, happy figure, bubbling over with elation and pride, who, when the young major eventually stood before him, stood to attention to hear the report, now and again gravely nodding his head, but with the twinkle in his eyes never far away.

The speech over, the emotion was released; a full minute's all-embracing bear hug, while the two men exchanged unknown words, all but drowned beneath the roar of shouts, handclapping, stamping of feet, whistling and singing that through TV and radio was rippling out to every country in the world. Tears glistened in 80-year-old Voroshilov's eyes; President Brezhnev was speechless with delight. After the Soviet national anthem, Khruschev directed Gagarin into the arms of his wife Valya, his parents, brother and sister, waiting, slightly dazed by it all, in a V.I.P. pen below a battery of cameras and microphones.

Everyone of importance in Russia who could be there, was there, straining to shake the hand, or catch a glimpse of, the man who had seen and done things that no mortal had seen and done before.

The airport scene had all the elements of a great historic event, literally of cosmic proportions. And yet it was also very down-to-earth and human. Fortunately no one had the idea of putting father Alexei or mother Anna into special clothes for the occasion. There they stood, carpenter and peasant, dressed in the rough clothes of the hammer-and-sickle age they represented, he wearing his carpenter's cap, she her peasant's shawl welcoming the son who only fifty hours previously had been unzipped from his astronaut's orange space suit and helmet. Father, not very comfortable among the great, doffing his cap now and again when someone smiled at him, rubbing his hands over the stubbly, shaven head. Mother fighting a battle with the tears of pride and joy that welled in her eyes and the need for courage and dignity worthy of such a son, such an occasion and such company. Valya, his gentle-faced wife, modestly in the background, her eyes glistening behind the spectacles.

Mother and wife need not have been ashamed of tears for this occasion. Tough President Brezhnev and old Voroshilov brushed away their tears too as the embraces and hugs and warm words of praise and welcome continued on the improvised tribune and the crowd strained forward to catch intimate glimpses of their hero. Then down from the tribune to be presented by Khruschev to the diplomatic corps – and what black-hatted, striped-trousered ambassador was not secretly a little thrilled to shake the hand that two days before had been at the controls of the spaceship.

Into an open, flower-bedecked car together with Khruschev and Valya, his wife, for a triumphal drive into the city. It was 'flowers, flowers all the way.' None could remember such a welcome and the general jubilation was said by Muscovites to be matched only by that on VE day. Official decorations for May Day had been hastily rushed up a few hours previously with City Council trucks laden with banners and flags and coloured lights racing around the city all night in a fever of activity. But the 'unofficial' decorations were provided by a million or so Muscovites who packed the last ten miles of the built-up part of the route from the airport, bouquets of flowers in hands, flags with rocket silhouettes, pictures of Gagarin, slogans and banners and crying: 'Now for the Moon,' 'On to the Planets,' 'Welcome Hero Yuri Gagarin,' 'Glory to Columbus of the Cosmos,' and so on. Along Leninsky Prospekt and its three solid miles of new houses and shops – each balcony with its red banner – down into the older part of the town. Gagarin with his easy smile; Khruschev happier than anyone remembered seeing him before; Valya with her gentle unwavering smile and moist, bespectacled eyes.

People swept forward, narrowing broad boulevards into tiny rivulets along which the police had difficulty in squeezing the triumphal cavalcade. It was Gagarin's day and the people had taken over the streets. A riotously happy, improvised holiday by public consent.

Red Square, where a meeting was scheduled after the airport reception, was a sea of people and riot of colour. Between a huge portrait of Gagarin at the History Museum end and the 70-ft. high model of a rocket soaring into space at the St Basil's Church end, the huge square was packed with just enough space for half a million paraders to file through after the speeches.

It was May Day and November 7 rolled into one. Party and government leaders with Gagarin as the focal point gathered on the Mausoleum tribune under which lie the embalmed bodies of Lenin and Stalin. Uniformed marshals and generals jostled for place with scientists, students and diplomatists in the granite stands below.

Nothing in Gagarin's ordeals of space training had prepared him for this. His own speech, to a crowd which madly cheered every sentence, was a brief one, mainly of thanks to party and government for having entrusted the first space flight to his hands; to the scientists, engineers and workers who built the spaceship, to all those who took part in preparing him for the flight. There was prolonged, tumultuous applause when he said: 'I am sure that all my fellow space pilots are ready to fly around our planet at any time. We can state confidently that we shall fly our Soviet spaceships on more distant routes.'

Then it was Khruschev's turn. He started his oration by listing the 'noble moral traits, courage, self-determination and valour'; praised 'this first person who for an hour and a half looked at our entire planet . . . viewed its tremendous oceans and continents . . . our pioneer in space flights . . .' Gagarin listened with the solemn, awed look of a man realizing for the first time that he had done something really big. 'If the name of Columbus, who crossed the Atlantic Ocean and discovered America, has been living on through the ages,' continued Khruschev warming up to his theme, 'what is to be said about our wonderful hero, Comrade Gagarin, who penetrated into outer space, circled the entire terrestrial globe and returned safely to Earth? His name will be immortal in the history of mankind.' And so on and much more.

Khruschev's words were aimed far beyond the hundreds of thousands in Red Square and the tens of millions elsewhere in the Soviet Union at their TV and radio sets. He was addressing a world audience of hundreds of millions (for the first time, by a happy coincidence, the Gagarin reception celebrations were carried on direct telecast to the whole of Europe – to England by the B.B.C., to West Europe by Eurovision, to East Europe by Intervision). It was a great historic occasion of which Khruschev was determined to make the most. And his voice rang with pride as he ran over the background to the Gagarin flight.

> Now when Soviet science and technique have demonstrated the highest achievement of scientific and technical progress, we cannot help looking back to the history of our country. In our mind's eye we cannot help seeing the years that have passed . . . We have defended our state in the fire of civil war even though we were often barefooted and half naked . . . When we stand beside the man who made the first space flight, we cannot help recalling the name of the Russian scientist and revolutionary, Kibalchich, who dreamed of flight to space but who was executed by the Tsarist Government . . . It is with special respect that we recall the name of Konstantin Eduardovich Tsiolkovsky, scientist, dreamer and theoretician of space flights . . .

It was when Khruschev started reading out the awards – 'Hero of the Soviet Union' – the first 'Pilot-Cosmonaut of the Soviet Union' – that the blinks started in Gagarin's eyes. They came faster when Khruschev started to eulogize his parents and the firm lips started to tremble at the warm tribute to his wife. The TV cameramen mercifully turned their camera lenses away for a while. It was a rather comforting moment to realize that a hero of outer space, conditioned to the most fearsome physical and psychological ordeals, can also produce tears; that the vibration stands and centrifuges had not annihilated emotions. 'A fine woman, Valentina Ivanovna,' said Khruschev. 'She knew Yuri Alexeyevich was departing into outer space but she did not dissuade him. On the contrary, she gave her heart's blessing to this noble exploit of her husband, the father of her two little children. Remember that no one could completely guarantee that the parting with Yuri Alexeyevich would not be the last one. Her courage and realization of the tremendous importance of that unparalleled flight show the great soul of Valentina Ivanovna ... She demonstrated her fine character, her willpower and her understanding of Soviet patriotism.'

There was terrific applause from the crowd when Khruschev referred to 'not very clever people on the other side of the ocean' who refused to believe the news of the first Soviet sputnik launching.

'Now,' he shouted, with a triumphant, ruddy smile, 'we can actually touch a person who has returned from the sky.' Khruschev dwelt for a moment on the wider implications of Gagarin's feat, what it meant for the future: 'The flight of the "Vostok" is only the first swallow in outer space. It soared aloft in the wake of our many sputniks and probes. It represents a natural outcome of the titanic scientific and technological work carried out in our country for space conquest. We shall continue this work in the future. More and more Soviet people will fly along unexplored routes into outer space and probe the mysteries of nature still further, placing them at the service of man and his well-being, at the service of peace. We stress,' he said, and he became very serious, 'at the service of peace. Soviet people do not want these rockets which can fulfil programmes laid down by man with such amazing accuracy, ever to carry lethal cargoes.' And he repeated his earlier pleas to 'the governments of the world' to take all possible steps towards 'general and complete disarmament.'

After the speeches – the monster parade. A mighty river of people with flags and flowers in hand and banners floating overhead, surging into Red Square. Every pair of eyes straining towards the trim, uniformed hero on the tribune. Impossible to miss him, wedged in between the beaming, ebullient Khruschev and a radiant Voroshilov. In the background the crenellated red walls of the Kremlin, the green-roofed cream palaces and churches, their golden domes and palace windows sparkling in the evening sun. How much history have those palaces and churches – and especially the noble Spassky Clock Tower that dominates the square – seen in their time!

But never a day like 14 April 1961, because the world itself had never known such a day.

Across the vast cobbled square the molten river poured, dividing up to leave that multi-coloured jewel of St. Basil's an island behind it, before joining up again for a brief descent to the Moscow River where it split up into tributaries carrying the components to their chosen place for continuing the celebrations.

Later that evening, the culmination of the day's rejoicing – a fabulous Kremlin reception. While some two thousand guests feasted and drank inside, the people thronged the streets and squares, and packed the bridges to admire the floodlit Kremlin towers. Etched against a sky exploding with myriad-coloured showers of fireworks and all reflected in the calm waters of the Moscow River. As the salvoes of the salute to Gagarin crashed out, the tips of the Kremlin towers were wreathed in smoke and with the bursting cascades of colour overhead it was one of those fairytale pictures that Moscow reserves for the very great occasions.

Inside the Kremlin, guests had gathered in the lofty St. George's Hall of the Grand Palace. Walls and pillars of milk-white marble, enormous gold and crystal chandeliers glittering overhead. Everyone who was anyone in Soviet public life was there. Delicate ballerinas and burly bemedalled marshals; composers and scientists; circus stars and space technicians; diplomatists and journalists – and of course all the Communist Party and government leaders.

When the scene was set – Khruschev arrived with Yuri and Valya Gagarin, and parents Alexei and Anna.

Khruschev, bubbling over with pleasure as he had been all day, guided the group to the space at the head of the hall, reserved on such occasions for the very honoured guests, with party and government leaders and foreign diplomatists in their wake.

The formal part of the proceedings was soon over. President Leonid Brezhnev, a former engineer with a rugged face dominated by huge shaggy eyebrows, read the decrees of the Supreme Soviet conferring on Major Yuri Gagarin the titles of Hero of the Soviet Union and Pilot-Cosmonaut of the Soviet Union. Amid thunderous 'hurrahs' and applause and much clinking of glasses, Brezhnev pinned on Gagarin's breast the Order of Lenin and the Gold Star Medal that go with the 'Hero' title, and then embraced him. A brass band struck up a quickstep march which is the signal at Kremlin receptions to down some quick toasts. From that moment, the atmosphere was riotously gay and relaxed. Normally staid, reserved government leaders competed with each other to kiss and hug the hero. Minister of Defence, Marshal Rodion Malinovsky, a massive bear of a man with iron-grey hair and a normally severe expression, swept the cosmonaut high up off his feet in a crushing embrace which must have recalled the boost period at take-off. There were toasts and more toasts, from the Chief of the Air Force, Marshal Vershinin, from Khruschev again, from representatives of workers, peasants and intellectuals.

The whole Gagarin family were there among the leaders, including the wife of one of Yuri's brothers. Khruschev insisted there and then on a group photo of the Gagarin family together with himself, Brezhnev, Voroshilov, Malinovsky and Vice-Premier Frol Kozlov.

By this time with toasts and music and general gaiety, the parents were as relaxed as anyone else. Clad in dark clothes now, more befitting the atmosphere of a Kremlin reception. Father Alexei looked uncomfortable in his more formal clothes, but pride in his son's exploits overcame any uneasiness at this – or perhaps it was suddenly being thrust shoulder-to-shoulder with the most important in the land.

Throughout the Kremlin reception, as at the airport, a balance was struck between the sense of historic importance of what was being celebrated and the human down-to-earth side of things. The space hero was put on a pedestal, it is true – the highest in the land. No Soviet citizen had ever been so feted and decorated in such a short time (the pedestal is no literary allusion. Khruschev, from the tribune in Red Square, promised a bronze bust of Gagarin would be set up in Moscow and a special medal issued to commemorate the first manned space flight). But every effort was also made to portray Yuri Gagarin as a very mortal bit of flesh and blood, a father, husband and son, with wife, parents, brothers and sisters like other ordinary humans. All entitled to a share of reflected glory. It would have been easy to have pushed him up to such cosmic heights that would set a spaceman apart from ordinary humans. As it was, most people, looking at that family group, watching their emotions, knowing their background, felt that Gagarin's feat was a great triumph for mankind itself. Soviet young men and women felt especially that there was nothing supernatural about Yuri Gagarin. Given the same chance and with the same grit to overcome training difficulties, they too could follow along the trail he had blazed.

Gagarin Day closed in Moscow with some of the greatest Soviet artists paying homage to the hero in a concert which followed the speeches and toasts.

Sviatoslav Richter, wearing the Lenin Prize medal awarded him only a few days previously for his great artistry, played Rachmaninov; ballerina Maya Plissetsskaya outdid her usual brilliance in a scene from 'The Little Hunch-Backed Horse.' The best song and dance ensembles in the country danced and sang their legs and heads off while the vodka and champagne flowed among the guests.

Long after the Kremlin reception was over and official celebrations had finished, the crowds danced and sang in Red Square; packed Gorky Street and the Moscow River Embankment. Till the small hours of the morning, the city was alive with laughter and song to complete a day that can never be repeated. A day and night of homage to the first mortal to reach for the stars.

[Chapter 1 of Wilfred Burchett and Anthony Purdy, *Cosmonaut Yuri Gagarin: First Man in Space* (Panther Books, London, 1961), pp. 11–20.]

5: *Yuri Gagarin with Wilfred Burchett, Moscow, 1961*

12

Gagarin: The First Interview with Western Journalists [1961]

With he and Purdy being the only Western journalists permitted to meet Gagarin, the following interview was one of Burchett's great scoops. Gagarin's achievement was inevitably the biggest story in the world, and readers everywhere wanted to know more about him and his flight.

He was born in Klushino on 9 March 1934, to parents who worked on a collective farm, although his mother was reportedly a voracious reader and his father a skilled carpenter. In 1955, after completing his technical schooling, he entered military flight training at the Orenburg Pilot's School, and was subsequently assigned to Luostari Airbase in Murmansk Oblast, close to the Norwegian border. In 1960, after an extensive search and selection process Gagarin was chosen with 19 other cosmonauts for the Soviet space program. Out of the twenty selected, Gagarin and Gherman Titov were eventually chosen for the first launch due to their excellent performance in training, as well as their physical characteristics – fully grown, Gagarin was 5 ft 2 in (1.57 m) tall, which was an advantage in the small Vostok cockpit. Burchett later also published a book about Titov.

It was on 12 April 1961 that Yuri Gagarin became the first human to travel into space in Vostok 1. While in orbit Gagarin was promoted 'in the field' from the rank of Senior Lieutenant to Major, and this was the rank given in the triumphant TASS announcement during the flight. Once safely returned, Gagarin issued a statement praising the Communist Party of the Soviet Union as the 'organiser of all our victories'. After the flight, Gagarin became an instant, worldwide celebrity, touring widely with appearances in Italy, Germany, Canada and Japan to promote the Soviet achievement.

* * *

On Friday, 9 June 1961, Gagarin interrupted his leave to see Burchett and Purdy in Moscow. It was his first and only meeting with Western journalists, face to face across a table. His press conferences had been huge, theatrical affairs, highly organized, with questioning restricted by time and security, with the atmosphere as impersonal as at a barrack-room briefing.

The private meeting was in marked contrast. It took place in a big, old-fashioned room of the State Committee for Cultural Foreign Relations, on the fringe of old Moscow.

Outside, it was hot; 80 degrees. In the courtyard Gagarin's official car was parked alongside Burchett's green-and-cream Ford Zodiac. One of the drivers brought out a deckchair and sunglasses and settled down in the shade of the high green hedge.

Inside, the room was cool and dark, but with a little tension in the air. While Gagarin was downstairs with the chief of the Foreign Press Bureau, the photographer, very slightly nervous, was pacing out distances for every possible situation. A tall, handsome young interpreter, also from the Foreign Press Bureau, said cheerfully: 'I never thought this would happen, you know,' and went on, 'even we don't know how this has been managed. It is difficult enough for our own journalists to talk to the major, and we have had applications for interviews with him from every country in the world. They have all been turned down.'

The arrangements for this meeting had, in fact, been fixed only two hours before, but the groundwork had taken weeks. The first request from the authors went to the Soviet authorities (in company with a thousand others!) only hours after the announcement that Vostok was in orbit. Soon scores of letters, telegrams, memorandums and telephone calls were passing; Purdy twice had to fly to Moscow from London at twelve hours' notice. *Isvestia* reported his arrival and the fact that the two men were 'working round the clock in two shifts.' While one wrote, the other carried out interviews. Sleep was forgotten for long periods. But all the time they were waiting . . . waiting for word that they could see the man who, to Westerners and all but a handful of Russians, is the most inaccessible in the world. One Moscow scientist jokingly told them: 'Now, if it was Mr. Khruschev, I'm sure you would be successful. He talks to journalists every day. But Yuri Gagarin. . .' and he shook his head.

Even the photographer was excited. As an official cameraman, he had taken pictures of the cosmonaut at several public functions, but he had never been the only photographer present, had never seen him relaxed, or closer than across a room. Gagarin had always been on a stage, but at 1.15 p.m. on that Friday, there he was, walking, sitting and talking with the audience...

Gagarin entered briskly, alone and smiling. The first impression was of his good-natured personality; big smile – a grin, really – light step and an air of sunny friendliness. He is short, stocky and powerfully built. But the key to his character, perhaps, lay in two other points: his handshake, and his eyes. His hands are incredibly hard; his eyes an almost luminous blue. 'Never,' said Burchett, 'have I seen eyes like that.' 'And never,' said Purdy, 'have I felt a grip like his.'

With the two writers on either side of him, Gagarin, wearing a well-cut dark blue suit, white shirt and silver tie and holiday sandals, sat down easily on a velvet sofa. He eyed the pile of papers – this manuscript – on the table, and pretended alarm. 'The next man to go up,' he joked, 'should be a writer!'

His attitude to questions was, like the very fact of the interview, unexpected. They had not been submitted, nor even asked for, beforehand. No one except Burchett and Purdy knew what was to be said. Yet in no single case was there hesitation in his reply, and the translations were instantaneous. Words tumbled out, facts and jokes and interjections, with pauses only to refresh his memory. He gestured with his hands constantly, trying to draw pictures in the air. 'My worst moment?' His right arm shot up. 'The first minute' – the hand swooped down – 'and the re-entry.' He tapped the table with his finger. 'But "worst" is a comparative word. There wasn't one "bad" moment. Everything worked, everything was organized properly, nothing went wrong. It was a walk, really.'

He talked with simple pride about the instruments and the ship itself, and the ground staff at Baikonur. 'The support I had, each man giving of his very best, gave me great confidence,' he said.

To whom did he speak on the ground? A scientist, a radio operator, or a fellow cosmonaut? Purdy explained that Shepard had reported during his flight to one man, a friend and colleague, because scientists said it would help him psychologically.

Gagarin thought for a moment. 'Well,' he said, 'I spoke to a lot of people from up there, not just one or two – many people. It made me feel pretty good. I remember them playing that song – "Moscow

Nights" – and some Tchaikovsky and ballads and army songs I knew. Somehow it didn't feel lonely at all.' He leaned forward, clasping and unclasping his hands. 'It's difficult to describe, but I really felt as if I had the whole country with me.' He couldn't help remembering at that time, he said, the staggering number of people who had put him into orbit, the scientists who, starting with Tsiolkovsky, had contributed to Vostok's triumph. Gagarin seldom referred to 'my flight'; it was always 'our flight' or 'the country's achievement.' Listening to him, watching his eyes, it was easier to understand that his formal speeches at Vnukovo Airport and in Red Square, speeches that were strangely unreal and artificial to Western ears, were in fact completely sincere; Gagarin is an officer, a space pilot and a party member, not an orator. Examining him closely, Purdy was amused and relieved to see other evidence that he was not completely perfect: a mole on his left cheek (was that taken into account?) and a minute cut where he must have nicked himself that morning, shaving.

Discussing Commander Shepard's trip, Gagarin regretted that he had not read the astronaut's own account of it – 'I'm supposed to be on leave, you know,' he chuckled. Nonetheless, he had followed the published progress of the American's training with great interest. From the start of their own programme, the Baikonur team had been reading and discussing the American methods in relation to their own. One thing had puzzled them, although it was a matter of no concern to the men themselves: why U.S. doctors preferred chimpanzees to dogs for human 'stand-ins.' The general opinion: 'They make better pictures.' And Gagarin laughed again when Burchett, quoting from American newspaper reports, asked why the manual controls of Vostok had not been used. 'The American view,' said Burchett, 'is that Shepard's flight was superior to yours in one way, in that he actually controlled it himself.'

'How much driving can you do in five minutes?' the major asked, almost incredulously. 'And what was the point of it? I could have guided Vostok had I wanted to; there was a dual control, we knew it worked, and that was enough. It was, after all, a secondary system, and I had many priority jobs in a very crowded schedule; I was busy every second, and I was travelling at eight kilometres per second. The tiniest error, say at the moment the braking system was switched on, just could not be permitted, and my mind was entirely occupied with these things. Manual control was not necessary or important.' Ground control did at one point ask him if he wished to 'take over' but he was absorbed in writing copious notes on instrument behaviour in zero-gravity, and declined the offer. The pilot-control was an exact duplication of the radio-control, and enabled him to undertake the whole landing and choose his landing spot as well, if he wished.

As with the scientists that the authors interviewed, the American Project Mercury was talked about by Gagarin without a trace of patronage or any jarring note of superiority. There was genuine admiration; though in discussing Shepard further, Gagarin could not resist adding: 'Please remember that ours was an entirely different kind of flight, for a different purpose. Vostok was a spaceship, built to go up and stay up. There was ten days' supply of food in that cabin. Shepard's was a ballistic trajectory. Still, it was a great achievement.'

He had seen pictures of the American capsule and instrument panel. 'But it's difficult to compare the two. Vostok's cabin was very big; the thrust of the engines was much greater. We had to go higher and faster for a much longer time with a much bigger rocket.'

Did he experience any sensations he had not undergone in training? 'A complicated question to answer. All the time there were different sensations, different feelings, of course. They lasted for seconds only, often, and there was really no time to analyse them. I was so busy; it was just work, work, work. Of course there was discomfort, there were great stresses on the body, but the training programme had been extremely rigorous and thorough, and included just about everything.' Weightlessness, he said, was 'interesting' but not uncomfortable. He is the only man in the world to have experienced this strange sensation for more than five minutes in flight, and, indeed, one of the objects of the flight was to see how man could stand up to a condition that could not be satisfactorily simulated on Earth. His report: 'No real problems.'

Gagarin talked earnestly for a few moments about his future. He wanted, he said, to go up again, and would shortly begin another course of training. This time he would know more than his instructors. What would he like to achieve next? 'Another flight.' Where? 'Well, anywhere it is necessary to go.' The Moon? 'A bit early to talk about that now, but I could fly a bit longer, much farther, in that ship. I have no doubt that there will be a Soviet citizen on the Moon one day, and we are all hoping that the day will not be far off.'

He wore only one decoration on his lounge suit – a badge that had just been presented to him, two hours before, by the Young Communist League. He is very proud of the honours that have been showered upon him, but always links them with the team who made it possible. One person is not so modest: his daughter Lena. 'At school, and to all her friends,' he laughed, 'she goes around saying: "My Daddy's a space man; my Daddy's a Hero of the Soviet Union!"'

Before he left, the young major collected another memento of his historic trip. Burchett's father, at 88 the oldest working journalist in Australia, was on holiday in Moscow at the time. In his luggage was a hunting boomerang, and he walked into the room with it just as Gagarin was leaving. 'Please take this,' he said, holding it out, 'as a symbol of safe return. It always comes back, and I hope you and your colleagues do too.' Gagarin, delighted, examined the precision-carved weapon closely, while one of the interpreters rapidly explained its use, and how experts could actually catch it on its return. 'I shall treasure it,' said Gagarin, swishing it a few inches through the air. 'It's a nice sort of symbol to have.'

[Chapter 11 of Wilfred Burchett and Anthony Purdy, *Cosmonaut Yuri Gagarin: First Man in Space* (Panther Books, London, 1961), pp. 118–123.]

13

Virgin Lands [1962]

Come East Young Man was Burchett's excursion into the virgin lands of Siberia, which no doubt reminded him of the 'virgin lands' of his native Gippsland in Australia. For those who believed that the Soviet Union was an 'Evil Empire', the book is pure propaganda. But for those who took a more benign view, the book was a positive assessment of the post-war and post-Stalin USSR, with its hopes, promises and contradictions.

As such, the book is a further representative, after *People's Democracies*, of a whole genre of writing in which Western left-wing journalists conveyed the optimism of many of the inhabitants of the socialist states to audiences used to the McCarthyite anti-Communism which dominated Western media at the time. There was a genuine belief among such writers that these new regimes offered a viable and rewarding alternative to a failing capitalism, and they attempted to convince their readership with extensive facts and statistics about the new societies.

* * *

At the small town of Ossipovichi, about sixty miles southeast of the Byelorussian capital of Minsk, a significant and moving ceremony took place in the early summer of 1960. Soldiers of the Fifth Red Banner Heavy Tank Division paraded for the last time in a sunny, grass-covered barracks square. Their commander, Colonel of the Guards Ivan Velichko, made a short speech reminding them of the fine record of the Division. From its birthplace in Tadjikistan the Division helped expel the Nazi invaders from the North Caucasus, chased them out of the Ukraine and Moldavia back across Eastern Europe – through Rumania, Hungary, Yugoslavia and onto Austria. Now the Division was to be disbanded – one of dozens of complete units being dissolved following a January 1960 decision to reduce the Soviet armed forces by another 1,200,000 men. Colonel

Velichko recalled Khrushchev's words: 'We need strong hands and warm hearts all over our country – in Kazakhstan, Siberia and the Altai Territory . . .'

The divisional banner which they had borne half-way across Europe was carried down in front of the tribune. Officers, non-coms and privates, representing their different units, stepped forward and knelt to kiss the flag. An order was given that it be consigned to the Soviet Army Museum in Moscow. Following a final march past their commander, the troops were dismissed. A Soviet tank division ceased to exist.

All the soldiers, all the non-coms and most of the officers were now demobilised. And forty percent of them had volunteered for the virgin lands.

I spoke with one trio of lance-corporals: Ivan Kokoshkin, Mikhail Zhukov and Mahmet Tulokov – stocky carefree youngsters of twenty-two. They had served two years, and were being demobbed a year ahead of time. They had volunteered to go together to the Altai regions, just across Kazakhstan's northeast border with Siberia.

What to do? I asked.

'We'll learn to drive combines,' said Kokoshkin, and Tulokov added with a laugh: 'Driving a combine or a tank's not much different – except for the results.'

They would go first to an Altai school for tractor- and combine-drivers and then be allotted to a sovkhoz.

'We're determined to stick together,' Zhukov said. 'Others have already formed bigger teams of drivers and mechanics. They've elected their own leaders from specialists and we hope to work together as a unit.'

An hour or two later, another ceremony took place at the railway station. Thousands of people had turned out to see the ex-soldiers off. There were some moving speeches from the local population. The words of one young woman stuck in my memory for a long time:

> Your leaving us shows again that our leaders are for peace. Peace! Peace is our good morning: our joyous day; our peaceful night. Success and happiness for all of you in your new life.

As they embarked aboard the waiting train, people surged forward smothering them with flowers and embraces – and good advice about raising bumper crops in the virgin lands. There were plenty of wet eyes among those departing and among farewellers as the train glided slowly away – carrying these young people to join the hundreds of thousands who, since 1954, have responded to the call 'Come East, Young Man!'.

It was a daring scheme – denounced by many at the time as a 'gamble' – to plough up and sow to grain ninety million acres of untried land; where there were no villages, no roads, no fields, no past experience to draw upon; and, its greatest deficiency, no people; where the climate set categorical limits on ploughing, sowing and harvesting periods: where a whole agricultural cycle had to be fitted in between the unfreezing of the earth and the blanketing of it with snow high enough to bury the tallest wheat.

It presented not only material, physical problems. Science and industry could do much. But even if the agro-biologists could produce frost-resistant strains that would ripen within the limits set by nature, and even if industry could produce the machines to plough and plant and harvest vast areas within the limits set by scientists and nature – what about the human element? How were they to get people to enter into such conditions of nature and climate? Especially since some nine million – mostly young people – had deserted the land for the cities in the early post-war years? In this case, one needed to know one's people – to have faith in them.

And this is something which Khrushchev had in plenty: The confidence in his own people, nourished by intimate contact with them. It was not a 'gamble'. People responded as he knew they would – quite as the soil responded in the way the scientists promised it would.

What this has meant in terms of bread for the Soviet dining table is best illustrated by the fact that Soviet wheat production increased by over 50 percent from 1953 to 1959 thanks to the virgin lands . . .

The atmosphere at Ossipovichi and the morale of that trainload of troops were impressive. All could have been going home, had they wanted to; 60 percent of their comrades were doing just that. I spoke to many such: Twenty-three-year-old Sergeant Igor Ilyukhin, who was returning to Moscow to finish a course as building engineer; Captain Lev Dulkin, off to his home town to work as a garage mechanic; Alexei Meshkov, staying on in Ossipovichi to build roads – and many others. Perhaps the morale of the east-bound ones was high because they had no idea what lay ahead? Perhaps after a short trial they would want to return home?

Shortly after the Ossipovichi visit, I spent several days at the Kamensk-Uralsk Sovkhoz in North Kazakhstan. Apart from the grain, meat and butter situation, the morale of the young people was of particular interest to me.

First – about the farm itself – huge for those parts. Just over 100,000 acres, of which about 40,000 were under cultivation; 30,000 acres of pasture; most of the rest covered with forest and lakes. Kuzma Grigoriev, the farm manager, a nuggety, energetic figure and one of the few on the farm to have been brought up in North Kazakhstan, talked of how things started.

'When the first group of us arrived in March 1955, this was snow-covered steppe,' he said. 'We reckon we killed the last wolf around here this past autumn. Our first group was one hundred and eighty men from Kamensk-Uralsk.[1] They had responded to the appeal and were first to get here, which is how the farm got its name. We put up tents and started to build houses. Timber was partly from our own woods, partly sent up from Kustenai, about 70 miles south. A couple of months later, the first tractors arrived and in the spring of 1953 we sowed 11,000 acres of wheat from which we harvested 1350 tons of grain.

'The same men that built the houses drove the tractors and combines. That was only the start. This year we planted 38,000 acres of wheat.'

I asked about the butter and meat aspect and manager Grigoriev explained that he had originally thought if they could produce grain it would be enough. But after the farm settled down – they had four hundred and sixty workers and their families – they added livestock to grain farming. Now the farm supported cows, young stock and fatteners for beef, 1400 cattle in all; 5500 sheep; 7900 poultry; 460 pigs and 100 horses. After agricultural zones had been defined for Kazakhstan, livestock received top priority. By 1965, the plan called for 2000 head of cattle, 10,000 sheep, 20,000 poultry – and no pigs.

Why no pigs?

'We are situated on a good, asphalt road that leads directly to Kustenai and Rudni. We can carry eggs easily without risk of breaking them. So we will concentrate on poultry – farms further away from the good roads will go in for pigs. Bacon or pork doesn't crack,' he laughed. 'The concept of our farm has changed, you see. Originally it was to produce cheap grain for our western areas. Our main job now is to supply our own cities with milk and meat, butter and eggs. Our farm is close to the city – and so our role has changed. Life itself forces that kind of decision.'

'Didn't factory managers in Kamensk-Uralsk protest about workers quitting for the virgin lands? Didn't they say this or that chap is too valuable in industry to waste on agriculture?'

'There were such cases,' replied Kuzma Grigoriev, 'but they couldn't stop anyone from going. If somebody had put his name down and insisted on going – nobody and no power could stop him. Don't forget it was the Party and Government that launched the appeal.'

I asked if any had become disillusioned and left, and he said, 'No. They are building something together – something new and growing. But ask them, yourself, why don't you?'

It was Sunday evening, and some yards from the manager's office people were waiting for the cinema to open. The first person I spoke with was twenty-six-year-old Victor Panchenko, a slim, alert, neatly dressed young man, whose home town was Voronezh. He had been demobbed from the army during an earlier armed forces cut – made at the time the appeal for the virgin lands went out.

'That's something for me, I thought,' he said. 'Virgin lands. A new future! So I put my name down – and was one of the first to arrive here. They were short of tractor hands. I had driven a tank – and had no trouble with tractors. At first I helped cut and hauled timber from the forest for housing. Then from 1957 onwards I was a radio technician. The farm's pretty big and we keep contact with the different brigades by radio.'

'Isn't that a fairly passive job for someone who has come to conquer the virgin steppes?' I asked.

'It's not just passing on messages. I have to follow things through. Some brigade needs a spare part. They contact me and I contact the depot and follow the thing through till the brigade signals they have got the part and it's the right one. My orders on such things have to be carried out – and quickly. I am very happy with this job – and with life here in general.'

I asked about personal plans and he explained that the army call-up had cut short his general education and he was starting a course the following year.

By chance the next person I tackled, Nikolai Borodkin, was also from Voronezh. His parents had been killed by bombing during the war and he was evacuated to Alma Ata with other children. In 1947 – when he was sixteen – he went to a school for tractorists and from there had been called up by the army. When he was demobbed in the summer of 1955, he decided to make for the virgin lands.

'I had married before entering the army and we had one child. But my wife never hesitated about coming here.' A plump fresh-faced young woman was clinging to his arm as he spoke, smiling her approval.

'Now we've got a second child. I borrowed 6000 roubles from the State to build a four-room house. We worked hard and paid it back the same year. We have a nice garden, a cow, pig and poultry – everything we want, really.'

Where were the children while the parents were at the cinema?

'There's a good creche and kindergarten here – but at the moment my wife's mother is looking after them.'

What did he think of the future?

'When you look back you can say that what's been done is good. I can show you pictures of how it looked when I came. Only tents. We're satisfied and like the pioneering life. Of course, there's room for improvement. The quality of building work needs to be improved – especially a better finish. It's a question we're discussing these days. We have to build up some of the weaker sections. But in general things are good.'

As a tractor-driver, Nikolai Borodkin averaged about 1100 roubles a month – most of which he could put away.

The third one I spoke to was Ivan Mekhov, a former worker at the Chelyabinsk tractor plant. He had made his application to settle on the virgin lands through the local trade union commit-tee. Within about three weeks, he had his discharge, documents, travel tickets, etc. At first he worked as a mechanic, and later as a combine-driver in the season, and as a tractor-driver and mechanic between harvests. His wife and three children were with him – they had a three-room house, built with a state loan. How much interest had he paid?

'If I pay back on time – within ten years – not only do I pay no interest but only 65 percent of the loan. It's a sort of state subsidy to encourage building.'

How did he like the life?

'Wonderful. Nothing like it. Cold in winter. But there's plenty of elbow room. Nature here is great – the woods full of mushrooms and berries. Plenty of wild duck about and plenty of fish in the lakes. There's no place like it. Wouldn't get me back to Chelyabinsk for anything.'

What did he do in his free time?

'Football – volleyball – motor-cycle racing.' Yes, he had his own motorbike. 'Also fishing, hunting and taking my wife to the cinema.'

The film that evening was *Mamlyuk*, based on the exploits of a nineteenth-century Ukrainian patriot. A different film was screened every evening six nights a week, unless the public demanded a repeat showing of a particular film. On the seventh night, Saturday, there was dancing in the local hall.

During the days that followed it became obvious that these three young men were typical of the place – young people who in a few years had sunk their roots deep into the virgin soil – modern, young farmers content to have something growing up under their capable hands. Proud of the past, satisfied with the present, confident of the future. There have been, and still are, all sorts of hardships and difficulties which they obviously did not want to discuss with an outsider. Life had been more than tough for the first year or two. But the relaxed, cheerful faces of the young men and women chatting outside that cinema told me their story . . .

I asked Kuzma Grigoriev, what about the articles that had appeared in the Soviet press citing examples of farmers who were putting their private plots and animals into the common pool, while here they were emphasising the benefits of private plots, cows, pigs, and so on. What did he think about abolishing the private plots?

'That's the ultimate goal,' he said. 'But that can only be done after a farm is well established and well organised. Remember that many of our young people came here because of the incentive for a small plot of land, a house and a cow. When we've got things running well, with milking machines, thriving vegetable plots and plenty of recreation facilities, the people will come around to it. They'll find out themselves it's a waste of time trying to be a private farmer and a wage-earning one as well.'

The virgin lands can absorb millions more people. When the last cut-back in the armed forces was announced, newspapers were flooded with appeals from ministries, economics councils and even individual farms in Siberia and Kazakhstan for the demobbed soldiers to come their way. One, published in *Izvestia* on 27 April 1960, was from L. G. Melnikov, Chairman of the Kazakhstan State Planning Commission.

He called for an extra 200,000 workers of different trades, and listed the vast riches of the Republic in natural resources, outlined future plans[2] and offered all newcomers work and housing and an opportunity to acquire the trade they want.

'Come to our hospitable Siberia. Great deeds await you!' was the appeal from the Komsomolets State Farm, near Lake Baikal. Among the farm benefits it listed were a hospital, four medical centres, 'a polyclinic to be opened this year', eleven schools, six clubs, three libraries and . . . 'during field work the average monthly earnings of machine operators are 1500 to 1700 roubles. All state farm workers have personal plots of land'.

The plots of land and good pay and other material incentives were important. But unless the people had had the pioneering spirit necessary to wrest the wealth from the virgin lands and the vision to realise its enormous benefits for the whole country, this gigantic endeavour would have failed. But it did not.

[From Chapter 4 of *Come East Young Man* (Seven Seas Books, Berlin, 1962), pp. 55–68.]

6: *Pyotr Maximov, one of the tens of thousands of Soviet youth who answered the call: 'Come East, Young Man!', 1962*

14

Lilac and Outer Space [1962]

On occasions Burchett managed to step outside the somewhat prosaic materialism of the new socialist states, and beyond the production statistics and population figures which often rendered this type of journalism rather turgid. This is the case in the following chapter of *Come East Young Man*, where he takes readers into a more philosophical realm by letting his good Moscow friend, the great Russian writer and humanist Ilya Ehrenburg, try to sort out the contradictions between the spiritual and material aspirations of *homo sovieticus*.

Ehrenburg was a prolific writer who was an important link between Soviet and Western intellectuals before and after the Cold War. A revolutionary and disenchanted poet in his youth, writing Catholic poems despite his Jewish background, he was also a friend of Bukharin and later Mayakovsky, and met and followed Lenin in Paris. Later he was hired to write Soviet propaganda, while occasionally defending his views with boldness against Stalin or government mouthpieces. He was a prominent member of the Jewish Anti-Fascist Committee and, together with Vasily Grossman, edited *The Black Book*, containing documentary accounts by Jewish survivors of the Holocaust in the Soviet Union and Poland. He is probably best known for his fiction, particularly his novel *The Thaw*, which portrayed Russian society under the post-Stalin reforms of Khruschev.

* * *

A letter, written in the autumn of 1959 to Ilya Ehrenburg by a Leningrad University student about a quarrel with her engineer boyfriend, sparked a deeply revealing controversy over questions which touch the very roots not only of Soviet society but of the whole modern world. The girl, whose name Ehrenburg discreetly left at 'Nina', wrote to the author about her bitter quarrel with Yuri – the engineer whom she loved deeply – over his attitude towards art, poetry, music and even ordinary human feelings. She had decided to break with him, and out of her heartache, she had written to Ehrenburg – not for advice, but for confirmation that what she had done was right.

Ehrenburg, noting that he often received such letters and usually answered them, felt this one reflected such fundamental issues that he replied in a 2500-word article in *Komsomolskaya Pravda*.[1] His answer sided with Nina. The paper was bombarded with letters, literally thousands of them; a selection was published under the title 'Discussion of the Moral Complexion of Soviet Man'. The discussion raged for almost four months to the intense interest of the public.

First, the essence of Nina's disagreement with Yuri, as disclosed in her letter:

> . . . When I read him a poem by Blok he listened impatiently, then said it was nonsense and old-fashioned, that we lived in a different age. When I suggested we should visit the Hermitage Museum together, he snapped that he had been there once and hadn't found it interesting, and again declared that I didn't understand the age we live in . . . He's a capable and conscientious worker. All his fellow workers have a high opinion of him. I could listen to him for hours when he talked about his work. He helped me to understand the importance of physics. But that's the only thing in life he recognises . . . outside of physics he approves only of sports. He says they are a healthful form of recreation, and again, that we must be a people of the atomic age . . .
>
> Even important events don't touch him. I was very upset by the Glezos trial.[2] 'Will they dare to execute him?' I asked Yuri. He said the trial of course was a disgrace. There had been a meeting at his place of work and everyone had voted in protest against the trial. Now others would have to carry on the job . . . When I tried to discuss our relationship, he either lost his temper or smiled and said I was trying to complicate matters . . . He'd be getting a flat at the beginning of the year and had asked me to marry him long ago . . .
>
> Once he read a satirical article in *Krokodil*[3] and announced triumphantly that it had poked fun at Chekhov's 'Lady with the Dog'. He'd never read Chekhov's story and when I told him it had depth and beauty, he laughed at me. He started calling me his 'lady with a

dog' and said he'd get me a lap dog so I could carry on 'psychological conversations' with more authority . . .

There were a great many things that long annoyed me about him. He told me he had a wonderful mother. Although she had been widowed early and gone to work as a storekeeper, she had managed to raise three children. At first I thought Yuri really loved her. He said he sent her 300 roubles a month. Then he mentioned casually that his mother wanted to visit him but that he had put her off. She was a fine woman, he said, but uneducated and he had nothing to talk to her about. I quarrelled with him and didn't see him for a month. Then he came round and told me I misunderstood him, but I knew I was right. He had stopped seeing his best friend of his college days because they no longer had anything in common. His friend was not getting anywhere . . .

The last time I saw him he declared sarcastically that I was crazy, that I failed to understand that in this space age only 'ladies with dogs' could be interested in novels, that I was old-fashioned and so on and so forth. In a word, we parted.

I am writing all this not to unburden myself . . . It is true that I still love Yuri, but if there's any weeping to be done I can do it into my pillow. I simply wanted to ask you what you think of Yuri's attitude. Do you think the arts are going to pot, and that love should be approached more simply, the way Yuri does. Sometimes I begin to wonder . . .

Ehrenburg, as a humanist and vigorous defender of the arts, obviously came down heavily on the side of Nina. He paid full tribute to the great advances – both positive and negative – of science: 'The tragedy of Hiroshima and Nagasaki and consequences of nuclear tests on the one hand; and on the other the artificial satellites of the Earth and the Sun, the first steps in exploring the universe, have made a far deeper impression on people of the mid-twentieth century than all the novels, paintings and symphonies.'

He gives full credit to the scientists, the engineers, creating material values for higher living standards. But . . .

The narrower the specialty, the more mechanical the work, the more important the role played by leisure. Man's spiritual make-up depends to a significant degree on the way he spends his free time. Besides the work a man performs, he needs social ideals, knowledge of the world, close contacts with the arts, and great love ... Progress in the exact sciences and technology, and ignorance of social problems drives society to marasmus or catastrophe. No one would say that Germany was a technically backward country when Hitler came to power. Without cultivated sensibilities, social progress and the growth of science cannot conquer crude morals and manners and a certain reversion to savagery ...

It is not enough to move a man into a modern home filled with conveniences and provide him with the latest radio and TV set, a soft armchair and peaceful leisure. A person must also have adventure, creative activity, deep sensibilities and great ideals!

There must be creative co-existence between the arts and science, is the essence of Ehrenburg's argument. 'Science helps us to discover certain laws, but art penetrates to spiritual depths no X-ray can reach.' Of Yuri, he writes that obviously he is an educated man who probably knows all about electrodynamics 'but his development has been one-sided. There is a direct connection between his lack of understanding of the arts and his failure to understand Nina; between his sneering attitude towards Blok's poetry and the Hermitage Museum and his attitude towards his mother and college friend.' It was a misfortune that Yuri did not realise that just as Nina learned much from him, he could have learned much 'from a girl who in the spheres of emotions is far more sensitive, more enriched and cleverer than he'.

Finally Ehrenburg wrote, 'It is a fine thing that this student at a Soviet teachers' training college finds "The Lady with the Dog" not a stupid nickname but a story of true love; that if she "cries into her pillow" she also suffered when a brave and innocent man was being tried in Greece. She has that humanity, that hatred of barrenness and indifference without which life becomes a series of dispirited motions.

'I know many young people,' concluded Ehrenburg. 'I have met many young men like Yuri. But I am sure the victory will be with those who possess passion, will-power and inspiration; with those who besides having knowledge, have big hearts.'

One would like to record that there was unanimous support for these wise, human and sensitive words from Ehrenburg; complete sympathy with the position of Nina and universal condemnation of the attitude of the strictly 'utilitarian' Yuri. But Soviet society, like any other, is a complex affair. Lots of young people are completely carried away by the breathless advance towards the stars. A number of the earliest letters that poured into *Komsomolskaya Pravda* supported Yuri against Nina and Ehrenburg.

A Moscow engineer, L. Poletayev, wrote in part:

Can one possibly say that life today is coming more and more into the tow of artists and poets? Nothing of the kind! Science and engineering are shaping the profile of our epoch and exerting increasing influence on tastes, morals and behaviour. The tempo of life is not at all what it was when so many masterpieces were created . . .

Our lives are guided by the creative force of reason and not by emotion; we are moved by the poetry of ideas, by theories, experiments and construction. That is what our epoch is like. Our times covet the whole of a man, without reservation, and we have no time to dote: 'Ah, Bach! Ah, Blok!' Both are undoubtedly outdated and hardly in keeping with our time. Whether we would or no, both belong to leisure and recreation and not to life.

Let us compare the puerile Nina – immodestly advertising her intimacies and her penchant for 'weeping into her pillow' (something she is inclined to be proud of) as well as her vague and fuzzy 'general development' and love of art – with Yuri: business-like, guided by a single purpose, knowing his work well, conscious of his aim. Which of these two is more useful to our society as a worker and a fighter? It seems to me the answer is obviously Yuri.

Whether we like it or not, the poets are losing their grip on our souls and have less and less to teach us. The most fascinating stories now spring from science and engineering, from bold, precise and merciless reason. To ignore this is to refuse to see what is happening. Art is receding into the background, to the sphere of rest and recreation. I am as sorry for this as Ehrenburg. Our dear Ninas are somewhat pinched and inferior today. Yuri, on the other hand, finds life easier for he happens to be where he belongs.

It seems to me that a society with many businesslike Yuris and few Ninas is stronger than one with lots of Ninas and few Yuris. So let us leave art to its admirers and those who go in for it – and stop hammering away at poor Yuri.

Perhaps it was symptomatic that Poletayev was an engineer, that the majority of Yuri's defenders were also engineers.

'How can I admire Bach or Blok?' asked engineer Petrukhin in his letter. 'What did they ever do for Russia or mankind ... Leave the arts to the dilettantes.' 'I can get along beautifully without art,' wrote Engineer Nekrassov. A college student, Levin, maintained that 'a decent physicist is twenty times more useful than any poet'. Engineer Koshelev, in a sneering disparagement of art in general, wrote, 'It is not by chance that ordinary people find it much easier to understand "the art" of kicking a football.'

But as the stream of letters swelled into a flood, the defenders of Yuri became an insignificant minority. The controversy revealed the depth of feeling of ordinary people all over the Soviet Union on matters affecting the heart and soul of man. Many letters contained moving, poetic expressions of faith in beauty and the noblest instincts. From the tens of thousands of letters, Ehrenburg finally perused a thousand selected at random as the basis for a final article to close the controversy. Of these only sixty defended the position of Yuri, Poletayev and the others. It is noteworthy that the majority of engineers who wrote in also disassociated themselves from the views of the 'utilitarians'.

Elvita Popova, a Young Communist League member wrote: 'Notwithstanding the terrific advance of the most exact science, electronics, I am confident that in outer space man will struggle, suffer and love ... Man will appreciate lilac in outer space too ...'

The point about lilac and outer space was seized on as a symbol to illustrate the harmony that must exist between the arts and the most advanced science if man was to continue to be a civilised being. Contributor after contributor expressed the conviction that despite the stormy go forward into the future, the arts would keep their place and advance hand in hand with science. As the discussion developed, it was clear that Nina and Ehrenburg had projected on to the public platform the whole question of aesthetics and the humanities and their place in the space age.

'I am sure that the first space pilot will be a man who knows Bach and Blok, who has read Gorky and Chekhov, who is fond of Pushkin and Gogol,' wrote B. Kirillov[4] from the remote town of Kizil-Arvat in Central Asia, 'because they, the great geniuses of music and literature, have since our childhood helped develop our courage and honesty, our love of people, our pride in what we have achieved. The first man to invade the cosmos will not merely be brave, but cultured.'

Another engineer, R. Leonidov, agreed that man 'will need a sprig of lilac in the cosmos as well', but he defended the importance of science with humorous, poetic fantasy; he warned that to keep the lilac alive in the dark and cold of the cosmos, the sprig would have to be protected by science. 'Shining containers filled with liquid oxygen will enable it to breathe. It will be kept warm by semi-conductors of solar batteries. Artificial gravitation apparatus will secure a normal circulation of the juices in its lustrous leaves. Slabs of lead and graphite will preserve it from the deadly currents of cosmic rays; and the superstrong envelope of the space ship will keep it from the blows of the swiftest meteorites . . .'

Leonidov had some gentle tilts at lovers of art who ignore science and technology. He expressed the conviction that 'these two mighty trees will grow side by side with branches interwoven'. And while he said he agreed with Poletayev that the physicists and engineers have come to be the 'masters of thought . . . shaping the face of our epoch', Engineer Leonidov concluded: 'For all that, we should once more like to emphasise that in the cosmos too, man will need a sprig of lilac; and in the pockets of their space suits, the astronauts of the future – real men and women of great science – will no doubt carry books of verses on their flights to the Moon, Mars, Venus and the stars!'

A chairman of a collective farm in a remote village in the Kursk region, I. Korobov, wrote that he thought he had every right to call himself a 'business-like person' as he had put a backward collective farm on its feet. There were no radios, no electricity when he arrived. 'Hard drinking and violence' was the rule on holidays.

'I hardly knew where to begin,' he wrote, 'but it occurred to me that music was something everyone needed, for it warmed the soul, softened people, made them somehow gentler, more responsive. One of my first cares therefore was a radio system enabling the peasants to hear good music. My first concern, in short, was spiritual food . . .'

He recalled the bitter war days at the front when a 'good heartfelt song was one of our best weapons, for through it we caught sight of the golden lights of the window-sills of our sweethearts a thousand kilometres away . . . One can break any machine but never a song . . .

'You can blow tanks sky high with mines and we did, during the war,' continued Korobov, 'but what barriers can there be to a song echoing the hopes of the people, a song of peace and friendship? There is no wall high enough to check its stride.'

Finally he excused himself for the 'sharpness' of his letter as he was 'really troubled when I read of such advocates of Yuri in the newspapers as the engineer Petrukhin who seems to be a man of very narrow and limited views, and for whom I am sincerely sorry'.

An assistant excavator operator from the Urals, Fedor Antonenko, full of derision for careerist Yuri, wrote: 'Many people who feel real joy when contemplating the beautiful . . . are not always able to define happiness exactly. But the Yuris never have that trouble . . . "There goes a happy man" this sort of person says when some colleague or other has got ahead on the job.' Antonenko thought Ehrenburg had treated Yuri far too tenderly.

From a state farm in the Kaliningrad region, V. Chebotova, looking into the future, predicted that 'under Communism each of us will command two or three professions, will know techniques and painting, and be equally versed in science and art. Our Communist labour brigades are preparing for this even now. The future will not belong to those with a lop-sided development'.

And so the letters went on. As the months rolled by the question of arts, aesthetics, technology and their interrelationship spread beyond the pages of *Komsomolskaya Pravda*. Long after the newspaper had dropped the subject, it was discussed by groups all over the country. The overwhelming majority of those who took part, condemned 'philistinism' and 'utilitarianism'. The discussions directed the thoughts of thousands, perhaps millions, toward the 'question of aesthetics and the arts'; on a much broader front toward questions of public taste, manner of living, human relations and so on.

It gave stimulus to wider discussion in other newspapers on all sorts of questions of bringing aesthetics more into line with the astonishing advances in science and technique. It acted as a necessary brake on a tendency among some of the technical intellectuals to drop values of the past and present in order to rush ahead and conquer nucleonics and outer space.

Ehrenburg touched on one aspect of this in his final contribution to the discussion when he wrote: 'We often see a discrepancy between a person's splendid qualities on the job and his inertness, lack of sensitivity and even coarseness in his daily life. The sooner we can get rid of these contradictions, the fewer the people who are spiritually narrow-minded and want to limit the culture of others, the closer we shall be both to the Moon and, what is more important, to Communism. How can the arts help us? Primarily by cultivating our sensibilities ... Perhaps we should drop Bach and Blok for a while and discuss our own mode and manner of life, our ethics and aspirations, and decide what we have accomplished and what remains to be done?'

An important shot in this new direction hinted at by Ehrenburg was fired a month later when *Izvestia* gave more than half the front page – the space usually reserved for editorials – to a letter from a group of skilled workers at the Moscow Frezer machine-tool plant. In publishing the letter, *Izvestia* announced editorially that this was the beginning of a crusade against shoddy goods, sloppy work and attitudes. Soviet products must not only be good – they must also look good. Other papers followed suit in a continuing campaign which ranged from attacks on tasselled lampshades, to a demand for brighter wedding celebrations, and on to 'service with a smile' in the shops. It amounted to a veritable overhauling of questions of taste, and manners.

Noting the advanced scientific and economic achievements of the U.S.S.R. the workers from the Frezer plant asked: 'Why are there still so many shoddy, ill-made goods? Why do we often spoil the joy of those moving into new flats with floors that buckle, doors that won't close, badly fitted windows? The newcomers have been dreaming of that flat for so long! Let's face it! Anyone can see that people are furious at such slipshod work. They reason this way: We've built rockets that fly better and further than any others; even around the Moon. First-class airliners like the TUs. An atomic ice-breaker – but we are making bad wardrobes, and sideboards so ugly you can't stand looking at them . . .'

The workers went on to criticise ill-cut clothing, the bulk and weight of radio and TV sets, and many other shortcomings – attributable, fundamentally, to people with the Yuri mentality who could see the Moon but not a sprig of lilac.

Even in early 1962, the Soviet press was hammering away at this very problem. And while the need for this justified criticism still exists, there is also a conscious drive from top to bottom to eliminate conservatism and downright bad taste in consumer goods.

An earlier, more official view on the need for 'more lilac' had appeared several months before the start of the Nina–Yuri discussion in *Kommunist*[5] under the title of 'Aesthetic Training in Shaping the New Man'. The author, Skatyershchikov, complained that of all forms of art, only literature had been studied in school; that it was now necessary to introduce music, art, appreciation of literature as well as training in manners and behaviour.

> Beauty in everyday life is an important aspect of aesthetic training. Our industry has achieved a high level of development. No material or technical obstacles hinder our country from carrying out designs or manufacturing any objects that can beautify our life . . . The press should help fight philistinism in our home surroundings, should help fight poor taste in the cut and colour of clothing and millinery, in the design of furniture and in general all the objects that surround Soviet people in everyday life!

A significant aspect of the lag in matters of taste to which the *Kommunist* article referred, was given me by a sensitive, cultivated Soviet woman whose own taste is impeccable.

'Don't forget that we are a generation that grew up in sacrifice,' she said.

We deeply believed that our generation was to sacrifice itself, building a new life from which future generations would benefit. We willingly accepted this. We still think that was right. We looked forward to little but austerity and hardship for ourselves. Grooming, pretty clothes, elaborate coiffures were out of place. They were for those who were not pulling their weight – the left-overs from the old bourgeoisie.

There was almost a cult, if you like, of the shabbiness of unremitting toil. Of course it lasted longer than we realized. There was the war. And rebuilding the fruit of two Five-Year-Plans which war destroyed. Culture in those years was of the public kind because it was the easiest to provide. We enjoyed good music, good theatre, good literature – perhaps the best in the world. But aesthetics in private life was considered 'bad taste' cultivated by those outside the mainstream of our work and sacrifices. And after all there was not much place for it when families were sharing apartments – even rooms.

Now we have built a good life. The new generation is here and has a right to enjoy it; but somehow old habits die hard. It has become a question of education, more than technique.

The education in aesthetics is now going on apace, partly through the press, partly through some 2000 people's universities which teach art appreciation and a generally more sophisticated attitude to life in two-year courses of Sunday lectures. There is a conscious, nationwide effort to ensure that the sprig of lilac will flourish and always have an honoured place in Soviet life.

It is interesting that although Soviet people themselves are highly critical of the lag between the arts and sciences, it is the relatively harmonious development of the two in the Soviet Union as compared to the West which strikes many visitors from abroad. C.P. Snow, the outstanding British novelist who visited the Soviet Union in the spring of 1960, commented specifically on the 'happy marriage' between the arts and sciences in the U.S.S.R. and found that in 'things of the mind' the Soviet Union was well ahead of the West ... which only confirms that, fortunately, it is not the Yuris who have the final say in such matters here.

Soviet 'lilac' – as all can testify who have visited the packed theatres and concert halls throughout the country, who have enjoyed the ballet, theatre and ensembles, the Oistrakhs and

Richters and the rich choice of violinists, pianists, instrumentalists – is one of those important built-in 'imponderables' of Soviet society that have to be thrown on to the scales when measuring living standards. The 'lilac' has been there for public enjoyment since the first days of Soviet power. What everyone now feels is that, as the rockets fly off at ever-increasing tempo into outer space, enough 'lilac' must be made available to place a sprig on every mantelpiece in every home. And a start toward this has been made.

[Chapter 11 of *Come East Young Man* (Seven Seas Books, Berlin, 1962), pp. 155–168.]

15

War Against Trees [1963]

Hopes for peace in the former states of Indochina promised by the 1954 Geneva Agreements soon turned into covert and then overt war as the US replaced France as the regional Western power to counter China and the threat of Communism. A united Communist Vietnam with Ho Chi Minh as president was not part of the American plan for the region. The 'Domino Theory' sold to Western public opinion as justification for intervention suggested that if one 'domino' (South Vietnam) fell to the Communists, other dominos would follow. It was the duty of America and her allies to stop the 'Red' and 'Yellow' hordes.

From Wilfred Burchett's perspective things stood very differently: US imperialism had replaced French colonialism and was preventing the peoples of Vietnam, Laos and Cambodia from achieving true independence and national reconciliation on their own terms.

In the first half of 1962 he visited the former states of Indochina and returned convinced that the US was preparing for full scale military intervention. For the next two decades he would denounce American imperialism and the Vietnam War from 'behind enemy lines' in countless articles, books, pamphlets, films, interviews, speeches and so on, which secured his fame and notoriety. He became, as his biographer Tom Heenan writes, 'arguably the war's most influential journalist'.

In introducing *The Furtive War* Burchett wrote:

> On questions of war and peace, it is difficult to be impartial and dispassionate. The book that follows sticks to carefully verified and verifiable facts that throw light on dark places in Southeast Asia. I was able to seek the opinions of Southeast Asian leaders most directly concerned with present day problems, including the Laotian princes; Prince Sihanouk of Cambodia; President Ho Chi Minh and Premier Pham Van Dong of North Vietnam; Professor Nguyen Van Hieu, Secretary General of the National Liberation Front of South Vietnam, and many others. If the book contributes to finding the end of the war trail in Asia, it will have served its purpose.

* * *

The Chemical Spray Campaign

The expression 'war against trees' was one that stuck in my mind, and in subsequent interviews with refugees and other travellers from South Vietnam I paid special attention to this. The picture that emerged is horrifying. Wide scale spraying of chemical agents from planes has been used not only against trees but against food crops with the deliberate intent of starving the peasantry into entering the 'prosperity zones' and 'strategic villages.' Food-killers have been sprayed on areas outside the concentration zones to destroy all surrounding vegetation and further back still to destroy all crops and orchards apart from those grown behind barbed wire.

The South Vietnamese people have now become guinea pigs for testing out new types of weapons, types developed by the U.S. government for the sort of 'local wars' which Pentagon ideologists like Henry Kissinger had been urging on Washington for years previously.

From experimental tests on plots of about 10 acres carried out in August 1961, chemical spraying was begun early in 1962 over areas of several hundred acres at a time. Apart from the insane attempt to destroy a mile-wide strip of trees along South Vietnam's borders with Laos and Cambodia, air-sprayed chemicals have been used to clear swathes alongside roads and rivers, to create buffer zones around the 'strategic villages', to clear the jungle from the *Hauts Plateaux* region – the highlands home of many of the ethnic minorities. From the 17th parallel demarcation line down to the southernmost tip of South Vietnam, chemical warfare has been waged against forests, plantations, orchards, and food crops.

An account, typical of dozens of others I heard, was that given by Pham Tri Thach, a fragile, middle-aged peasant woman from Phuoc Tan village in Bien Hoa province. I met her at the 17th parallel, shortly after she had floated across the Ben Hai river at night, clinging to the stout trunk of a banana palm. She had made her way across from one of the southernmost provinces, hitching rides where she could on trucks and boats, but for hundreds of miles she had slogged it out on foot till she reached the Ben Hai.

'Planes came over on several mornings between January 12 and 18,' she said.

Not only over our village but the nearby ones of Tam Phuoc, An Loi, and Tam An. I saw them the first time on the 12th. I was on my way to market when a plane came down quite low with what looked like whitish smoke coming out of its tail. There was another one about the same height half a kilometre away. When the 'smoke' drifted over me, I thought at first I was going to choke. My chest started to burn. All the way to market I had difficulty in breathing. I had to keep stopping to sit down. After a while my nose started bleeding. When I got to the market I found some other women suffered the same thing. Two of them were bleeding from the mouth as well. Others had burning pains in the chest.

Everyone talked about it at the market. We thought it must be some new thing to kill insects. But afterwards, on the way home I noticed all the young rice plants had shrivelled up. Leaves on the banana palms were hanging limply alongside the trunks. There was something peculiar about the leaves on papaya and other trees.

When I got back to the village, I found that one of my neighbors, a woman of my age, was paralyzed. She had also had severe nose bleeding and vomiting. She was paralyzed for several hours. By evening she was able to move about all right, but had severe pains in the chest and difficulty in breathing. She had been hoeing in the fields and started to run when the plane came right over her head. She and others who were in the fields said the plants shrivelled up five minutes after they had been sprayed.

Next day the banana palms were dead and the leaves had fallen from all the fruit trees. They died afterwards too. From the other villages we heard that several other people had been temporarily paralyzed and many others had chest pains.

A wizened up old fisherman, with a face like a ripe walnut – one of a group which had fled north in a flimsy raft-like boat of lashed bamboo poles – told of how planes at the end of the previous December had sprayed a ten-mile stretch of coastal land.

'Two planes came,' he said, 'and sprayed up and down just as if they were ploughing a field. We were fishing just off the coast and wondered what they were up to. By the time we got ashore, the banana palms were dead and the leaves of other fruit trees were hanging limp. The folk ashore were complaining of pains in the chest. Afterwards the leaves dropped off all the trees. Some of them died but on others the leaves grew back again. The worst affected were the fruit trees, bananas, papaya, mandarins, and others. They all died.'

The worst report came from two villages along strategic Route 15, which leads from Saigon north to the 17th parallel. On January 14 and 15, planes systematically sprayed rice fields, plantations, and orchards. The result, according to a former minor functionary of the Diem administration now an exile in Cambodia, was the destruction of 230 acres of rubber trees – two whole plantations – 50 acres of citrus trees, 190 acres of other fruit trees, 35 acres of coffee, 287 acres of rice fields, and 87 acres of vegetable gardens.

'Thousands of days of work and many years of growth destroyed in two days by American planes,' said the former functionary who must be nameless as his family remains in South Vietnam. 'The official reason was that vegetation must be destroyed to protect the road from Viet Cong attacks, to deny them a hiding place. But the real reason was to destroy the people's livelihood so they would be forced to abandon the villages near the road and move back into the so-called "prosperity zone".'

A similar action to clear a half-mile wide strip each side of the road between Saigon and Cap St. Jacques resulted in the destruction of several hundred acres of mainly French-owned rubber plantations. The French and Vietnamese plantation owners in this case created a big scandal, demanding heavy compensation, and the 'war against trees' was halted for a time – at least in that area. But according to reliable reports the Americans have stocked sufficient chemicals to spray an area 1500 miles long by six miles wide. Normal procedure is to photograph the target area from helicopters before and after spraying, presumably to verify the results.

The chemicals used against vegetation are only one of a number of new types of warfare the Americans are trying out – Asians as usual on the receiving end.

As to what is being used – and prepared for future use – there was a revealing article in *Newsweek* of 21 August 1961. Among the new weapons and equipment being shipped to, or designed for Southeast Asia, writes *Newsweek*, are:

A 'microjet' rocket, a tiny projectile about an inch long, that can be fired from a plastic tube no bigger than a drinking straw. The needle-like nylon rocket has a range of 4000 yards, a velocity of 4000 feet per second. The weapon in effect is a modern adaptation of blow-gun darts, and by mounting a cluster of straws together, a Gatling gun effect can be created. 'It's almost a silent killer and it's the deadliest little weapon I've ever seen,' says a guerilla expert . . .
An explosive gas that could be released over the enemy. Hugging the ground, the gas is set off by any spark in the same way that dust in a grain elevator ignites. 'In a fraction of a second,' says a researcher, the stuff goes boom and it pulverizes everything in sight.'
Canadian-made de Havilland 'Caribou' transport planes that can be effectively used from improvised airfields for close support of troops. The Caribou carries 24 paratroopers or three tons of cargo at speeds up to 200 mph or as slow as 70 mph. Vietnam is getting some of the first off the assembly line.[1]

Among other types of chemicals that *Newsweek* did not mention is one . . . sprayed in combat areas, [it] lies like soap suds on the ground and explodes at a grenade burst or if a tracer bullet is fired into it. A variant of the anti-vegetation chemical is one which when sprayed on ponds or lakes kills the fish and ducks and other birds that feed on the fish.

From descriptions by eyewitnesses from many different parts of South Vietnam, the general effect of the anti-vegetation chemicals seems to be the following. Within a few hours of being sprayed, plants like rice and maize are completely dried up; root crops like sweet potatoes and manioc deteriorate markedly within 24 hours; quick-growing vegetation like banana palms and papaya trees die within 24 hours, the banana palm simply collapsing on the ground. Forest trees and some of the hardier fruit trees lose their leaves and bark after a few weeks, but unless the same trees are sprayed several times in succession, the leaves grow again. There seems to be a difference in the strength of the chemicals used, as some accounts spoke of leaves of rice plants shrivelling up within a matter of minutes, others in hours. Also some of those I spoke with thought the chemicals that killed the fish and ducks were the same as those used against vegetation.

On 16 March 1962, *Agence France Presse* (AFP) carried the following despatch from Saigon:

> The first American attempts to wipe out the thick vegetation along the main communication routes in South Vietnam by means of powerful chemical agents does not seem to have given the expected results. Two months after the beginning of these experiments, only the upper foliage of the forests have been 'killed'; the leaves burned a brownish hue have still not fallen, while under the big trees, the jungle which offers a much-sought cover for the Viet Cong, remains as thick and vigorous as ever. Officially, one is merely told that the experts have not finished evaluating the results of the first attempts and that there is no reason to believe that the experiment has been conclusive.

Further attempts will doubtless be made, it is added, when the experts' recommendations are known. The main aim of the operation, it is recalled, is to try and free the main communication routes and also, if possible, create a vast stretch of territory denuded of all vegetation along the frontier between South Vietnam and Laos.

AFP sets the beginning of the experiments about January 14 and 15, the time of the two attacks on the two districts mentioned earlier and made in a region difficult to conceal. With the extremely tight restrictions on Saigon correspondents, it is possible that the earlier experiments and the scale of the chemical warfare have been kept secret from them. It is not an operation that American military chiefs are very interested in publicizing. War against trees and food crops, and experiments in chemical warfare against Asian peoples are not the way to win friends anywhere in the world. Especially not in Asia where the overwhelming majority of the people live so close to the soil. The battle to fill the family rice bowl is too intense for any Vietnamese peasant to feel anything but raging fury towards those who perpetrate such acts. To wage war against nature as well as against the Vietnamese people adds macabre elements to U.S. intervention. Using Asians as victims for tests of new weapons fits into an all too-familiar pattern which stretches from Hiroshima to the nuclear weapons tests in the Pacific.

New Phase of U.S. Intervention

Chemical warfare is of course only one sidelight of U.S. military activities in South Vietnam. The new phase of direct involvement started with the visit of Vice-President Lyndon Johnson to Saigon in May 1961 with a letter from President Kennedy offering stepped-up U.S. aid. A communique issued on May 13, after three days of talks between Johnson and Diem, mentioned eight points, although press despatches said the program included 15 items. Some were kept secret. In the rather evangelical language of the communique, it was stated that both governments had agreed to step up existing military and economic aid programs 'and to infuse into their joint actions a high sense of urgency and dedication.' The United States would finance additional armed forces, and would provide 'Military Assistance Program support for the entire Vietnamese Civil Guard forces.' The two governments 'should collaborate in the use of military specialists,' and 'the assistance of other Free Governments . . . against Communist guerilla forces would be welcome.' More financial aid was of course promised and it was agreed that both sides 'would discuss new economic and social measures to be undertaken in rural areas, to accompany the anti-guerilla effort.'

Other points not mentioned in the communique, but leaked to the press, included the despatch of U.S. 'guerilla experts'; more 'advisers' to train troops and police; U.S. engineers to repair guerilla-wrecked bridges and to build roads and airstrips; more cash to add another 20,000 men to Diem's army.

Following Johnson's visits, U.S. military experts started swarming on Saigon like vultures on a dead cow. By November 1961 there had been no less than 44 military missions visiting South Vietnam, expert in everything from 55 methods of silent killing to tightening the stays in bullet-proof vests. The two most important were those headed by Dr. Eugene Staley in July and by Kennedy's special military adviser, General Maxwell Taylor in October.

Staley himself is almost the personification of the central figure in Graham Greene's famous book, *The Quiet American*. A mousy sort of person, with trim grey moustache, an economist who likes to pass for a 'liberal,' he emerged on the South Vietnamese scene with missionary-like fervor to 'save the country from communism.' With clinical efficiency he set to work to draw up a plan which a Hitler or an Eichmann would have been proud to have dreamed up. Details of this scheme so meticulously prepared by the 'liberal' economics expert have not been announced officially, but the most monstrous provisions, which have little to do with either economics or liberalism, are well known.

Apart from calling for an intensified effort to form concentration camp villages, mentioned earlier, Staley's plan provided for:

1. Pacification of South Vietnam within 18 months and intensified sabotage in North Vietnam by air-dropped spies and commando groups.
2. Following pacification, to build up the army on a regular, modern basis, intensify sabotage in the North, and organize commando bases in the North for future action.
3. Develop the economy of the South and attack the North.

To carry out the first stages, Staley recommended: (a) increasing the regular army from 150,000 to 270,000, the militia from 68,000 to 100,000, and gradually transform the militia into regular forces; increase the police from 45,000 to 90,000 and develop various local guard and militia units to free the police for mopping up and regular military operations, (b) to organize a network of 'strategic villages' and 'prosperity zones' with a series of 'no man's lands' to isolate South Vietnam from her neighbors and the 'prosperity zones' from each other; (c) to launch a series of military actions to destroy the resistance movement.

The plan was accepted, and to carry it out President Kennedy stepped up military allocations for South Vietnam for 1961 from the original $125,000,000 to $216,000,000 and for 1962, to $400,000,000. No peasants anywhere in the world had so many dollars per capita lavished on their extermination.

General Maxwell Taylor was sent from October 19 to 25 to work out supplementary details of the Staley Plan in view of a decision taken a few days earlier by the National Security Council (which directs military policy in Washington) on direct U.S. intervention. Taylor's proposals called for:

1. Diem's army to be reorganized structurally and placed under direct U.S. control. The powers of lower echelons would be increased and units would obey the orders of American 'advisers' of the MAAG (Military Aid and Assistance Group) without reference to Diem's own Headquarters staff.
2. Small units of the U.S. army would gradually be transferred to Vietnam.
3. The number of U.S. 'advisers' would be increased. Deliveries of arms, including various new types would be stepped up to re-equip the Diem army.
4. After the frontier between South Vietnam and Laos was sealed off with the 'no man's land' as provided by Staley, troops would be stationed along the frontier and then a corridor would be established linking South Vietnam with Thailand through Laos. There would be a single command embracing Thailand, Laos, and South Vietnam; Cambodia would then be completely isolated and subject to increased pressures.

This program was approved by President Kennedy and the National Security Council on November 15. The 'Blue Book' was hastily knocked together for release a few weeks later, and on December 11 the first U.S. combat units – still technically classed as 'advisers' and 'instructors'– arrived in Saigon.

During the latter part of November and early December, large quantities of war material, including helicopters and fighter-bombers, started arriving in South Vietnam, unannounced by Washington or Saigon but reported in the world press. The correspondent of the London *Times*, for instance, reported on December 8, that supplies delivered by the United States within the previous few weeks 'range from fighter-bombers aircraft to trained dogs for hunting down terrorists.' Four days later, the *New York Times* reported the arrival of two U.S. helicopter companies comprising 'at least' 33 helicopters with 400 U.S. pilots and ground crew. These would be 'assigned' to Diem's army but would remain under U.S. control and operation. American combat troops, from 11 December 1961, were thus directly involved in combat operations in an undeclared war against the South Vietnamese people.

From 2000 U.S. 'instructors' at the beginning of 1961, the number went up to 7000 by mid-1962. Apart from training Diem's troops, U.S. military personnel work out operational plans, direct combat operations, fly the fighter and bomber planes that protect such operations, release the bombs and fire the machine-guns, transport Diem's troops by helicopter to carry out terror raids against recalcitrant villages, and hunt down guerillas with German police dogs. The latter had been requested by Diem after U.S. experts carried out a demonstration in which two dogs – the sort the Nazis used to force their victims to quicken their pace into the gas chambers – had discovered eight 'Viet Cong' in a refuge 30 miles northwest of Saigon. Robert Trumbull reported in the New York Times of December 6, that 'high South Vietnamese government officials who witnessed the demonstrations' were so 'highly impressed with this performance, the South Vietnamese government has asked the United States to provide 1000 dogs.' One wonders what sort of training a dog has to receive to distinguish between a peasant and a 'Viet Cong'! In fact these dogs are to be used as American slaveowners used bloodhounds in the past to track down their runaway slaves – to hound down any peasant who lives or moves outside the concentration camp villages.

Intervention was formalized on 8 February 1962, with the establishment of a U.S. Military Command in Saigon, headed by General Paul Donal Harkins – also an old Korean hand – Chief of Staff of the U.S. Army, Pacific area. Harkins set up a headquarters staff big enough to handle three combat divisions, according to the U.S. press.

All the moves preceding the setting up of the Command and much of its actual activities were shrouded in secrecy. What little was known of what was going on was pried out of tight-lipped Pentagon planners – including the President – by congressmen and journalists anxious to know if Kennedy was pushing the United States into another Korea.

Such anxiety was expressed in many U.S. periodicals. The Christian Century of 25 April 1962, for instance, accused President Kennedy of concealing the facts about South Vietnam just as Senator Kennedy accused President Eisenhower eight years previously:

Give us the truth Mr. President [the Protestant weekly said in an editorial] . . . What justification has the President for sending U.S. troops, reported to number nearly 5000, plus ships and planes to a country 10,000 miles away?

According to the Geneva Convention of 1954, South Vietnam can have no more than 685 military advisers from a single nation and it is forbidden to import military personnel from any foreign country.

A nice question arose for Washington when the first Americans were wounded. The elaborate pretense that no Americans were engaged in combat had to be maintained. On the other hand, the wounded were demanding their Purple Heart medals. But these are awarded only to those wounded in action 'against an armed enemy of the United States.' The first sergeant to have been wounded in action was denied his medal, because as the *New York Times* reported on April 24, 'Washington does not recognize this as a combat zone for Americans.' The report went on to say that 'Eight of twenty planes of the United States Light Helicopter Company have holes from Communist bullets. The crews cannot follow the subtlety of State Department thinking and are indignant.' A few days later, Washington overcame its legal scruples and decided to award the medals. In the same quiet, furtive way in which the whole intervention operation has been handled, the South Vietnamese people are now classified as *an armed enemy of the United States.*

Lest there be any doubt as to the direct U.S. participation in the furtive war, there was an interesting despatch from the *Agence France Presse* correspondent in Saigon, on 16 March 1962:

American instructors sent to South Vietnam within the framework of U.S. military aid to this country sometimes take part in combat operations against the Viet Cong. According to the U.S. Embassy in Saigon, this does not at all imply that it is the United States that wages or directs the war in South Vietnam. Their role, as set out in official State Department directives to their U.S. Embassy in Saigon, is solely to provide material aid and logistics support to the Vietnamese armed forces, to train and advise them . . .

However it is recognized unofficially that it is sometimes difficult actually to distinguish between 'pure training' and 'active participation' in combat operations. Training, it is stressed, is not always done on the training ground but sometimes also on the battlefield. Thus certain instructors may be led to advise a commando unit in actual combat. It is the same thing in the huge project for training pilots. It happens that planes leave on combat missions with an American pilot-instructor at the controls and a young Vietnamese pilot. In such a case the instructor has to carry out his task to advise, by showing in fact how to do it.

On the same day Reuter quoted U.S. Defense Secretary McNamara at a Washington press conference as saying that two-seater training planes have now replaced single-seaters in the Vietnamese Air Force. 'Such training,' said McNamara, 'occasionally takes place in combat conditions.' Asked whether American pilots actually use the machine-guns or drop bombs on Communist guerilIas, McNamara is quoted as replying: 'Americans have received instructions not to fire unless they are attacked.' Pressed to say whether this applied to planes as well, the U.S. Defense Secretary said 'yes,' the firing to which he referred applied to planes as well as to forces on the ground.

In other words before the pilot strafed or napalmed a recalcitrant village, he should enter into the plane's log that he had been receiving 'ground fire' – that is, if he really believed the scruples of McNamara or the Pentagon. To ensure better efficiency was not the only reason for U.S. pilots at the controls. As the AFP despatch pointed out, 'the training results have not been at all bad if one judges by the accuracy with which the rebel pilots recently bombed the Presidential palace.' But because Diem feared to let any Vietnamese pilot at the controls of a plane loaded with bombs and rockets, the twin-seater combat planes were introduced within a matter of weeks after the bombing of Diem's palace.

Another interesting sidelight on the cloak-and-dagger nature of U.S. intervention was the arrival in Saigon on 15 April 1962, of Allen Dulles, former chief of the Central Intelligence Agency. He came as a member of a Pentagon 'study' group to check on, among other things, according to the *New York Times*, whether 'the approximately 6000 U.S. military personnel . . . really know why they are here and what they are doing.'

For a typical account of 'what they are doing,' Dulles could look up the *New York Times*. Under the headline, 'US 'Copters Aid Attack on Red Force in Vietnam,' he could gladden his heart and pride with the following despatch, datelined Cai Ngai, Vietnam, 9 March 1962.

United States Army helicopters carried a Vietnamese battalion in a successful raid today against this Communist stronghold near the southern tip of Vietnam. Five helicopters were struck by Communist bullets and one was disabled . . . [As for what sort of a 'stronghold,' the despatch continues] Cai Ngai, a clutter of huts along a canal 20 miles southwest of Ca Mau in An Xuyen province, fell easily after a brief fight. Three Communist guerillas were killed in a bamboo thicket at the edge of a village. Strafing by Vietnamese fighter planes killed an estimated 25 more who were seen to flee the encirclement . . . About 20 suspected Viet Cong guerillas were seized.

But as usual the main enemy force got away. It slipped through the trap even though the airborne attackers had achieved excellent surprise in their vertical envelopment of the village . . . The Government troops failed to exploit the Viet Cong state of shock. They bunched up and dawdled in drainage ditches and under the shade of coconut trees until an American adviser cried out in exasperation, 'Let's move this thing forward!'

To anyone reading between the lines, an attack was made against an ordinary South Vietnamese village. Fleeing peasants were mown down by American piloted fighter-bombers. A few were killed and a few more seized. The South Vietnamese troops were reluctant to take part in further butchery but were prodded into action by an American officer. This is a scene repeated daily over large areas of Vietnam, especially in the Ca Mau peninsula where the most intense U.S.–Diem effort was made in the first half of 1962 to herd the peasants into concentration camp villages. One wonders whether the U.S. 'advisers' have no qualms that the day might come when South Vietnamese troops will turn their guns on the foreign officers and make common cause with their intended victims. The

French could probably give them a few tips about this. There are signs that this is already starting.

After an attempt had been made – allegedly by students – to assassinate U.S. Ambassador Frederick E. Nolting Jr., in Saigon, and several Americans had been wounded by grenades in that city, Saigon has taken on more and more the face it wore at the height of the war against the French. The *New York Times* reported on May 21 that 'buses for servicemen have wire screened windows to deflect missiles. Some restaurants have taken the precaution of installing wire netting across their front windows ... The (U.S.) embassy is planning to renew next week its warning against travel outside Saigon.' Just like old times, the French colonialists were saying.

In connection with the grenade thrown at the U.S. Ambassador, a brilliant poet and professor of mathematics, Le Quang Vinh, and three students were sentenced to death and eight other students sentenced to from five years to life imprisonment. The grenade incident was used as a pretext to terrorize Saigon students in particular and intellectuals in general. Students had been agitating for some time for the Vietnamese language to replace English and French as the sole languages for instruction in South Vietnam's higher educational establishments. Also they had been demanding that an effort be made to build more schools. In Saigon, highly favored in comparison with other centers, over half the children of school age had no education because there were neither schools to attend nor teachers to instruct. Le Quang Vinh, who had received his higher education in France and the United States, supported the students' demands, a sufficient cause for his arrest.

At his trial before a Saigon 'special' court, on 23 May 1962, despite the standard severe tortures he had undergone, he used the court room to denounce in no uncertain terms the fascist nature of the Diem regime and the iniquities of foreign intervention. He and the other 11 accused all denied any knowledge of the assassination attempt.

It was obvious that the U.S. Ambassador only had to lift his little finger to spare the life of Le Quang Vinh and the others. The sentences were monstrous even had they been guilty of the incident, in which no one was injured. To expect humanitarian considerations to move the chief agent of U.S. intervention in South

Vietnam would be unrealistic, but one would have thought that political considerations might have moved Ambassador Nolting. The savagery of this sentence united thousands more students and intellectuals against Diem and the Americans.

To emphasize that they had come to stay and to compensate for the privileges denied them by the guerillas of looking for fun outside Saigon, the Americans started to build picnic grounds with barbecue pits, bowling alleys, an 'Olympic-sized' swimming pool, tennis courts, radio station, and the like. Trees being planted in 1962 were expected to shade American invasion troops in years to come, but they feel so insecure even in Saigon, despite the U.S. military patrols that prowl the streets of the capital day and night, that it was decided to set up special housing units for the garrison troops and other personnel of the fast-developing new colonialists. This, reported the *New York Times* on 21 June 1962, 'would also ease the extraordinary difficulty of providing security for offices and men now scattered throughout Saigon in converted hotels and apartment blocks. The proposed units would form a compound more easily protected against grenade throwers.'

Involvement of the Control Commission

A 'threat to peace' there is indeed in South Vietnam, but not, as the 'Blue Book' claims, because of any activities of, or from the North. The real threat comes from 10,000 miles away – in Washington's Pentagon building.

The Americans did manage however to pull something off with the 'Blue Book.' At the press conference at which Dean Rusk presented this dubious document, he said that he was confident that the International Control Commission would take up many of the matters raised in the book. President Kennedy, he said, had raised the question with Prime Minister Jawaharlal Nehru during the latter's visit to Washington the previous week. As the United States loudly proclaimed, it had never signed the Geneva Agreements, and indeed encouraged its puppets in Laos and South Vietnam to denounce them as often as possible. Accordingly, it was hardly Kennedy's place to discuss with anyone the work of the ICC (established only to control the application of the Geneva Agreements).

Among other demands Kennedy had pressed at the meeting with Nehru was that India immediately send a 'strong man' to Vietnam as Chairman of the Commission. Accordingly, Mr. Parthasarathy, whom Nehru had just named India's representative at the UN, was hastily despatched to Vietnam, on what must have been a disagreeable task.

The Americans were impatient. Their intervention had already started and despite the furtive way in which the start had been made, there were raised eyebrows in many capitals normally complacent about any U.S. moves. The *New York Times* of 28 April 1962, had reported that Washington was 'putting pressure' on India to produce a report that would show evidence of subversion, sabotage, and terrorism on the part of North Vietnam.

> On the diplomatic front [reported Washington correspondent Max Frankel] the United States is still trying to prod the Indian member of the three-nation International Control Commission to denounce North Vietnamese 'subversion' and 'interference' in South Vietnam. This, it is believed, would be the best way of combating Communist contentions that the fighting amounts to a civil war between a 'reactionary' government and national 'liberators.' Officials cited this policy to rebut reports that President Ngo Dinh Diem was considering the idea of evicting the commission as ineffective and as a cover-up for Communist activities.

Fake a report or get out, the Americans were telling the Control Commission just as Diem later told U.S. correspondents, 'Produce paper victories, or get out.'

Even if 'subversion' and 'interference' were at the root of the problem, which they were certainly not, these terms are nowhere mentioned in the Geneva Agreements, the implementation of which the International Commission was in Vietnam to control. But clauses specifically mentioned in the Agreements were being violated day in and day out by the United States itself and by the Diem regime.

Nevertheless, to the discredit of those responsible for its compilation, a majority report, with Poland strenuously objecting, was produced which dutifully rubber-stamped many of the charges made in the 'Blue Book.' As an example of the quality of the ICC majority report, it is stated that it has been impossible to check the 'accuracy' of reports of 'alleged' American military aid. The Americans had quite officially spoken of 5000 'advisers' and the U.S. press by the time the report was published had put the figure at 7000. But the ICC report, in an outrageous attempt to diminish the importance of U.S. intervention, said its teams from 3 December 1961 to 5 May 1962, had 'controlled the entry of 72 military personnel and observed but not controlled, 173 personnel,' plus military planes, howitzers, armored cars, etc.

The prestige of the ICC could not but suffer in producing a document so obviously aimed at justifying America's undeclared war against the people of South Vietnam.

[From Chapter 3 of *The Furtive War: The United States in Vietnam and Laos* (International Publishers, New York, 1963), pp. 60–76.]

The Tragedy of South Vietnam's Ethnic Minorities [1964]

My Visit to the Liberated Zones of South Vietnam was a collection and adaptation of articles Burchett had dispatched to the New York *National Guardian* during his visits to Southeast Asia in the early 1960s. The following chapter begins his examination of US 'Special Warfare', a subject he was to expand on subsequently (for example, see Chapter 18). In this case he deals specifically with the experiences of ethnic minorities in Vietnam.

There are more than 50 identified minorities in Vietnam, most of which live very different lives in the highlands from the dominant ethnic Vietnamese who populate the coast and the lowlands. The variety of languages and religious practices among Vietnam's minorities reflect the country's ethnic complexity and explain the difficulties they have presented for various Vietnamese governments.

After the mid-1950s, North and South Vietnam dealt with the minorities differently. The Hanoi regime understood the traditional separatist attitudes of the tribal minorities and set up two autonomous zones for the highlanders in return for their acceptance of Hanoi's political control. In contrast, the Saigon administration under Ngo Dinh Diem opted for direct, centralised control of the tribal minorities and incurred their enduring wrath by seizing ancestral lands for the resettlement of displaced Catholic refugees from the North.

After Diem's assassination in 1963, successive Saigon administrations granted a modicum of autonomy, but the 'strategic hamlet' program largely embittered its minority participants. In an act of resistance, some tribal leaders gathered in 1964 to announce the formation of the Unified Front for the Struggle of Oppressed Races, and some understanding of the motivation behind this can be gleaned from Burchett's description of their experiences in the following chapter.

* * *

One of the most horrifying aspects of the 'special war' being waged in South Vietnam is the massive attempt to wipe out the ethnic minorities. The 'quick' method of physical annihilation having failed because the tribespeople finally took to arms to defend their homes and families, the 'slow' method of U.S.-type 'reservations' is now being tried. The Americans have plenty of experience with both methods in dealing with their own 'redskins'. I have talked with scores of tribal leaders and ordinary tribal members in widely separated parts of the country and their stories bear a deadly and horrible similarity. The attempts to wipe them out or kill them slowly in concentration camps is mixed up with a really macabre plan of reshuffling vast masses of the population. People from the plains forced at gunpoint to emigrate to the mountains, tribespeople forced to move from the mountains down to the plains, where even the air is stifling for them. This was a process that started immediately after the ceasefire agreements went into effect.

It must be borne in mind that the ethnic minorities in Central Vietnam – as indeed in the main resistance bases in the Viet Bac in North Vietnam – played a vital role during the resistance war against the French. This was sufficient for the Diemist regime to launch a specially ferocious drive against them, the moment the armed units of the resistance had withdrawn to the North according to the Geneva Agreements. Le Quang Binh, a member of the Quang Ngai provincial executive of the Liberation Front, told me that in one small district of his province, Son Ha, 4000 former resistance members from the Hre minority were arrested in December 1954 alone: 'Important suspects were dragged to death behind automobiles,' he said. 'Others were buried alive in batches of 20 and 30. They would tie them together in groups of three or four, kick them into a ditch and start shovelling the earth over them. There were terrible, muffled cries as from buffalos or cows, the earth heaved for a while, then all was quiet. We knew of this and rushed to the spot as the execution squads left, and by tearing the earth away we managed to save some before they suffocated. All the lands distributed to the minority people during the resistance war were grabbed back and divided up among Diemist agents. The repression in Quang Ngai was terrible for everyone, but it was doubly and trebly terrible for the minority people.'

It was not surprising that the first resistance spark was struck in Central Vietnam, by the tiny Cor tribe, led by a 90-year-old chieftain in armed struggle after over 500 of a total of 4700 had been tortured to death or executed. This was early in 1959.

'In the repression that followed,' said Le Quang Binh, himself a veteran resistance cadre, with iron-grey hair and a strong, gaunt face, 'the Diemists launched 230 mopping-up operations in the north-west part of the province from June 1959 to the end of that year. They concentrated two army divisions in one district of 200 sq. kms, in a kill all, burn all, destroy all operation. They killed anything that moved and burned over 200 hamlets to the ground. In Tra Bong district (where the Cor uprising took place) every house was burned. Over 32,000 persons were homeless – a huge number in the minority areas where villages are very small and spaced far apart. People fled to the forest and made temporary shelters, living on wild roots and whatever animals they could trap. Their buffalos, pigs and chickens were wiped out. But from that moment, they prepared to wage a violent struggle with rudimentary weapons to protect their lives and property. Fortunately because of the cover that nature gives, relatively few lives were lost in this ferocious campaign.'

Over 300 kms to the south-west of Quang Ngai, in Darlac province in the 'High Plateaux' area, the story was similar. Here I spoke for instance with Ama (Father of) Tien, a native of the Rhade minority and an officer in the Darlac provincial armed forces. 'Our peoples in the north-west part of the province, where I come from,' he said, 'absolutely refused to have anything to do with "strategic hamlets". We are used to a free life with plenty of space – how can we live cooped up behind barbed wire? One day the Diemists showered my village of Buang Ket and two others with leaflets demanding that we move into "strategic hamlets" they had set up at the district centre. Of course no one moved, so a few days later they sent planes over again – but with bombs this time – and wiped out our villages. We had expected this, so the whole population had fled to the forests and no one was hurt. But all the houses were destroyed. Napalm bombs were dropped on our fields and the ripening maize was destroyed.'

Ama Tien, a slim wiry young man, dark-complexioned and with otherwise splendid teeth filed off at the edges to make a nice straight line as is the custom of his people, said that in May 1962 'the Diemists used all means, infantry attacks, more bombings and strafings, helicopter-borne troops to herd our people into the "strategic hamlets". At gun- and bayonet-point and by burning the houses, they did force a few people in. But most of the younger ones fled to the forest to take up arms. And every now and again there is a mysterious fire in one of the hamlets and all the inmates rush off to join us in the forest.'

One of the most moving stories I heard was also from Darlac province, quite close to the capital of Ban Me Thuot, which is also the chief town of the district that bears the same name. In this district, the tribal people in the late 1950's had been driven from their villages by one of the U.S.–Diemist mad schemes to set up 'agricultural settlements', glorified concentration camps to which about 25,000 Vietnamese political 'suspects' had been herded from the plains. Tribal lands were seized to provide coffee and rubber plantations on which the 'suspects' were to slave, villages were bulldozed out of existence. But the minority people had built up new villages and were working new cultivation patches.

At the end of 1961, a scheme was concocted to concentrate them in a 'model' strategic hamlet area at Boun Ea Nao, only 3 kms from the capital. Incidentally this was a scheme very close to the heart of General Maxwell Taylor, the U.S. President's chief military adviser. He visited the site every time he visited South Vietnam. The minority people hated the whole idea, thoroughly mistrusted Diemists and Americans alike. Every village in the district was supposed to send 10 'elders' and other responsible inmates to a training centre to receive instruction in 'new' religion and also in the use of modern firearms. The chief instructor was an American colonel in pastor's clothing who called himself simply 'Eay Teo' or 'Grandfather Teo'. He described himself as a 'new' American and had a very smooth line (I was informed about all this by a local village 'elder', a very dignified and intelligent person whose name and village may not be revealed because he is still in the area).

'We are "new" Americans', the instructor assured them. 'We are against those Americans who helped the Diemists suppress the people. We are here to help you become really independent – to become autonomous, in fact. But in order to be really independent you must not help either the Diemists or the Viet Cong. We will give you everything, rice, salt, cloth – even bicycles – and arms to defend yourselves . . .' For a while the tribespeople were a bit confused. Some Americans helped Diem, others claimed to oppose him. And these 'new' Americans looked just like the 'old' ones, the same skin and hair. They seemed to be military men, but they dressed like priests. 'We are not priests,' insisted the instructor, knowing full well that priests would be identified with French colonialism. 'We are sent by Christ to help you, but ours is a "new" religion, the religion of the "new" Americans.'

The tribespeople argued back: 'But you look just like the "old" Americans that even now help the Diemists kill our people.'

'You see' said Eay Teo, who I have no doubt was from the US Psychological Warfare Department, 'it is this way. The "old" Americans and the Diemists were like a cat. The Viet Cong is the mouse. You minority people are the rice paddy. The mouse smuggled himself into your paddy, so the cats came to kill the mice. But in doing so they also harmed your paddy. But if the mice don't come to the paddy, the cat will also not come. No harm will be done to the paddy either by the mice or the cats.'

The tribespeople talked this over among themselves, but were still very suspicious. They still did not want to be concentrated. Nor did they want to accept the arms the chief instructor kept pressing on them. So they gave their answer – no concentration and no arms.

'If you refuse to carry arms to protect yourselves and "old" Americans and Diemists come to kill you, we will not be responsible,' said the 'new' Americans. And sure enough within a few days of the final refusal, a regiment was sent into the area, five villages were burned to the ground and 20-odd tribespeople, mainly children and old people, were killed. The villages were now ordered to send their representatives again to Ban Me Thuot, but before going they contacted local resistance cadres and asked for advice.

'They found it difficult to advise us on such a terribly important question,' my informant said. 'At their level they could not take a decision at that moment, because they always tried to find solutions that would reduce our sufferings.'

Over a thousand tribespeople assembled at the meeting place. They were ringed round by a battalion of Diemist troops. 'Eay Teo' was there of course, together with the provincial governor and chiefs of districts. Formalities were minimal: 'Either you agree to concentrate or military operations start against all villages in the district tomorrow', said the colonel-priest.

'We were all very depressed,' the 'elder' said. 'Many of us had passed through the smoking ruins of villages, others had been made homeless or had lost relatives. It seemed there was nothing to do but agree. But then an old man, I Bru of Boun Dju village, climbed up on a house platform and demanded to speak. He was nearly 70 years of age.

'"We ethnic minorities always lived with our ray (cultivation patches), our forests and brooks and trees. Now you are going to concentrate us. In that case we will die out slowly. You have your troops around us. Better pull the triggers and kill us all together now." The district chief strode up to him. "If you disagree with the Government and the Americans, you will all be killed, foolish old man. And if you continue to speak like that you will be killed on the spot."

'"If you are killed," cried old I Bru, "you lose your villa, your plantation, your car, your beautiful women. If I am killed, I lose this only," and he snatched off his loin cloth and threw it at the district chief.

'There was tremendous excitement. Everyone rushed forward to save the old man, shouting "No concentration". Officials were swept off their feet. Then Eay Teo climbed up on the platform and said "Why all this noise. We only asked you here to have your opinions. Now you may go home."'

The 'elder' with whom I spoke went off to inform the LNF cadres what had happened. 'There were tears in their eyes when we told them of the heroism of old I Bru,' he said, 'and they sent an armed unit back with me to bring the old man to safety. They were sure the Diemists would kill him that very night. But we arrived too late. Troops had come from a nearby post and dragged the old man away. He was killed the same night.

'Next day, people from over 20 villages met to honour the old man. The enemy also came and said "Why this big meeting? How do you know the old man is dead?" We replied "He was a man who always did good for our people. But last night a tiger took him, so we pay him our last respects."'

At the meeting the tribespeople unanimously took a pledge that they would carry on the fight as the old man had done and that 'Only when there is no more forest and when the brooks have dried up will the Rhade people allow themselves to be concentrated. But that day will never come. As we know for thousands of years the brooks never dry up and trees may be cut down but others grow in their place. Our community may die out but others will grow up and prosper like the trees.'

The tribespeople won their battle against being concentrated, but later their villages that remained near Ban Me Thuot were fenced around and turned into 'strategic hamlets'. As my 'elder' informant expressed it, 'They may fence in our villages, but they cannot fence in our hearts. They belong to the revolution.'

Stories similar to this I hear every day, as often as I have the chance to sit down and talk with the ethnic minority people.

[Chapter 4 of *My Visit to the Liberated Zones of South Vietnam* (Foreign Languages Publishing House, Hanoi, 2nd edn, 1964), pp. 29–37.]

17

Interview with General Vo Nguyen Giap
(April 13, 1964)

Over the years he reported from Vietnam, Wilfred Burchett developed a warm personal relationship with the North Vietnamese leadership, based on genuine affection. He was a frequent visitor to Hanoi during the American War and would often have breakfast with President Ho Chi Minh in his residence, or a private chat with General Vo Nguyen Giap, as well as the occasional 'official' interview with them and other senior figures. The following chapter reproduces one such interview (published in Vietnam, the translation is as appears in the original publication).

In 1954, General Vo Nguyen Giap masterminded the bloody 57-day siege against a French garrison in Dien Bien Phu in northwestern Vietnam, battle which signalled the coming end of colonialism. This Communist Viet Minh victory was the first by an Asian resistance group against a colonial army in a conventional military conflict. It ended the myth of Western invincibility, led to the ignominious withdrawal of the French from Vietnam, and inspired anti-imperial forces worldwide.

Fourteen years later, Giap triumphed in another epic battle, the Tet offensive, widely considered the turning point of the American War.

* * *

W. Burchett – Could you please comment on the recent declarations by Washington and Saigon concerning the extension of the war in South Vietnam into an attack on the Democratic Republic of Vietnam?

General Vo Nguyen Giap – My comment? Well! It is clear and categorical. Any act of aggression against the DRV by the Americans and their lackeys would be an act of suicide. All our people, both in North and South Vietnam, will stand up as one man to annihilate them. Even the hottest heads in the Pentagon have no doubt about it. That is why we think that they will think it over not only twice, but several times, before attempting such an adventure which would be quite dangerous for them. In any case, we are vigilant.

W. Burchett – That is clear and categorical . . .

General Vo Nguyen Giap – Of course . . .

W. Burchett – What was the extent and importance of sending groups of commandos from South Vietnam into DRV territory, and what was the aim of those incursions? Did those activities increase during the past few months?

General Vo Nguyen Giap – I can tell you that all sabotage commando units sent by the Americans and their lackeys against us have been completely annihilated. Generally speaking, they came in squads. In most cases they were annihilated by the civilian population and by our self-defence forces. Those commandos sought to commit acts of sabotage, and especially to ferret out military information, and also to rally certain groups of malcontents which only exist in the imagination of those who sent them. Of late the Americans and the Khanh government have redoubled their efforts in this matter.

W. Burchett – Ah yes . . .

General Vo Nguyen Giap – In their criminal actions, they wanted to make use of the complicity of Phumi Nosavan and Chiang Kai-shek. I can assure you that their failures will only be more bitter. Their men will be annihilated, yes, annihilated.

W. Burchett – What are the main characteristics of the present military situation in South Vietnam?

General Vo Nguyen Giap – That, for one, is a big question. The main characteristic of the present military situation in South Vietnam is that in their undeclared aggressive war of a special type, as the Americans call it, they have run up against the unshakable will for independence and freedom of an entire people. A real people's war is waged in the southern part of our country, under the leadership of the Liberation National Front, a sacred war, the second war for national liberation of our people, which is mobilizing the largest masses of the population from town to country – the minority nationals, people of all religions, of all sects and patriotic social strata. That war is winning even the sympathy of the patriotic elements still within the enemy's political administrative and military organizations. That is the main characteristic, it is a people's war.

The second characteristic is that the situation in South Vietnam over the recent period has entered a new stage marked by the following features: the balance of forces has unceasingly been tipped gradually, but inevitably, in our favour, in favour of our compatriots, to the detriment of the Americans and their flunkeys. The Staley–Taylor plan has gone bankrupt. The famous policy of 'strategic hamlets' which in the eyes of Washington constitutes the most conclusive experience of what they call an anti-people's, anti-guerilla war, on which the Americans and Ngo Dinh Diem pinned all their hopes, is crumbling under the waves of political and armed struggle by our compatriots. Meanwhile, the overwhelming majority of our compatriots, rallied around the Liberation National Front, support its programme of independence, democracy, peace and neutrality. And the South Vietnam Liberation armed forces have not ceased to grow, and have won victory after victory. By the way, I would like to say that the Americans and Nguyen Khanh have well organized, to the benefit of the South Vietnam Liberation armed forces, the quartermaster and supply services for USA-brand weapons.

W. Burchett – I have noted that not only the arms – both American and local – but also the machines used by the liberation forces to manufacture weapons, are American made. That surprised me a great deal.

General Vo Nguyen Giap – That proves the Americans have much experience in the organization of the quartermaster and supply services.

Well! Washington is now looking for a way out, but the only possible way out, the only solution, our President Ho Chi Minh has told you this morning.

W. Burchett – Yes.

General Vo Nguyen Giap – That is to respect the will of the South Vietnamese people. That is the only way out, is it not? As the President rightly put it, to put an end to the war, there is only one solution: to respect the will of the South Vietnamese people. That will was clearly expounded by the Liberation National Front in these words: that the South Vietnam question must be settled by the South Vietnamese people themselves on the basis of national independence, democracy, peace and neutrality. The prerequisite must be the complete withdrawal by the Americans of their military forces and armaments, and the respect by the US of the 1954 Geneva Agreements on Vietnam. Well, let the Americans go home!

W. Burchett – Yankee go home! Very well.

General Vo Nguyen Giap – In any case, sooner or later, they will have to pack up, we are sure. They are in brief the characteristics of the situation. You have been to South Vietnam, and you have seen with your own eyes how the situation has progressed, haven't you? I congratulate you on what you have aptly said of the situation. You have drawn quite a correct conclusion that the liberation army is invincible, the people's war will certainly be crowned with success ... Yes ... invincible.

W. Burchett – I am sure of it. It is impossible to be there and not to be persuaded of it. We agree, completely agree. I think the Americans, too, agree.

General Vo Nguyen Giap – They are no longer discussing whether they will lose or win, but when their defeat will come.

W. Burchett – The last and very important question. Ten years have elapsed since Dien Bien Phu. How do you draw the essential lessons from that historic battle?

General Vo Nguyen Giap – This year, our people and army will celebrate the 10th anniversary of the historic battle of Dien Bien Phu. From the experience of the national liberation war of the Vietnamese people, particularly from the Dien Bien Phu victory, I think we can draw the following conclusions:

Firstly, the Dien Bien Phu victory constitutes not only a great victory for the Vietnamese people but also for progressive mankind, a victory for all the weak peoples who are struggling against colonialism in all its forms, old and new, for independence and freedom, a great victory for the forces of socialism, democracy and peace all over the world. The Dien Bien Phu victory proves that in the present international circumstances, guided by a correct policy, united in a resolute struggle for independence and democracy, against imperialism and colonialism in all its forms, and enjoying the approval and support of the world's people, an oppressed people, however weak it may be, will certainly win final victory. In any case, the events that have taken place during recent years have substantiated this conclusion. The peoples of Cuba, Laos, Algeria and other countries have stood up and won victory. This is the first conclusion.

The second conclusion is that in the struggle for national liberation, in face of the acts of violence and war of the imperialists and old and new colonialists, the oppressed peoples of the colonial, semi-colonial and dependent countries have only one path: to counter such acts of violence and war by resolute political and military struggles, by political violence, by the armed violence of the entire people. The political and military struggle of the entire people, the people's war, the people's army, the national united front of the whole people, constitute the path of national salvation and victory.

I wish to add that in South Vietnam the war has never ceased since 1959. One may say that over the past years, the United States and the Ngo Dinh Diem administration have waged a unilateral war, perpetrated countless acts of violence and massacres against the peaceful population. Yes . . . At last, our compatriots in South Vietnam realized that there was no other way than to stand up to struggle for national salvation. Since then, they have been using political and military violence against the acts of violence and war of the enemy.

The third conclusion is of great interest to our people and of vital importance for us. If in the past, the Vietnamese people defeated the French and American imperialists, especially on the Dien Bien Phu battlefield, in the just struggle for liberation they are now waging against the extremely barbarous 'undeclared war' unleashed by the imperialists and their stooges, our compatriots in South Vietnam, despite the great many difficulties they have to overcome, have recorded big successes and will certainly win final victory. The Vietnamese people's struggle to liberate South Vietnam and reunify their country will certainly be victorious. We have unshakable confidence in this victory. Please tell world public opinion that the Vietnamese are one of the peoples who most cherish peace, and have been waging a protracted war of liberation in extremely difficult conditions. Our compatriots in South Vietnam are now in their 20th year of war. Our people, our compatriots in the South, are struggling for their liberation, for peace, a genuine peace, a peace in independence and democracy.

I think that a fourth conclusion can be drawn. We know that Dien Bien Phu opened the way for the conclusion of the 1954 Geneva agreements which re-established peace in Indochina and recognized the independence, sovereignty, unity and territorial integrity of Vietnam, Laos, and Cambodia.

For these reasons, we can draw the conclusion that all negotiations with the imperialists must be backed up by a resolute struggle in all forms against their perfidious designs. Only when the people's forces have grown in their struggle are the imperialists compelled to renounce their privileges and interests and recognize our legitimate rights.

Hence one can also draw the conclusion that by their protracted, hard and heroic resistance war, by their fights and the great victory won on the Dien Bien Phu front, the Vietnamese people struggled not only for national independence but also for peace in Vietnam and South-East Asia, a peace which the Americans are seriously sabotaging in South Vietnam and Laos. Have you been to Laos?

W. Burchett – Not in the recent past, nor in these last months. I have been there several times earlier.

General Vo Nguyen Giap – In Laos, since 1954 there had been peace, then the national coalition government ... But the Americans toppled the national coalition government and fomented a civil war, didn't they? What they call 'civil war' is in its essence a war of aggression aimed at turning Laos into an American colony and military base. They have systematically and cynically violated the Geneva Agreements. At last the Laotian people, a peaceloving people who follow Buddhism, had to rise up once more to carry out armed and political struggles. Only after many years of military and political struggles and after many defeats inflicted on the pro-American Phumi Nosavan troops, could the new Geneva Agreements be reached. The Americans however are seeing by every means to undermine these agreements.

7: *General Vo Nguyen Giap, Defence Minister and Commander-in-Chief of Vietnam's People's Army, Hanoi, 1965*

I am coming now to the fifth conclusion which has a more general character.

By their impudent manoeuvres, camouflaged or not, by their schemes of intervention and aggression, the US imperialists have completely unmasked themselves in the eyes of the people of Indochina as well as of the world. They have shown themselves to be a brutal and cynical aggressor of the peoples of Vietnam, Laos and Cambodia, an international gendarme, and the most dangerous enemy of the world's people and the national liberation movements. That is why the world's people should intensify their struggle and make the broadest united front against US imperialism. We are convinced that in all parts of the world, in Asia, Africa and Latin America, however perfidious and Machiavellian their schemes to enslave the peoples may be, the US imperialists will in the end certainly suffer an inevitable, bitter failure. The struggles of the peoples of Asia, Africa and Latin America will certainly win final victory.

These are in a nutshell the conclusions we can draw from our war for national liberation and the Dien Bien Phu battle. Ten years have passed and many events have taken place. I think these events in Indochina as well as in other countries of the world confirm these conclusions.

[Chapter 16 of *My Visit to the Liberated Zones of South Vietnam* (Foreign Languages Publishing House, Hanoi, 2nd edn, 1964), pp. 139–147.]

18

A Fortified Hamlet [1965]

In November 1963, Burchett embarked on his 'greatest journalistic enterprise since Hiroshima'. He spent six months travelling in the jungles of South Vietnam with 'Vietcong' guerillas in areas controlled by the National Liberation Front of South Vietnam. He lived with the NLF fighters throughout this period, marching with them, inhabiting their network of tunnels, and dodging attacks on them.

The articles, photographs and the book, *Vietnam: Inside Story of the Guerilla War* that resulted from this historic visit propelled him back into the front pages of the Western news media and publishing houses. His discussions with the tribespeople in the mountains and the ordinary Vietnamese in the lowlands of the country were new to Western audiences, and combining these insights with his interviews with American POWs gave this book a unique value as a record of the war, and marks it as one of Burchett's best.

In the early 1960s the US began to apply the principle of 'Special Warfare' in South Vietnam to fight the Vietcong. The father of this theory was General Maxwell Taylor, who was advisor to President Kennedy when he first began to advocate it in 1961, and later became chairman of the Joint Chiefs of Staff. The program involved Ngo Dinh Diem's Saigon regime supplying cannon fodder, the US supplying equipment and advisors, and peasants and ethnic minorities being relocated into 'strategic hamlets' to separate them from the guerillas. As the following chapter indicates, however, the NLF had a network of hamlets of their own.

* * *

Among those I met the following day were two dimpled and demure girl guerillas, whose names in Vietnamese meant 'Blossom' and 'Lissom' respectively. They were both from the same village and the district guerilla leader had mentioned them as having helped, with five lads from their village, to repulse a company of enemy troops.

They were in spotlessly clean black cotton shirts and trousers; hand grenades dangled from their U.S. webbing belts and each had a U.S. carbine. They looked 15, but 'Blossom' said she was 19 and 'Lissom' assured me she was 22.

'Blossom' was the real heroine of the action and she made it sound quite simple. 'When the enemy came very close, I rushed from one firing position to another firing my carbine and one of the puppets fell each time I fired. We all shifted our positions so they would think there were a lot of us. Actually most of our self-defense unit was away that day and we were only seven,' she explained in a light, babyish voice. 'The enemy started to set up a machine gun to fire at one of our positions, so I ran there and threw a hand grenade. It killed the gunner and put the machine gun out of action. By then the enemy had nine killed and wounded and they withdrew. Later they fired some shells but they did no damage.' That was all. It seemed incredible to me that a company, 80 to 100 men, would break off an engagement with nine casualties or that they would not have tried to take the positions by assault.

Then I was taken to have a look at the 'fortified village' which the two girls had helped defend. The defenses consist of a maze of tunnels, about 20 miles in this one hamlet, I was told, leading into spacious fire positions which cover every approach. They are big enough for someone of Vietnamese size to run doubled up from one fire position to another, as 'Blossom' had described.

I was taken to inspect a single clump of bamboo and told to look very carefully for anything suspicious among the roots. I found nothing. Then I was taken into the tunnel and to a firing position which could accommodate three or four people. Someone took a stick and poked it through what seemed to be blind slits with earthern gun rests behind them. The slits opened up to cover the road along which we had cycled a few minutes earlier into the hamlet. Again I was taken to the bamboo clump and there my attention was drawn to the tiny slits which had been opened up among the bamboo roots, impossible for anyone to detect at even a few yards.

Other firing positions which I inspected were also perfectly cam-ouflaged and as the guerillas changed places constantly, even if the gun flash or smoke gave a position away, it would be little use firing at it. All roads, paths and canals approaching the village were adequately covered. To jump for cover at the time when the firing started was inevitably to fall into a terrible series of traps, most of them deep pits with bamboo and steel spikes; others with grenades and anti-personnel mines made in a local arsenal. I understood why an action was broken off after nine casualties. To take even the outer perimeter of such a fortified hamlet would be a very costly affair. If attacking troops were to penetrate the tunnels, all sorts of hand-operated traps would go into action. The attackers would probably be diverted to a section which would be blown up with everyone in it. If an assault force attacked in the centre it would be fired on from the flanks, if it attacked the flanks it would be fired on from the centre; if it overran the outer perimeter and penetrated further, the second and third and fourth lines of defense would go into action. If the odds were too overwhelming, the guerillas could pull out altogether through the system of escape tunnels which might lead into the forest, to a river bank or to a neighboring hamlet.

The 'fortified hamlet' of 'Blossom' and 'Lissom' was the first of such perfection I had visited. I was later to visit other tunnel systems which linked a whole group of hamlets and had over 500 firing positions and successive traps to block off sections in case flame-throwers or some sort of poison gas was used. A hundred thousand work hours had been put into building the tunnel defenses of some of the hamlets. They were built almost entirely by the young people of the villages, the older ones keeping up supplies of rice, tea and fruit while they worked often from dusk to dawn.

'The enemy builds big posts with huge watchtowers to try and control the countryside,' said the military chief of Saigon–Gia Dinh. 'We build our fire positions as close to the ground as possible and the rest underground, because our people are defending their own homes. They need to see the enemy – over their sights – only when he comes with evil intent to the gates of their hamlets. The enemy cannot move along the roads and paths near our villages without being continually in the sights of our guns. This is what we mean by people's war.'

There were about 4300 such fortified villages in South Vietnam at that time, mostly in the Mekong Delta region, but they were being added to every day in Central Vietnam. It seemed to me that those who devised them had pooled the experiences of General Vo Nguyen Giap and his creeping system of trenches used so effectively at Dien Bien Phu, the tunnel system used by the Chinese guerillas in Hopei province during the anti-Japanese war in which whole counties were linked by underground defense and communications networks, and the system of defensive tunnels built by the Korean–Chinese forces across the waist of Korea near the 38th parallel. If one such hamlet could keep a company at bay – and I heard of plenty of cases where even battalions were repulsed – one only has to multiply by 4500 the magnitude of the task of any regime or any military machine in trying to reconquer them.

From midnight onwards on the night after the meeting with 'Blossom' and 'Lissom' there was intermittent artillery fire, but none coming close enough to make us leave our hammocks – they were slung in a rubber plantation. At dawn the firing was more intensive and coming our way. *Mesdemoiselles* were also very active, showing a special interest in our little corner. About the time the Saigon morning papers were delivered to my interpreter, one of those tiny envelopes arrived. It was for the Saigon–Gia Dinh military chief who happened to be with us – a brisk, cheerful man with that alert, decided way about him that marks a good staff officer in any army. After studying the note, he scribbled a reply; showing both to my companions and buckling on his Colt, with a few terse words and a sunny smile he strode away.

'A company of parachutists moved into the other end of the plantation about midnight,' said Huynh, my journalist–interpreter. 'We have had them under observation and they are moving this way at the moment. We had better put you in the secret trenches.' By that time, there was considerable activity all around. The doctor was checking his medical pack, and our baggage – always packed for instant moves – was being carried with some speed deeper into the plantation. 'They're still about a half mile from here,' said Huynh laconically. 'We also have some troops around. We'd better not dawdle because bullets will soon be flying.'

I did not favour spending an unlimited period in the secret underground tunnels which were not tailored for my girth. A compromise solution was found by letting me move into a well-camouflaged semi-circular trench, with communication trenches leading well to the rear. The parachutists in mottled green camouflage uniforms were advancing, cautiously, weapons at the ready in two groups, one about fifty, the other carrying some mortars, about thirty. There were three U.S. advisers with the larger group.

At about a hundred yards distant, they sighted two trenches with some Front troops in them. The parachutists flopped down and opened up with heavy machine guns, from both columns. The Front forces replied with a short burst from each of two heavy machine guns, wounding three paratroopers. From where I was I saw the Americans drop into a trench at the first shots and could see their hands gesticulating, urging the unit to advance. But the troops wavered a moment, then swept up their machine guns and the mortars they were just setting up and started retreating into the trees, the Americans scrambling to their feet and leading the way once the retreat started. They fled so precipitately that they left their lunch rations in the trench. Guerillas followed them up and little envelopes started arriving with news that the parachutists had withdrawn one, two, three miles – back to their training base at Trung Hoa. There had been no casualties in the Front trenches, and the position in which I was installed had not fired at all.

A local guerilla leader came over as soon as the 'all quiet' was received and a few excited words were exchanged between him and the unit commander of the regular forces which had done the firing. 'The guerilla is angry because they fired so soon,' the interpreter explained. 'He wants to know why they fired at 100 yards, instead of 10 or 15 yards like the guerillas. The whole unit could have been wiped out and their arms captured.' The unit commander explained that his aim was to scare them, not to wipe them out. His job was to protect a 'foreign friend'. If they had been wiped out and the Americans killed, there would have been a big action to recover the bodies, the village would have been bombed as a reprisal and such results would violate instructions to give 'maximum security' to their foreign charge.

The locals explained that the parachutists were trainees who were just about to 'graduate'. The exercises under simulated battle conditions which I had heard a few days earlier were the

8: *'Blossom' and 'Lissom', 1964*

last but one phase before graduation. The last was an actual combat engagement, usually against lightly-armed local guerillas. To
their surprise, this batch had run into regular troops who also had
heavy machine guns. Doubtless those particular graduates were put

through another conditioning process of simulated battle conditions before being sent out to face enemy fire again. 'In any case the trainees run after we fire a few shots,' the guerilla leader said, 'but we usually get some of their weapons.'

About an hour later, as we cycled through the hamlet near which the action had taken place, a girl from the local information office was striding through the street with a megaphone, announcing that an attack by enemy forces had been repulsed and that news 'of casualties and booty will be announced later.'

The incident in the rubber plantation was the start of an exciting few days in the Saigon area and I was able to sense something of what 'living integrated with the enemy' meant.

[From 'Struggle in Saigon', Chapter 2 of *Vietnam: Inside Story of the Guerilla War* (International Publishers, New York, 1965), pp. 43–47.]

19

Patriots & Mercenaries [1965]

The circumstances prevailing at the time Burchett wrote *Inside Story of the Guerilla War* help to explain the optimistic assessment of the liberation struggle which fills its pages. By early 1965 it had become clear to the Americans that their cautious policy in Vietnam was not working. South Vietnam was at the point of collapse and it was increasingly understood in Washington that a continuation of existing policies would necessarily lead to defeat for the US and for South Vietnam.

The US response was to greatly increase its troop levels in the South (184,000 by the end of 1965; 385,000 by the end of 1966) and to initiate Operation Rolling Thunder, the sustained aerial bombing of North Vietnam. It was at this moment that the war moved into a new phase. Strategists in Washington took some time to realise that increased troop numbers were not likely to win this battle, and it may have been useful for them to read the assessment of the relative motivations of the combatants in the following chapter.

* * *

A Terrorist Squad

My journalist–interpreter friend excused himself for having awakened me. My watch showed 10.44 p.m.; I had been dead to the world in my hammock for a good two hours. 'Three compatriots have arrived with a very interesting story,' he said. 'Can't it wait till morning?' I asked, and he replied that it was really an 'exceptionally interesting story,' and the three were only resting for an hour before they took off again.

So I swung out of the hammock and was guided to a little clearing where the tiny bottle lamps had been set up on tree stumps, the flickering flames lighting up the faces of three exhausted looking but triumphant men. Almost exactly three hours previously they had exploded a 25-pound bomb inside Saigon's 'U.S. Only' Capitol Cinema. According to the official account of the results, as I heard it over the 'Voice of America' next morning, three U.S. servicemen were killed and 57 wounded.

Two of the three before me were former peasants from the Saigon outskirts, the third a former factory worker, and I shall refer to them as No. 1, 2 and 3. No. 1, the worker, was the master planner and also organized the escape: 'We had previously blown up the MAAG (Military Aid and Advisory Group) headquarters,' he said. 'That was in July 1963. Another group had tried to blow up this cinema but failed because they tried to attack it from the rear. And still another group had exploded a bomb in a U.S. baseball stadium the week before. Our task was to succeed where the others had failed at the Capitol. We had decided to do this after the Lunar New Year ceasefire period, but when American planes napalm-bombed a big meeting in Cu Chi district on New Year's Day, we decided to teach them a lesson. Also we thought they should be punished for the coup they had just made in putting Nguyen Khanh in power. By that they wanted to show that they were the real masters in Saigon; we wanted to show that the people are still there too. So we decided to attack within the ceasefire period which they had violated.'

As they described it, while Nos. 1 and 2 created a diversion at the side entrance, No. 3, the second peasant with the rather exalted face of a poet, walked through the main entrance with the explosive. 'Because of the shooting outside, the Americans inside were alerted,' No. 3 said. 'Two jumped on me as I entered and started to strangle me. Because I had the explosive in my arms, I could not defend myself. But I managed to pull the detonator and as it spluttered the Americans were stupefied with fear, and ran up some stairs. There is just ten seconds after pulling the detonator before it explodes. I had time to put it down between the aisles and walk out, closing the grenade-proof steel doors after me just as the explosion took place.'

'You intended to blow yourself up with the two Americans?' I asked, and he eyed me calmly and said, 'Of course.' Looking at him, I thought of the descriptions in 19th century Russian literature of the poets and intellectuals who sacrificed their energies and talents, and often enough their lives, in trying to blow up the tsars. No. 3 was of that category. What pushes people to such deeds, I wondered, scanning as much of their tense faces as the bottle lamps would permit, their profiles etched against the impenetrable black of jungle night on which a newly born moon made no impression at all. There was silence for a moment, except for the monotonous cry of an intensely boring night bird which never ceased its metallic two-note cry between dusk and dawn.

'There are thousands of militants like us in Saigon,' said No. 2, 'ready to sacrifice ourselves at any moment, but we want to kill five or ten Americans for every one of us.'

'Were there women and children in the cinema?' I asked.

'We don't make war against women and children,' blazed forth No. 2. 'But what do they care for our women and children? In that cinema are only the pilots that go out day after day in their planes and blindly bomb and strafe our villages. Do they ask if there are women and children inside the houses they napalm? They bomb and fire on every living thing they see.'

No. 1 explained that a 12-year-old sister of the one who had planted the explosive had been killed with 15 other children in the strafing of a school in Cau Xe.

I was interested in knowing enough about their lives to understand what impelled people into such desperate ventures. No. 1 had spent five of the preceding nine years in Diemist prisons: 'In front of my eyes I saw my comrades, the finest men that ever lived, tortured to death for no other reason than that they had been patriots in the struggle for independence,' he said. The hamlet of No. 2 had been bulldozed out of existence to make way for airfield extensions north of the city. After that he had worked as a coolie on an American military base. 'I will never forgive them for what they did to our women,' he said. 'I saw things that no human being should see. As long as they remain on my soil while I live, I shall take my revenge. For my own sister and my own compatriots, our young women violated, comrades tortured and massacred.'

It was time for them to move on. As they swung their small packs on their shoulders, I asked where they were heading. 'We are going to a rest area,' said No. 1, 'and there we have to work out something special to mark May 1. In Saigon we have a tradition of celebrating

May Day.' I thought of them later when the radio reported an audacious coup in which a 14,000-ton U.S. aircraft-transport was sunk in Saigon harbour in the small hours of May 1 and a second bomb exploded killing and wounding Americans who came to investigate salvage possibilities. This happened despite exceptionally strict security precautions and mixed U.S.–Vietnamese anti-sabotage patrols set up following the Capitol Cinema incident.

Hatred of the Invaders

Huynh Tan Phat had earlier explained to me that terrorist attacks against Americans were part of Front policy. 'We have the spontaneous support of the population for such actions,' he said. 'We attack only cabarets, cinemas, sports grounds, restaurants reserved exclusively for U.S. military personnel. They have to put up barbed wire and anti-grenade grilles, as the French did in their time. This helps to expose their real situation – that they live in mortal fear of the population. Of course it would be impossible to carry out such actions with a handful of isolated, individual terrorists, but it is possible with the support of the whole population who always find means of sheltering them. It has happened several times when someone has been hurrying away after such an action, before the police got on his trail, that an unknown person has pushed him inside his house or shop and hidden him; or pressed money in his hand and said: "Take this for a taxi."'

A couple of weeks after the Capitol Cinema incident, the Front broadcast a warning for Americans in Saigon not to take their wives and children to public places reserved for Americans. The terrorist attacks were for 'men only.'

In the days when France was involved in her 'dirty war' in Indochina, there was no lack of American leaders who saw things in a realistic light. The late President Kennedy's remarks on 6 April 1954, when he was still the 'Senator from Massachusetts', were realistic enough: 'To pour money, material and men into the jungles of Indochina without at least a remote prospect of victory would be dangerously futile and destructive . . . No amount of American assistance in Indochina can conquer an enemy which is everywhere, and at the same time nowhere; an "enemy of the people" which has the sympathy and support of the people.' This quote has become rather famous today when it is truer than when it was uttered ten years ago. But there was an observation equally apt made a year earlier by Adlai Stevenson, published in Paris (*L'Intransigeant*, 21 May 1953) after his visit to Indochina. Following some correctly gloomy appraisals of the situation, Stevenson, now chief U.S. delegate at the United Nations, commented:

> One sees here in a startling way one of the major difficulties the French are up against. How to persuade the peasants in their rags that these Germans, these French, these Senegalese and these Moroccans are fighting for *them* against the Vietminh, who after all are of their race and their country?

It was a good question then and a good question for Adlai Stevenson, Dean Rusk and President Johnson to ponder over today. How to persuade the peasants in their rags that these Americans, these Kuomintang Chinese, these Filipino and Australian and other troops are fighting for them against the 'Viet Cong', who after all are of their own race and country? It would still be a good question even if there were Vietnamese from north of the 17th parallel fighting side by side with their southern compatriots. The point is that the peasants in their rags have long ago answered this question in their own hearts and the acts of the young terrorist group only underlines this. They regard the Americans as interventionists and aggressors, no less odious than other invaders in Vietnamese history.

I came across a grim story while I was in the Tay Nguyen which illustrates the point. It was related by H'Blong, a young tribeswoman from the Rhade minority, now a Liberation Front cadre responsible for information in her village, in Lac Lac district of Dak Lak province. 'There had been many enemy raids,' she said, 'lots of people had been killed, livestock slaughtered and stolen. American advisers were many in this area. Our people were very angry and we started resisting, first by traps and spikes to stop them plundering our houses. But still the enemy persisted and our young men set up self-defense units. We had no guns, only crossbows and poisoned arrows.

'Once when a surprise raid was made against our village, all but two lads, who were too young to be in the self-defense team, were away in the fields. They saw a column of enemy troops approaching and hid themselves on the village side of a river which the enemy troops had to wade across. When they were in the middle of the stream, the two fired their arrows and hit two Americans and four Diemists. They died immediately from the poison arrows. The rest went back and opened fire with their machine guns from across the river. The boys kept their heads down and waited. The enemy troops started to cross again and when they got to the same spot, our boys fired and more of the enemy fell. The enemy thought this was a large-scale ambush and fled. They greatly fear poisonous arrows. The dead were left behind, so the lads went and dragged them on to the bank and collected the weapons. On the Americans were two daggers. Then they raced off to the fields and told what had happened. Our people had heard the shooting but they could not believe that these two lads, who were not considered old enough to be in the self-defense corps, could have defeated such an enemy force. Everyone came down to the river.

'There, sure enough, were the dead bodies. But the two Americans had been stabbed through the heart. "Why did you stab the Americans when they were already dead?" we asked. "And why only the Americans?"

'"Because the Vietnamese are our people. They do wrong because they are misled," replied one of the boys. "But the two Americans are foreigners. They have come from far away, crossed the ocean with the clear aim of harming us. It is these big noses that put the Diemists up to doing so much harm. So, we stabbed them with their own daggers, even though they were dead." The two boys are now members of our self-defense unit,' concluded H'Blong, 'and the enemy never attacked our village again.'

I accept this as the grass roots feeling that even what may seem to be the most primitive of minds recognize the primary source of their miseries and act accordingly. When planes are shot down and it is bits of blond-haired skulls that are plastered over the fields, when American 'special forces' experts direct the slaughter of buffalo and chickens, things become crystal clear – as Adlai Stevenson recognized, when it was the French and not the American presence involved.

American POW's

Quite another view of the situation, both as concerns morale and an appreciation of what the war is all about, came from four American war prisoners whom I met in what was doubtless the beginnings of the first camp for U.S. POW's to be established in Southeast Asia. They were all sergeants-first class, and were captured at the Hiep Hoa 'Special Forces' training camp on the night of 23 November 1963, when guerillas overran the camp, destroyed all its installations and made off with enough arms to equip an over-size Liberation Front battalion.

Considering that these are the men especially selected to train Vietnamese in anti-guerilla or 'counter-insurgency' operations, as their textbooks spell it out, it was interesting that all four had been captured without arms in their hands; that not a single shot seemed to have been fired in defense of this key training center; that of 12 Americans allotted to the camp only five were there when the attack took place, the rest 'whooping it up' in Saigon.

Kenneth Roraback, a veteran of the Korean War with 15 years' service in the U.S. army, was the only one of the four awake at the time of the attack, around midnight; he was writing a letter to his wife. 'What actually happened?' I asked. 'They called our place a training camp,' said Roraback, a dour-faced person with thinning hair and bushy eyebrows. 'In reality, like a lot more, it was just a sitting target to be wiped out at any time. It was a well planned, well executed night attack, all over in about 15 minutes.' To my question as to what action he personally took, he replied: 'I ran for the trenches.'

'Did you take a weapon?' I asked.

'There was no time.'

'Was any resistance organized?'

'It was impossible. Everything was burning, there were "Viet Cong" all over the place, streaming in over the ramparts, around all the buildings.'

The other three – Camacho, a swarthy Texan; McClure, a Negro specialist on demolition; and Smith, a medical assistant and radio operator – were all in bed and all gave about the same account as Roraback. 'A perfectly organized night attack,' said Smith. 'I was awakened by explosions right behind the barracks. There was a mortar barrage. I think they were using white phosphorous. Everything was ablaze within minutes. There were explosions in the bunkers. I raced for the trenches. Within a few minutes the "Viet Cong" were there, too. They tied up my arms and led me out over the ramparts.'

None of the four had taken weapons with them. I could no more imagine a guerilla rushing for the trenches without a weapon in his hands than I could imagine an elephant flying. Their arms are set up right alongside their nylon hammocks in which they sleep and they would automatically grab their weapons even if they fell out of their hammocks. The four POW's had been on the move for months after capture, sometimes in sampans, mostly on foot, zig-zagging around, heading in all points of the compass until they had little idea where they were. They were now in a safe rear area.

I asked Roraback if air raids had bothered them much in their travels. 'Planes were over for a strike soon after the attack. Whether they did any good or not, I don't know. The main thing, thank God, I was not touched. A couple of days later a B-26 came over and made 12 strafing runs. Whether anyone was hit or not, I don't know. In any case, like I said before, the main thing, thank God, I was not touched.' My thoughts went back to the three that had attacked the Capitol Cinema: 'thousands of us ready to sacrifice our lives at any moment, but we want to kill five or ten Americans for every one of us.'

Each of the four sergeants assured me, in separate conversations, that they had been well treated and each expressed surprise at this. 'My captors were considerate from the moment I was taken,' said Roraback. 'I expected to be shot right away and I guess this showed in my face. When it didn't happen at once, nor on the second day, I figured they were taking us a bit further away to shoot us.'

'Why did you expect to be shot?' I asked, and Roraback looked a little confused. 'Well, I considered it normal,' he said after a pause. 'Guerillas don't have conditions to look after prisoners. But they saw I was afraid and did everything to calm my fears.'

'How were you able to communicate? Did you have a common language?'

'No, but they patted my back, waved their hands in a sort of friendly way in front of my face, stroked my arms and generally made signs that I shouldn't worry.'

One could guess why Roraback and the others were worried, because they knew very well that any guerilla captured is almost invariably tortured to death immediately, and the 'Special Forces' to which they were attached were amongst the most savage in their behaviour. One only has to look at photos published on the front pages of American newspapers of 'Viet Cong' prisoners to know why these men were worried. On the front page of the 24 May 1964 international edition of the *New York Times*, for instance, there is a photo of an almost nude Vietnamese, lying on the ground, his hands tied together over his head and attached by a long cord to a U.S. tank. The caption laconically informs the readers that the 'Viet Cong' is about to be dragged around by the tank, including through a river, as a preliminary to 'making him talk.'

McClure was wounded in the attack by mortar fragments. 'I had first-aid treatment next day and the fragments were removed four days later,' he said. 'They treat us real well – that's the main thing. No rough stuff of any kind. I never thought to be treated like that, a real surprise.'

'The treatment has been fair,' said Smith, 'considering guerillas don't have proper facilities for taking care of POW's. They do the best they can under the conditions.' And Camacho observed: 'They treat us very well, but it's difficult for them to supply us with the food we're used to.' I was surprised to find that U.S. soldiers still seemed to be convinced that a white man cannot live on rice instead of bread as the basic diet, but this was the main problem for the four prisoners. Following the high death rate among U.S. POW's in Korea, compared with virtually none among British, French, Turkish and other nationalities, much publicity had been given to the fact that all U.S. soldiers destined for Asian service were to be conditioned to eating rice. One would have thought that, especially for guerilla 'specialists,' a prerequisite would be the ability to 'live off the country.'

Liberation Front policy in the past had been to give captured Americans a few weeks of 'explanations' as to what the struggle is about and then set them free. Judging by the way the little camp, where I met the four sergeants, is organized, it seems many more American POW's are to be catered for, and release in future may be a matter of negotiations. The uniforms of the four had been taken away and replaced by two sets of tailored black shirts and trousers. They had been given soap and toothbrushes, were able to take a bath once a week and 'when they want us to shave, they bring us a shaving kit,' as Camacho expressed it. Each hut has an air-raid shelter and a high bamboo palisade surrounding it. They sleep on the standard Vietnamese bamboo bed. Camp authorities told me that although 'with the best will in the world we can't set up a bread factory in the jungle,' they would try and vary the diet in deference to the American stomach.

Their surprise at seeing me coming out of the jungle could not have been greater than if I had dropped down from Mars. As they had been out of touch with the outside world for months, I asked each if they had any special questions. I was astonished at their lack of interest. Camacho assumed a dead serious, almost tragic air when he asked if he could put one question. 'Do you by any chance happen to know who won the world heavyweight boxing championship?' By chance I had heard the result over the radio: 'Yes, Clay beat Sonny Liston in the 7th round with a technical knockout.' A smile spread over his face as he thanked me and marched off with an almost beatific expression.

I asked Roraback what he thought about the war, now that he had had several months to think about it. After explaining that as a military man he had no right to discuss 'political' matters, he said: 'It's all a mystery to me. I've no idea what it's all about. Of course, as a legally constituted government, Saigon has the right to put down the guerillas and ask us to help them. But there are two sides to every question and the guerillas also have the right to try and overthrow the government if they don't like it. But as to who is right and who is wrong, who will win or lose or what the whole thing is about, I have no idea.' The others replied similarly. They had 'no idea' what the war was about or why they were really there. They all insisted on their purely 'advisory' role.

Very different were the interests of the young soldiers and cadres of the Liberation forces. Questions ranged over the whole world and discussions lasted far into the night. They were especially interested to know what the outside world knew and thought about their own struggle and to know about national liberation movements in other parts of the world. They may often have been hazy about geography and the status of many of the countries they named, but they knew what they were interested in, and it was not the world heavyweight boxing championship that was on the top of the list.

When I asked Roraback how he occupied his thoughts – the POW's had nothing to do except keep their individual, tiny bamboo huts clean – he said: 'I think of all the things I'll do when I get home. I've built, in my imagination, a barbecue pit; put shelves in the kitchen; made six model planes for the kids and three radios. It's the only way I can keep my mind occupied.'

It was typical of the way things are in South Vietnam that both Smith and Roraback had been wounded, in an action at Can Cho a few days after they had landed in South Vietnam. 'My wife was mad with anxiety when I left,' said Roraback. 'So many friends and acquaintances of ours had been killed, badly wounded, or just missing, once they left for South Vietnam. The first word she got about me was that I'm wounded. And four months later that I'm captured.'

The question arises why do people who have no ideological interest in, or knowledge of, what this war is about, volunteer for such dangerous, unpleasant duty? For that, one has to look at their pay. Roraback's basic pay of $335.00 per month, jumped up to $858.40 a month while he is in South Vietnam and the other three each received from $450 to $500 per month extra for the South Vietnam service, which must make them about the highest paid mercenaries ever, in relation to their rank. Their Liberation Front opposite numbers, from rank and file troops to regimental commander, get 40 piastres per month – a little over one dollar at the official rate and about 40 cents at the real, black market rate. But the difference between patriots and mercenaries on the field of battle reminds one of the dog explaining why he had failed in a hard race to catch a hare. 'That hare was running for its life, I only for my dinner.' The Vietnamese are fighting for their lives, the Americans for their dinners, and that means the difference between victory and defeat in the type of struggle being waged in South Vietnam.

[Chapter 7 of *Vietnam: Inside Story of the Guerilla War* (International Publishers, New York, 1965), pp. 96–106.]

9: *Wilfred Burchett with a member of a Vietnamese village self-defense corps, 1964*

20

At Ground Level [1966]

In 1965, the US committed troops to South Vietnam and began bombing the North. The Pentagon's thinking was that to win in the South they had to bomb the North into submission – tacitly admitting they were losing the war against the Vietcong.

From his base in Phnom Penh, Wilfred Burchett made frequent trips to the South and North, often with French film producer and filmmaker Roger Pic. From the perspective of the North Vietnamese and the National Liberation Front, by taking the war to the North, the US had effectively re-united Vietnam and created a single front. Burchett was absolutely convinced the US would never be able to break the will of the Vietnamese people, and he believed they would inevitably lose the war. He stressed this point repeatedly in articles, books and films.

Vietnam North was one of several books in which he sought to answer the questions he poses in the Introduction: 'How does an underdeveloped country of 17 million, with an overwhelmingly agricultural economy, envisage waging – and winning – a war against the richest, most highly industrialized, most militarily powerful country in the world? Why the confident smiles on the faces of Ho Chi Minh, Pham Van Dong, Vo Nguyen Giap and the others?'

* * *

At a Hanoi concert, during the first part of my visit, I met for a moment General Vo Nguyen Giap, North Vietnam's brilliant Defense Minister and Commander in Chief. He knew I had just returned from the coastal areas where the battle for roads and bridges raged daily. 'So you've seen what American air power is worth?' he said, adding with a contemptuous laugh: 'Nothing!' Later, in a recorded interview he gave his views on this subject in greater detail. From a military viewpoint, his sneer was justified. Otherwise, how explain that 18 months after the best American planes and pilots were sent to destroy the few hundred miles of road and railway that led to the 17th parallel, they were still attacking the same bridges, the same junctions and crossroads, the same radar stations, even the same miniscule targets such as the fishing town of Dong Hoi and the islet of Cong Co, both just north of the 17th parallel?

Traffic rolled down Highway No. 1 almost normally. I found myself moving at almost the same speed as during my last trip toward the 17th parallel, two years previously. I found some of the bridges I had seen in 1964 damaged, others untouched. But I also found more bridges than formerly, including some over rivers where there had never been a bridge before in all of Vietnam's history! American bombing of the traditional ferries made new bridges necessary, and more efficient. They were not the sort of bridges the American pilots were looking for or would find even if they were looking, or could destroy if they did find. The Vietnamese call them floating bridges – a variant of pontoons, except that instead of the roadway being supported by boats, it rested upon huge bundles of unsinkable giant bamboo. Built in easily transportable and joinable sections, they could be assembled quickly at nightfall, towed away at daybreak, and reassembled next evening at any one of a dozen or so crossing points to which branch roads of the main highway now led.

'Our leaders laid down,' explained Doan Trong Truyen from the State Planning Commission, 'that transport and communications are the central and most urgent task in wartime. Our slogan must be: "The enemy destroys, we repair. The enemy destroys again, we repair again and ensure transport and communications." To achieve this,' continued Truyen, 'means a bitter fight between us and the enemy. We have a whole army of workers concentrated on this. They not only repair damage; they also build new strategic communications networks, new highways and bridges. We've been able to keep transport moving, both for civilian needs and the war. There was a certain slowing down when the attacks started in February last year until about July when we got organized. From July until now (May 1966) the volume of transport, even from Hanoi to the 17th parallel, is greater than ever before.'

For anyone who knows North Vietnam, and I had been visiting the country regularly from the start of the Dien Bien Phu battle in 1954 until my previous visit in 1964, it was evident that what Doan Trong Truyen said was correct. On the major and secondary routes, more traffic was moving than ever before. Not only that, but goods and equipment were arriving on time.

For years, everything connected with the country's economy has been planned, and that includes transport. Today also the transport convoys, from trains and trucks to junks and bicycles, work to a strict timetable. Transport companies enter into pledges to deliver specific volumes of goods at specific places on specific dates. I am assured that the pledges are invariably met even in the most intensively bombed areas. In entering into such pledges, allowance is made for a certain average of time lost due to bomb damage, and this is a fairly precise figure – precise because the road-menders also give pledges and have their plans too. They know how long it will take to repair the maximum damage the bombs can cause on any given sector. With such a system the planners at the centre only have to start feeding goods into the transport pipeline in volumes required and on appropriate dates – adding their own margin of error – to have them flowing out in the right quantities, at the right times and places. These were the sort of calculations that General Vo Nguyen Giap had to make for Dien Bien Phu in 1951, under more difficult circumstances when he had to calculate in terms of human backs, ox-carts, bicycles and a single, terrible mountainous road with no organized economy behind him. Nothing that US air power can do, or has been able to do in a very considerable and costly effort so far, can alter this. Washington knows this, despite the optimistic communiques that continue to pour out of Saigon.

'In fact we ought to be "grateful" to the Americans,' continued Doan Trong Truyen of the State Planning Commission.

Their bombs forced us to jump ahead and do things in a few months that would otherwise have taken years. Certainly we did more in 1965 to improve transport and communications than we had done in the previous three or four years. For instance, we had discussed for a long time the question of improving the railroad from Pingshiang on the Chinese frontier. Major improvements were planned for 1965, the last year of the five-year plan. By the end of 1964 we had prepared a plan which provided for these improvements but in the end we shelved it because we felt we had not the manpower available. But when the bombs started to fall, we pulled the plan out of the filing cabinets and the whole job was completed in a little over four months. The improvements are not just a wartime necessity but very important for peacetime developments.

On one single stretch of railway and highway along the coast, over 2000 tons of bombs have been dropped and quite small bridges along this stretch have been attacked 20 and more times each. But roads and railways still function normally. Damage is often repaired before the smoke clears away. Our notions of time to repair bridges has changed radically. Normally there would have been lots of paper work. After the expert inspections, estimates of structural damage, various draft projects for the repairs sent to numerous department heads to chew over, reports and recommendations from procurement, financial and other experts would come up to ministerial level. Several ministries would become involved. Paperwork alone would take months. Some of our specialists sent to look at a damaged bridge with our old way of looking at things – in the first period of the attacks – said: 'Six months, maybe a year.' But battle-hardened workers on the spot said: 'Nonsense. We'll repair it in a month.' The specialists were scandalized. But, in fact, traffic was moving again within a week. There have been many similar cases. More recently the workers have rationalized, systematized their experiences. With stocks of standardized structural parts which they have designed themselves together with some of our experts, they have repaired or even replaced damaged bridges within one day.

This is very demoralizing for American pilots when reconnaissance photos taken after bridges have been claimed destroyed, show them in place again! A vitally important fact in this is that the repair gangs, often headed by fledgling graduates of the engineering faculty of Hanoi University or Polytechnic institute, have full authority to go ahead with repairs without any reference to departments or ministries.

In traveling around the country, I noticed many roads that I had never seen before. At times I came across groups of young people, often enough working by the light of blazing bamboo torches or small roadside fires at night, hacking away at rocks and trees, hauling earth in wicker baskets, pushing and pulling at road-rollers, for miles on end. On this, Doan Trong Truyen had the following to say:

> During the past year, new strategic highways have been built between the various zones, and a whole network of new inter-zonal, inter-provincial and inter-district highways and roads have been built, giving us numerous alternate routes in every direction. As with bridge construction and repair, this work has been decentralized. Previously it all came under the Ministry of Communications; now it comes under zonal, provincial and district authorities.

Our road lay through fields of flourishing sweet potatoes, the lush, deep green foliage giving promise of a bumper crop. Water pounded along at a furious rate in a yard-wide irrigation channel, parallel to the road, filtering through at regular intervals to the rows of potatoes. We were approaching the Ban Thach dam.

Suddenly a thought struck me. Shouldn't these be rice fields and not sweet potatoes? There was no lack of water, which sweet potatoes hardly need. And Vietnamese peasants regard the latter as a second-rate crop compared to rice. I asked the district committee chief who was acting as guide.

'Quite correct,' he said.

> This would normally be rice land. But for months past the Americans have been bombing the Ban Thach dam. It irrigates around 50,000 hectares of rice fields. So far we've been able to save it. They badly damaged the sluice gates once. On another occasion they breached the dike walls, but the peasants rushed out and plugged the breaches. We'll fight to the utmost to save the dam. But if the worst comes to the worst . . .
>
> Ever since the first attacks the local co-op members have worked might and main to build subsidiary dams and irrigation systems to trap as much of the water as possible and save it for the rice fields. They have levelled off the fields and raised the terrace banks to trap the water wherever possible. But this bit of land we're passing through now is too high. If the dam is seriously breached we couldn't get any water here, so we decided to plant it to sweet potatoes – we'll get a food crop off it even if the worst happens.

At the sluice gates and small hydroelectric station, workers were working away at wrecking machines, salvaging undamaged parts, trying to put together one whole machine from two wrecked ones. There were bomb craters all around the sluice gates and the retaining walls, where the water backed up before hurtling down to the turbines. There was nothing remotely resembling a military target within scores of miles. Electricity from the small station powered local irrigation pumps, the dam and power station being exclusively for food production.

At a sister dam at Bai Thuong, two jet fighter-bombers roared over while our little group was actually on the dam embankment. Heavy anti-aircraft guns opened up, and little black clouds started immediately scampering after their tails. The roar of the jets and the guns and the crashing explosion of a few bombs they dropped, were merged into almost a single sound. It was all over in a second or two, the planes not diving or circling but hurtling straight ahead in a single, futile bombing run. The bombs crashed into some rice fields and a bamboo thicket, sending up spouts of soil and smoke and carving out huge craters which peasants, who had flattened themselves in the fields as the planes passed, started filling in immediately. A lone sentry on the dam embankment laid aside his rifle as the planes passed, and went back to an enormously long fishing line which stretched down into the seething waters far below. A hamlet of brick houses, under the trees of which we parked our jeeps, had been bombed to rubble in previous attacks . . .

One of the most senseless examples of bombing I was to come across in Thanh Hoa province was on the road to Sam Son, a seaside resort where lots of rest homes for workers have been built up in recent years. A few miles before Sam Son itself, there was a fine Old Peoples Home, half a dozen or so red-tiled, brick buildings. It had also been bombed to rubble in a series of raids in July 1965, and doubtless the destruction of another 'naval barracks' was registered in the Pentagon records. If it is true, as reported in the American press at the time, that President Johnson personally approved every target to be attacked in North Vietnam to insure that no civilian losses would be incurred, one can only assume that either the President had particularly bloodthirsty moods or American intelligence is pitifully inadequate. Between 12 June and 22 August 1965, eight major hospitals and sanatoria were attacked, many of them repeatedly, until in each case every building was destroyed.

The attacks on the Quynh Lap leper sanatorium and research center were particularly scandalous. It is difficult to find an excuse for this, even if one accepts that the US is justified in any attacks at all against the DRV with which it is not in a state of war. Dozens of ordinary publicity magazines and scientific journals in the DRV had published photographs of the big leprosorium set out among filao trees on the coast, in Nghe An province. At the time of the first attack on June 12, there were over 2000 lepers dispersed in some 160 buildings of the sanatorium: 139 of them were killed and 80 seriously wounded. Every day for the following ten days, the attacks were repeated, sometimes several times a day, until virtually nothing was left. Losses were particularly heavy because many of the lepers were cut down by machine-gun bullets as they tried to hobble and crawl to safety on stumps of arms and legs.

As the attack continued day after day, Vietnamese cameramen were able to get to the spot and shoot a horrifying documentary film which shows white-clad attendants with lepers slung across their shoulders, others on stretchers with bombs exploding all around them; bodies blasted off the stretchers, attendants blown off their feet, but recovering their charges and staggering on through the bomb blasts to shelters among the rocks.

If the rubble of the Quynh Lap leper sanatorium and the Thanh Hoa TB hospital are symbols of a ruthless and senseless, to say the least, use of air power, the Ham Rong bridge across the Ma River, at Thanh Hoa, is the symbol of the efficient defiance of the Vietnamese people.

At the time I last crossed it, at the beginning of March 1966, it had withstood many hundreds of attacks; some 3000-odd bombs had been hurled against it and hundreds of rockets and bull-pup missiles. It is a vital bridge, carrying road and rail traffic on the main north–south communications route. Its defenders claim they had downed 69 planes before the Americans apparently decided to give up. At the time I left North Vietnam, the bridge was still intact, with numerous battle scars on its girders and structural elements, but trains and truck convoys still moved safely across it. I interviewed

Commander Denton of the US Navy, shot down on his very first mission over North Vietnam while attacking the Ham Rong bridge. He fell smack into the Ma River. In the interview he refused to say what he was attacking or where he fell. But by chance I had earlier met one of his captors, Nguyen Thi Hang, the beautiful young woman commander of a local self-defense unit which had taken part in 30-odd battles defending the Ham Rong bridge. 'He threw away his knife and pistol while he was still parachuting down,' said Nguyen Thi Hang (Miss Moonlight), 'and he went into the river with his hands up. We fished him out and tied him up.'

At first when the word 'battle' was employed to describe an air attack, I objected: 'You mean air attack,' I said. 'No,' came the reply, 'we consider such actions as battles between our forces and theirs.' And when I had the first detailed descriptions of what went on and saw for myself the dispositions taken and later saw a few actions, then it was clear that 'battle' is the precisely correct term. Every air attack is met with immediate and fierce resistance. Pilots are correct when they complain they have to fly down through several levels of fire to get at their targets. Which explains why they have never smashed the Ham Rong bridge and dozens of other less important ones against which they have made scores of attacks.

Any important target is protected by heavy and medium anti-aircraft guns. But if pilots come down low enough for precision attacks, they run into a deadly curtain of small-arms fire from hundreds, sometimes thousands of rifles and light machine guns in the hands of workers, peasants and students, from the million or so Vietnamese organized in self-defense units. The dearest desire of every one of these is to get an American aircraft in the sights of his weapon. The enemy has been anonymous for too long. Death has come from afar. There is a feeling of exultation when the chance comes to fight back. It has become a nationwide duty to study plane silhouettes, to memorize characteristics of speed and altitude: to recognize planes by their sounds; to know how many lengths ahead of a certain type one must aim if it is in level flight and at which point of the nose to fire if it is dive-bombing.

Can small-arms fire be effective against America's supersonic fighter-bomber? One has only to visit the central plane 'cemetery' where a certain number of the downed planes have been collected, and examine the wreckage to know that the answer is yes. Many of the wrecks are riddled with holes of various caliber, including ordinary rifle bullets. The curtain of small-arms fire has two major advantages. First, it throws diving planes off their course. At least that seems the only logical explanation for the fact that 70 per cent of the bombs aimed at the Ham Rong bridge fell on the nearby hamlet of Van Phuc, which is now a mass of cratered ruins, while the bridge still stands. The attacking pilots, including one of America's greatest aces and bridge destruction experts, downed over the bridge, never held to their dives. They were already pulling out of their dives to avoid the deadly curtain of inter-woven small-arms fire, when they released their bombs. Of those that held to their course, 69 according to the defenders' figures went down with their planes or limped out of their dives to fall elsewhere. Only a fraction of the pilots could even use their parachutes. The other advantage of the massed small-arms fire is against planes that skim in from the sea low over the fields for a sneak attack, hoping to avoid radar detection and classic anti-aircraft fire. The fact that tens of thousands of peasants and workers are permanently at defense positions, makes this very difficult. The sheer volume of fire, coming from hands that do not tremble and eyes unafraid to look planes straight in the face, force the sneak-attackers to zoom up to heights where they have to reckon with medium and heavy anti-aircraft guns. The element of surprise is lost.

In their attacks, the Americans are caught between various contradictions. To bomb with precision requires slow, propeller-driven planes, which can turn in relatively tight circles and go on down to place their bombs – if not with the same precision as the guerrillas can plant their plastics, at least fairly precisely on their targets. But such planes are dream targets for the anti-aircraft gunners and even North Vietnam's embryo air force. To avoid the heavy losses they took in the first months of the air-ground battles, and even to avoid the handful of MIG-17's which the North Vietnamese send up from time to time, the Americans are forced to send their fastest fighter-bombers. Flying high and fast over their targets, usually in a single run, these are incapable of precision bombing. They try and compensate for this by dropping huge quantities of bombs indiscriminately with the hope that the law of averages will come to their aid and some will hit the target. The same is true of the B-52 bombers so far used against North Vietnam.

The first much publicized raid, 'the biggest of the war,' was against the Mu Gia pass where Route No. 12 leads into Laos. The pass and road were said to have been smothered with bombs, artificial landslides provoked, the road put out of action. Vietnamese on the spot told me that in fact 109 bombs were dropped of which four fell on the road, the rest exploding in the jungle. The road was cleared within a few hours, a fact the Americans seem to have recognized only two weeks later when they discovered the road was still functioning and bombed it again, with the same negligible results.

But what the pilots miss with their bombs is certainly made up for by the paperwork of those who draft communiques. I was astonished to read an item in *The New York Times* of 9 May 1966, quoting the American military spokesman in Saigon as saying that all railroads and highways leading into Hanoi had been cut and the capital was isolated:

Most of the arteries were sliced in a series of air raids in mid-April, the spokesman said, but what the military considered the final import link, the highway and railroads running northeast to Nanning, China, was blocked yesterday (Sunday, May 8).

May 7 was, in fact, the day I left Hanoi, and I have no way of knowing whether a 'highway and railroad' running north-east to China was 'blocked.' I have good reason to believe that if it were 'blocked' on Sunday it would have been 'deblocked' by Monday. But as for the rest, between mid-April and the early days of May, I was traveling almost daily in all directions from Hanoi and all roads and railroads were functioning normally. There were a dozen or so other correspondents also traveling around and I never heard of a single case of any 'arteries' being 'sliced.'

If American taxpayers could see the military results of the fabulous expenditure of their money by American air power in North Vietnam they would be shocked to the core, at least to their pocketbooks, even if they were not affected by the moral aspects of it all. For expert American justification of General Giap's contemptuous 'Nothing!' there was an article in the 5 April 1966, number of *Look* magazine by General Matthew B. Ridgway who commanded the United Nations forces in Korea and presumably knows his subject.

'Korea,' he writes, 'also taught that it is impossible to interdict the supply routes of an Asian army by air power alone. We had complete air mastery over North Korea, and we clobbered Chinese supply columns unmercifully. Unquestionably, we inflicted serious damage upon the Chinese and greatly complicated their problems of reinforcement and supply. But we did not halt their offensive nor materially diminish its strength. The Chinese, like the Vietnamese, traveled light, with each man carrying his ammunition, his food and his weapon on his back ... In Korea, I saw whole sections of railroad bombed into scrap iron by aircraft and yet the enemy rebuilt the tracks in a single night and the trains ran the next day ... It is easy for the civilian mind to be seduced with talk of 'easy' conquest through air power. But the crucial battles are still won by foot soldiers ...'

As I was on the receiving end of US air power in Korea for two years, traveling up and down the main supply route which led from Sinanju, on Korea's Yalu River frontier with China, down towards Kaesong–Panmunjom, at least 20 times while covering the Panmunjom cease-fire talks, I know that what General Ridgway now discloses is correct. Moreover, the daily Air Force communiques on destruction of truck convoys were a source of hilarious amusement to the Koreans and Chinese. Time and again when the Air Force claimed to have destroyed 300 or 400 trucks, not a single vehicle was hit. During my 20-odd night rides over that route, I saw only a single truck hit and that was on my first trip. Traffic moved at night and although the night bombers were always around, bombing and strafing at something or other, they were useless. And having been on the receiving end of American air power in both South and North Vietnam, I can add my snort of 'Nothing' as far as military results are concerned in Vietnam, to that of General Giap and it seems of General Ridgway also.

Implicit admission of the failure of American air power to disrupt communications was made by Defense Secretary McNamara in giving the reasons for the strikes against the fuel depots in the Hanoi–Haiphong areas at the end of June 1966. 'Enemy truck movements to South Vietnam doubled during the first five months of 1966 compared with the same period in 1965,' he said. 'Further, the daily tonnage of supplies moved overland has increased 150 per cent, and personnel infiltration 120 per cent during 1966, compared with 1965 averages. This has led to a greater reliance on petroleum.' This greatly increased north–south movement of supplies took place despite the 15 months of day and night bombing of bridges and communications routes. It seems predictable that the bombing of fuel depots will take its routine place in the daily communiques, along with the bridges destroyed, the roads and railway lines cut. It may well be that within a year of the strikes against the Hanoi–Haiphong fuel depots, there will be an attempt to justify another mad escalation effort by claiming that the movement of supplies has doubled again as compared to 1966.

The absurdity of American claims was perhaps never better illustrated than by President Johnson's solemn announcement that in that single, first raid on 29 June 1966, 57 per cent of North Vietnam's fuel reserves had been destroyed. By what fantasies of American intelligence such a precise figure was arrived at – when the pilots themselves stated that smoke prevented assessment of results – only President Johnson could know. In fact, the major part of North Vietnam's fuel reserves, for many months previous to the strikes, had been distributed throughout the country, deep underground and well out of reach of American bombs or rockets. Attacks against the Hanoi–Haiphong depots had been anticipated ever since the first bombings of the North took place in February 1965.

If President Johnson and his Pentagon experts believe that leaders as experienced as the North Vietnamese would leave 57 per cent of their fuel supplies in the exposed Hanoi–Haiphong depots, they are making the same woeful miscalculations that have marked every stage of their escalation policy.

Only seven weeks earlier, Pentagon and Saigon spokesmen were claiming that all road and rail links with Hanoi had been severed. But in his press conference to justify the raids against Hanoi–Haiphong, McNamara had discovered that 'the enemy's military effort is further attested to by his action to improve infiltration-network routes. Some of these routes are new, some have been upgraded for all-weather truck use. By-passes have been built and bamboo-trellised canopies have been rigged over some jungle roads to inhibit aerial observation.' And as for previous predictions that the air strikes in the North would force the 'Vietcong' in the South to break up into smaller units and go back to guerrilla warfare, McNamara said that 'as a result of the greatly increased movement of men and supplies by trucks and powered junks [the latter despite the presence of the mighty Seventh Fleet in Vietnamese waters] there has been a shift from a small-arms guerrilla action to a quasi-conventional military operation involving major supplies, weapons and heavier equipment.'

It was not only on the military front that the American bombings proved ineffective. On the civilian front life and work continued [as] normal. Despite the greatly stepped-up raids during May 1966, the spring harvest was reaped, transported and stored, deliveries to the state completed strictly according to the planned timetable.

General Ridgway, incidentally, in the article previously cited also touched on the moral problem, questioning 'The increasingly significant ignoring by our planners of the consequences of omitting the moral factor in considering the use of the immense destructive capability which now exists in the world . . .' And, he adds, 'It is my firm belief that there is nothing in the present situation or in our code that requires us to bomb a small Asian nation "back into the Stone Age" . . . There must be some moral limit to the means we use to achieve victory.'

The Vietnamese would certainly question that American air power could ever 'achieve victory,' but General Ridgway deserves credit for having touched on the moral aspects of a situation in which the mightiest industrial and military power in the world uses its destructive power against a small, poor and technically backward country like Vietnam.

[From Chapter 1 of *Vietnam North* (Laurence & Wishart, London, 1966), pp. 11–29.]

10: *Anti-aircraft defence: village girls in training (North Vietnam, 1966)*

21

A Spurned Olive Branch [1967/1977]

Today, yes, it's the grasshoppers that dare stand up to the elephants.

Tomorrow it's the elephant that leaves its skin behind!

Grasshoppers and Elephants was the book in which Wilfred Burchett attempted to sum up his more than two decades of reporting the French and American wars against the people of Vietnam, Cambodia and Laos. As he describes it in the Introduction, 'in the book that follows, I have tried to place in perspective the role of the people, not only in that historic offensive [the fall of Saigon] which resulted in the final and total victory of the forces of national liberation, but throughout the decades of struggle and sacrifice which led up to that final offensive and made victory certain. It is the product of numerous first hand observations of that struggle, starting with my first visit to the Liberated Zones of the North at the start of the battle of Dien Bien Phu in the spring of 1954, and ending with two months in the Liberated South in the summer of 1975, with many visits to the North and the Liberated Zones of the South in between.'

With these conflicts largely concluded, the book was written at a point when he had some hope that his beloved Indochina could finally enter an era of peace. But this was not to be. China would shortly turn against Vietnam, and the Khmer Rouge in Cambodia would attack their own people. Nations Burchett had fearlessly supported in his writing were soon to be at each other's throats.

* * *

28 January 1967 was an occasion of which all journalists dream – an exclusive interview with the right man, in the right spot, on the most burning question of the day, one that was the main focus of international diplomatic activities.

Hanoi was the place, Foreign Minister Nguyen Duy Trinh the man, peace or continuing war in Vietnam the issue. As for the timing, it was just twelve days before there was to be a four-day truce, to celebrate Tet, the Vietnamese lunar New Year. It was a time of intensive diplomatic activity, with initiatives from the Pope and UN Secretary-General U Thant; with Polish and Italian diplomats negotiating in Saigon; French and North Vietnamese diplomats in contact in Paris; American and Soviet diplomats in Moscow on the eve of Prime Minister Alexei Kosygin's visit to London to confer with Prime Minister Harold Wilson as – amongst other things – his Co-Chairman of the 1954 Geneva Conference on Indochina. Amateur American peace-seekers were also in Hanoi – all activities aimed at trying to move the confrontation in Vietnam from battlefield to conference table.

Pushed by public opinion at home and abroad to get the war ended, President Johnson and his Secretary of State, Dean Rusk, had made repeated statements that one or the other of them was 'ready to go any place any time' if there was the slightest chance for a negotiated peace and that the U.S. bombings of the North which had started systematically in February 1965 would be halted if there were the slightest sign, 'private or public, official or non-official' that Hanoi was ready for the conference table. In response to one of U Thant's repeated remarks that a halt to the bombings would create the proper atmosphere for talks, the U.S. delegate to the United Nations, Arthur Goldberg, had said on the last day of 1966 that the United States was 'ready to order a prior end to all bombing of North Vietnam, the moment there is an assurance, private or otherwise, that there would be a reciprocal response towards peace from North Vietnam . . .'

A short, stocky man with a very stubborn face, foreign minister Nguyen Duy Trinh devoted most of his replies to my written questions to hammering the United States for having launched the air war of destruction against the North, stressing the firm determination of his people and government never to yield to force. The real message came in his reply to my last question:

'The United States has spoken of the need for dialogue or contact between itself and the DRV. Would you comment on this?'

'The United States has made such statements, but in its deeds it has shown the utmost obduracy and perfidy and continues the escalation, stepping up and expanding the aggressive war. If it really wants talks, it must first unconditionally halt the bombing raids and all other acts of war against the DRV. It is only after the unconditional cessation of U.S. bombing and all other acts of war against the DRV that there could be talks between the DRV and the United States.'

This was interpreted in diplomatic circles around the world that Hanoi had given President Johnson the clear signal he said he was awaiting. To make it quite clear, Mai Van Bo, head of the North Vietnamese diplomatic mission in Paris, informed Pierre Etiene Manac'h, who then headed the Asian Department of the French Foreign Office, that his government wanted Washington to understand that the Nguyen Duy Trinh interview was very important and that talks could really follow an unconditional end to the bombings. Manac'h, one of France's most brilliant diplomats, relayed the message to John Dean, first secretary at the U.S. Embassy, in the presence of Senator Robert Kennedy, then on a fact-finding tour in Europe. A few days later, Premier Kosygin was due to arrive in London, and it was clear that Vietnam would be a primary subject of discussion. The world awaited with considerable interest President Johnson's response.

At a dinner with Nguyen Duy Trinh following the interview, I found him very skeptical as to any immediate results. To my off-the-record question as to why the DRV (Democratic Republic of Vietnam) had not used a thirty-five day bombing pause starting at the Tet celebrations the previous year to make such a gesture, he replied that the Americans would have interpreted that as a weakness –

We couldn't stand up to the bombings. They would have hit us harder. And a year ago, to be quite frank, we were not quite sure how we were going to cope. A year ago we were still moving our essential industries underground, de-centralizing the economy. While we were certain that we would survive, there were many unknown factors and difficulties. Now we know we can cope. The industries we dispersed are producing. We can repair roads and bridges faster than the Americans can destroy them. Our people are more united than ever. We can maintain and even increase food production; we can keep transport moving and can fulfill our role as the great rear base for the struggle in the south. We understand quite well the risk we have taken in proposing talks.

Washington is certain to interpret this as a sign of weakness. Double, treble the dose, they think, and we crack. That is their mentality. They interpret any gesture of ours in favor of peace as a sign that we are at our last 'gasp' and so they should strike harder. It is difficult to explain this to a lot of our friends. The fact that we have made this gesture today is only possible because we are strong and completely confident of our ability to carry on despite the worst the U.S. imperialists can do.

The interview was perhaps the most explicit, but not the only gesture that Hanoi made at that time. Ten days earlier, President Ho Chi Minh had received the well-known American pacifist, Rev. A.J. Muste, together with Rabbi Abraham Feinberg of Toronto and the former Church of England Bishop of Johannesburg, Dr. Ambrose Reeves. Addressing himself to Rev. Muste, President Ho Chi Minh said:

> President Johnson has stated that he will talk to anyone, anywhere, and at any time, about peace. I invite President Johnson to be our guest, sitting just where you are now. Let him come with his wife, his daughters, his doctor, and his cook, but let him not come with a gun on his hip. Let him not bring his admirals and his generals. I pledge on my honor as an old revolutionary that Mr. Johnson will have complete security.

As soon as they returned from seeing the President, Rev. Muste told me what had been said and asked whether he could possibly have been joking. I replied that Johnson only had to take the invitation at face value and see. But however we wanted to interpret it, this was the clearest and most sincere appeal to get a dialogue started, and that President Ho was not one to joke about such a serious matter. At about the same time, there were two distinguished U.S. editors in Hanoi, Harry S. Ashmore, who had won an unprecedented double Pulitzer Prize by his reporting on the racist horrors at Little Rock, Arkansas, and William C. Baggs, editor of the *Miami News*, both of them leading lights in the Center for the Study of Democratic Institutions. They were received by President Ho and were impressed by the conciliatory mood in Hanoi, relaying their views to President Johnson via Undersecretary of State Nicholas Katzenbach. Harrison Salisbury, assistant managing-editor of the

New York Times, was also in Hanoi that fateful January and in a four
and a half hour interview with premier Pham Van Dong, became
convinced that the DRV leadership was ready for negotiations, but
that the American military was not:

> I was told while I was still in Hanoi, by someone who had recently
> been in Saigon, that the American military establishment there would
> not accept negotiations at this time, no matter what Hanoi did. 'They
> think they have Hanoi on the run,' said this man. 'They are not going
> to quit now. They want to pour it on. If it's poured on hard enough,
> there won't be any Hanoi to bother with.'
>
> I don't know if that accurately reflected the thinking of the Amer-
> ican military establishment in Saigon, but I encountered this line in
> Washington in some quarters on my return . . .[1]

President Johnson's reaction to all this was astonishingly close
to that predicted by Nguyen Duy Trinh. At a TV press conference
on February 2, the President backed away from all his previous
proposals and called for 'reciprocity' in exchange for a bombing
halt, something which he knew in advance was unacceptable to
Hanoi. He spoke of 'mutual steps' of de-escalation, but the point
was that Hanoi was not bombing the United States – it was the U.S.
that was bombing North Vietnam. Johnson said he hoped for 'some
new steps' from Hanoi. 'In all candor', he said, 'I must say that I am
not aware of any serious effort that the other side has made, in my
judgment, to bring the fighting to a stop and to stop the war.'

In other words, halting the bombings so that talks could start was
not on, although this had been precisely the U.S. position, repeated
time and again, in the months that preceded the Nguyen Duy Trinh
interview. A few hours after the Johnson press conference, I sent
the following dispatch from Hanoi to the Tokyo daily, *Yomiuri
Shimbun* – which appeared in its Japanese and English editions:

> For the moment, Hanoi is confident that it has demonstrated its good
> will and is still hoping, despite Johnson's press conference remarks that
> Washington will show some modicum of good will . . .
>
> Hanoi's statement on talks was made to test the sincerity of Washing-
> ton's frequent expressions of a desire for peace through negotiations.

Hanoi feels it has opened the door with Nguyen Duy Trinh's statement and that it is up to Washington to make the next move.

If Washington is ready to stick to his (Johnson's) earlier pronouncements, he must definitely halt the bombardments, start the talks and see what steps are possible next . . .[2]

I warned that it would be a 'major blunder' if Washington interpreted the gesture as a sign of weakness but that Hanoi 'is prepared for a hawk-like reaction . . .'

On February 6, Premier Kosygin arrived in London and in his first discussion with Wilson, he stressed the importance of the Nguyen Duy Trinh interview, correcting the absurd hair-splitting semantics argument of the State department that the foreign minister had said that talks 'could,' and not necessarily 'would,' start if the bombings were halted. Talks 'would' start, said Kosygin.

In his book, Harold Wilson describes how Kosygin, in their first private talk, 'directed the conversation straight to Vietnam':

I set out the position as we saw it, bringing Mr. Kosygin up to date on the latest Washington position and the state of opinion in the United States. I referred to an interview given in Hanoi on 28 January to an Australian journalist, Mr. Wilfred Burchett, and confirmed as authentic by the DRV party journal . . .

Basing himself on public statements, and particularly the Burchett interview I had cited, he (Kosygin) could see similar phrases in public utterances by President Johnson and Mr. Dean Rusk. Warming to his subject, he said that if we, he and I, could take together the North Vietnamese statement (by the DRV Foreign Minister in the press interview) as a basis and say to the President – together or separately, privately or publicly in the communique or in a special message – that the statement was an acceptable basis for discussion, then this was the best move for us to take, leading to bilateral talks. He specifically agreed that because of Tet the present time was the most appropriate one. He said – and this again was new – that our task was to advise and to assist the U.S. and the DRV to meet and discuss their problems at the negotiating table . . .[3]

A formula was agreed upon, under which the North Vietnamese would give a secret assurance that if the bombings stopped, no new troops would be introduced into South Vietnam and the Americans would stop reinforcing their forces in the South. The U.S. agreed and a letter was prepared, authenticated by the U.S. Embassy and, stated Mr. Wilson, 'I was assured that there had been the fullest consultation with the State Department at top level.' Mr. Wilson quotes the U.S. Ambassador to London, David Bruce – later briefly to head the U.S. Delegation to the Vietnam Peace Talks – as being most enthusiastic:

'Prime minister' he said, 'I think you've made it. This is going to be the biggest diplomatic coup of this century.'

> Then at about 10 p.m. (Feb. 9th) the telephone rang. It was the White House – Walt Rostow had tried to phone Michael Palliser who had gone home with flu, and had been told to ring Downing Street. The gist of his message was that on the President's instructions our text had been re-drafted. A new text would come over the White House–Downing Street teleprinter starting now, and should be the one to be used with the Russians . . .

The new text stated that the U.S. would order a bombing halt 'as soon as they were assured that infiltration from North Vietnam to South Vietnam *had stopped*.' There were other changes too, such as public instead of secret assurances by Hanoi, the whole amounting to what Harold Wilson saw as 'a total reversal of the policy the U.S. had put forward for transmission to the Soviet prime minister'.

Of possible explanations, he wrote:

> One, which I was reluctant to believe, was that the White House had taken me – and hence Mr. Kosygin – for a ride. Two, the most likely, that the Washington hawks had staged a successful takeover . . .

That was the end of the 'biggest diplomatic coup of this century' and the next day Wilson was complaining to Johnson that he must realize 'what a hell of a situation I am in for on my last day of talks with Kosygin.' The bombing pause on which such hopes had been set lasted just as long as the Wilson–Kosygin meeting. By the time Kosygin was on his way home, U.S. bombers were over North Vietnam again and hopes for peace were once more blasted to bits. All that Wilson and Kosygin got was the customary snub reserved

11: *Wilfred Burchett and his wife with Vietnamese Prime Minister Pham Van Dong and President Ho Chi Minh, 1965*

for all those who – no matter how high their status – tried to take the Vietnam War away from the Pentagon.

If all this is mentioned in some detail, it is only to underline that at every stage of the Indochina conflict – going all the way back to Dien Bien Phu – the United States could have had an infinitely better settlement from its viewpoint than the rat-like desertion of sinking ships that took place in Phnom Penh and Saigon in April 1975 and in Vientiane a month later. It is obvious – from his book – that Harold Wilson was smarting from wounded pride even years later and it is hard to imagine that Alexei Kosygin felt any less hurt. They had fallen into the trap which snapped tight on many distinguished U.S. diplomats – that of believing that U.S. policies were those which were publicly proclaimed by U.S. presidents and secretaries of state – when half the time these were soporifics to calm public opinion at home and abroad. That the Wilsons and Kosygins, or Fanfanis in Italy and De Gaulles in France, earnestly worked away to produce solutions which they were convinced were those the White House wanted, was the least of the worries of the Johnsons, Nixons and Fords. The bombings had been halted for just five days – too impossibly short for any serious diplomatic follow-up of the Nguyen Duy Trinh opening. The tonnage was steadily increased until, within six months, it was running at about twice the figure at the time of my interview with the foreign minister.

In the meantime the State Department pundits were still fobbing off peace-seekers with the 'uncertainties' of the 'could' instead of 'would' formula on talks possibilities. In the summer of 1967, I returned to Hanoi and asked Nguyen Duy Trinh whether it was worthwhile doing another interview and correcting the mood of the verb. 'No,' he said with his typical stubborn smile, 'they still think they can break us with their bombs. So let them do their worst. Only when they see that their bombs can never break us is it worthwhile having another try. That may take many more months.'

[From Chapter 8 of *Grasshoppers & Elephants: Why Viet Nam Fell* (Outback Press, Melbourne, 1977), pp. 115–122.]

22

Personal Leader [1968]

In 1965, Wilfred Burchett moved his base from Moscow to Phnom Penh to be closer to the 'action' in Vietnam – and as far away from Moscow winters as possible. He had formed a partnership with French filmmaker Roger Pic and their exclusive films in both North and South Vietnam and interviews with Vietnamese leaders made world headlines. Burchett's writings on Vietnam were becoming increasingly influential in the US and Europe, where his *Inside Story of the Guerilla War* was a bestseller. Burchett was worried that a full US invasion of North Vietnam would drag China into military involvement, and possibly the USSR and its satellites. He envisaged a repeat of the Korean War scenario – with the risk of a nuclear disaster – so in the spring of 1967 he revisited North Korea.

Burchett was also fascinated by the ideological questions being raised in North Korea, and this was what spurred his interest in the North Korean leader. He writes in the Introduction to *Again Korea* that 'still another question interested me. There were signs that the North Korean Workers Party under Kim Il Sung was following a line of its own in the international Communist controversy, rejecting total adherence to the views of either Moscow or Peking, while seeming to aim at reconciling what was fundamental in each position. I was also interested in rumors of a "triangle" of ideas between Pyongyang, Hanoi and Havana, a kind of "third line".'

* * *

When I arrived in Pyongyang, at the end of April 1967, Kim Il Sung had just turned 55. The Korean press was celebrating his formation of the first anti-Japanese armed units 35 years before. At 55, this veteran revolutionary leader is still a young man of exceptional mental and physical vigor with experience as a practical leader that few world statesmen can rival.

One of the things which impressed me most before I met him was the extent to which he had personally supervised seemingly every detail of the postwar reconstruction. I had visited a dozen or so factories and farms, and to each of these places Kim Il Sung had come, not just once, but many times to see how things were going, to study conditions on the spot, to discuss with workers and peasants and learn of their problems as the first step toward solving them. At the Pyongyang textile plant, for instance, he had come no less than 28 times. The phrase 'the development of our factory is inseparable from the personal interest shown by Premier Kim Il Sung' seems to be a nation-wide truth. Before he developed his theses on the socialist agrarian question, he went to one village in Konson-ri county and stayed there for 15 days, living with the peasants, digging down to the very roots of their problems, the insufficiencies of party and government work, the fundamental aspirations of the peasantry – just as formerly he made no military move without the most detailed reconnaissance of the objectives to be tackled.

During the war years I had not met Premier Kim, and he referred to this within the first minutes of our meeting: 'I wanted to meet you then,' he said, 'but you were at Kaesong and I was busy at that time elsewhere.' He certainly was. He had the biggest fight on his hands that any Korean leader in history has had. But he left it at that: he was 'busy!' I could visualize him sitting down with peasants under a tree, perhaps chewing on a bit of straw, getting them to open their hearts. He has the warm, human touch, the simplicity of the great, and a down-to-earth manner rare among men in his position. This comes through in his speeches. Even dealing with such unromantic problems as heavy industry, there is always some little aside, to remind his listeners, especially if there are bureaucrats among them, that the end result of everything is to make life better and gayer for everyone. Machines are not being built for machines but to lighten and brighten the human lot.

'When we in North Korea eat well, dress well and live comfortably, when all of us have jobs, and labour has become much easier, what an influence all this will exert on the people in South Korea,' he said in a 1958 speech on communist education. 'Even the spies sent in by Syngman Rhee will not be able to conceal what they have seen in the North. Everybody has a job, work has become easier, incomes are high, all eat and dress well and live comfortably.' And in the same speech: 'We must advance faster than other people for we have lived too long in poverty ... Wherever you go in European countries you will find the roads well paved and even the rural people living, for the most part, in brick houses ... But as for us, we lived in shabby, straw-thatched hovels from generation to generation.' In his speech on 23 October 1962, urging fulfillment of targets for the seven-year plan, he said this 'will enable all of our people to lead an abundant life, inhabit tile-roofed houses, eat rice and much meat and wear good clothes. This means that the long-cherished desire of our working people will be accomplished in our time – a most happy and proud circumstance for us.'

The seven-year plan, launched in 1961, has not yet been fulfilled; it will span another three years because of urgent defense needs. But tile-roofed brick houses have become the rule over virtually all the countryside and peasants now eat rice all year round. The only thatch-roofed houses I saw were the two museum pieces belonging respectively to the families of Kim Il Sung's father and mother.

In the drive to bring the countryside nearer to the cities, Premier Kim has picked the county seat as the model for the new urban-type village into which the cooperative farms should transform themselves. The county seat 'must be built in a beautiful, neat, cultured and hygienic way so that the villages may follow its example. In every sphere ... with its cultural and welfare facilities, schools, hospitals, cinemas, bookshops and libraries ... the county seat must be an example for the farm villages and a model of the new, socialist way of life.' This is typical of the concrete way he expresses problems and guides the Korean people forward. Managers of the cooperative farms I visited all spoke of this service Kim Il Sung had given. They had built or were planning to build and introduce city-type facilities wherever possible and give an urban-type profile to their life. The introduction of the eight-hour working day and the freeing of mothers from much household work by the excellent nursery–kindergarten facilities has done much to make this possible. The peasants have leisure now and want the facilities to enjoy it.

A better deal for women in the countryside has been another of Kim Il Sung's constant themes. In a speech on cooperative farm management at the end of 1962, he complained that 'At present, many able-bodied men are loitering about with briefcases under their arms, on the pretext that they are some kind of leaders or are doing some highly technical job. So the farm work is left almost entirely to women. As far as possible, the women in fact should be given the lighter jobs and the men the arduous ones. If possible, clerical work such as compiling statistics and book-keeping should be left to the women and all the men should do field work.'

Style of Work

Fifteen years as a guerilla leader, sharing the daily life and dangers on an absolutely equal basis with his men and women fellow-partisans, have left an indelible imprint on Kim Il Sung's style of work. He is just the opposite of an armchair theoretician. In early 1959, in an attack on bureaucratic methods of work in the Korean Workers' Party and the former Communist Party, he said,

> If a few thousand revolutionary core elements who had taken part in the Korean revolution as guerrilla fighters had been preserved and if at least one of them had been allocated to each cell at the time the party was formed, the bureaucrat Ho Ga Yi[1] could not have spread his bureaucratic style of work which . . . led many people to believe that party work was something that should be conducted only by a sort of administrative method and by issuing orders. This has never, from the first, been the correct method of party work . . .
>
> It need hardly be said that the guerrilla units, being an armed force, carried out military activities upon orders. But military orders had to be explained patiently at party meetings until all accepted them consciously and everyone was determined to do his utmost to carry them through. To save their meagre ammunition, the guerrillas fought the enemy with bayonets, facing up to all dangers. With military orders alone, without persuasion and education, such heroism could hardly be expected. There was no means of control over guerrillas except their own will. There was no such thing as jail or lockups . . . It was persuasion

and education that were of exceptional significance. Education was conducted even during meals, marches and battles . . .

The prestige of the chairman of a party organization should be maintained by his real ability of leadership, not by brandishing party authority . . . You should not try to boost your prestige with the help of a big desk and an armchair. No red tape is needed for our party work.

Bureaucrats are anathema to Kim Il Sung. He has waged vigorous campaigns to rid party and government of that style of work acquired, as he once told leading party officials, because 'all that many of our comrades had seen and learned was the working method of Japanese imperialist officials.'

It is almost certain that the success of imposing his own style of work at all levels in party, government, factory and farm management, has been decisive in building up the country at such speed. The country in fact bears the strong imprint of the personality of Kim Il Sung, and he bears the strong imprint of the militant revolutionary environment of his most formative years and most of his youth and adult life.

[From 'Kim Il Sung', Chapter 9 of *Again Korea* (International Publishers, New York, 1968), pp. 101–105.]

23

The Tet of Peace [1973/1977]

The following chapter from *Grasshoppers & Elephants* demonstrates Burchett's writing at its best, his ability to integrate the personal experiences of ordinary people with the developments of great political events. The Paris Agreement was of huge historical significance, but here Burchett also describes what it meant to the people of Hanoi.

The Agreement was based on a draft written in October 1972. In a meeting with Henry Kissinger, North Vietnamese negotiator Le Duc Tho had agreed that the Saigon regime could remain in power. Kissinger held a press conference in Washington during which he announced that 'peace is at hand.'

When South Vietnamese President Nguyen Van Thieu was presented with the draft of the new agreement, he was furious with Kissinger and Nixon and refused to accept it without significant changes. He then made several public and radio addresses, claiming that the proposed agreement was worse than it actually was. Hanoi then believed it had been duped into a propaganda ploy by Kissinger. On 26 October Radio Hanoi broadcast key details of the draft agreement.

As U.S. casualties mounted throughout the war, American domestic support for it had deteriorated, and by 1973 there was major pressure on the Nixon administration to withdraw. Consequently, the U.S. brought great diplomatic pressure upon the South Vietnamese to sign the peace treaty even if the concessions Thieu wanted could not be achieved. With the U.S. committed to disengagement (and after threats from Nixon that South Vietnam would be abandoned if he did not agree), Thieu had little choice but to accede.

On 15 January 1973, Nixon announced a suspension of offensive actions against North Vietnam. Kissinger and Tho met again on 23 January and signed off on a treaty that was basically identical to the draft of three months earlier. The agreement was signed by the leaders of the official delegations on 27 January at the Majestic Hotel in Paris.

Le Duc Tho and Henry Kissinger were jointly awarded the 1973 Nobel Peace Prize for their efforts in negotiating the Agreement. However, Tho declined to accept the award, stating that there was still no peace in his country. Tho is the only person to have turned down the Peace Prize.

* * *

There were ugly gaps in the walls, and missing roofs and windows at Hanoi's Gia Lam civilian air terminal, but friends who I feared might have perished in the 'Kissinger bombings' were there, flowers in hand, to greet me. Along the road leading from the airport we were slowed down by a curious procession of vehicles: army trucks, horse and ox-drawn carts, handcarts hauled and pushed by people of all ages, all piled to capacity with beds, cupboards, and chairs – the modest furnishing of an average Vietnamese home with old people and children seated on top or jammed in between. Weaving through this odd assortment of transport were men and women pedalling bicycles, usually with children perched in baskets in front and behind. It was all part of the Great Return. Bombing north of the 20th parallel had been halted for over a month, but aircraft batteries, manned on each side of the road, showed that nothing was being taken for granted. The press and radio had made cautious references to the possibility of a peace agreement finally being signed. This was sufficient for homecomers to start converging on the capital from all directions.

Gia Lam itself, an industrial suburb on the northern side of the Red River from Hanoi, was a mass of rubble, the big railway repair depot reduced to twisted steel and collapsed roofs through which one saw rusted wrecks of burned-out trains.

Rubble choked the footpaths and where facades of houses and shops still stood there were gutted ruins behind. Our car bump-bumped its way across one of the several pontoon bridges with the ruins of the big Long Bien bridge in the background, one span drooping into the river, a great gap where another had been – twinkling blue flashes testifying that welders were at work at what one felt was a puny effort compared to the magnitude of the task.

The animation and vitality of the people and the spick-and-span cleanliness of the streets as we entered the city proper was in sharp contrast to the depressing destruction along the road from the airport.

I arrived in Hanoi on the eve of the great Tet of Peace, one that will never be forgotten by those who participated. Tet is like the western Christmas and New Year combined, a time of family reunions, of New Year hopes and plans, and as much rejoicing as the family budget permits. The narrow streets around the central market on the morning after my arrival were packed with early morning shoppers and ablaze with flowers, especially peach branches and tiny orange trees laden with miniature fruit glowing like little lanterns. Peach branches or orange trees – both if possible – are essential for a proper celebration of Tet. Never had there been such a profusion of flowers and everything from goldfish floating in glass spheres (both in a great variety of sizes) to paper flowers and dragons, festoons of firecrackers – everything that shone and made for good cheer. Market stalls were piled high with fruit and vegetables, with the glutinous rice cakes and pastries that are specialties of the occasion. The crowd in the streets quickly swelled so that even cycling became impossible. Most of the young people – girls as well as boys – were in the olive-green uniform and camouflaged pith helmets of the Vietnam Peoples Army. But there were also thousands of families freshly reunited – children perched high on parents' shoulders, faces shining like the persimmons and oranges at the feast of color and good things on every side.

Suddenly there was the sound of banging drums and clashing cymbals and the crowd parted to receive a truck, swathed in red banners, from which young people handed out copies of an extra-special edition of the morning paper. Unprecedented huge, red-banner headlines, announced the Peace Agreement had been signed. As the trucks passed at snail's pace with many a halt, hundreds of hands reached out for the papers, and shoppers took a few minutes off to read the unbelievably good news. The documents had actually been signed in Paris some 12 hours earlier, but with so many dashed hopes in the past, nothing was announced on the radio, or published until confirmation and full texts had been received from the DRV delegation.

As similarly decorated trucks and mini-buses slowly made their way along the main market streets handing out the good news, the loudspeaker system which for the previous eight years had so often sounded the grim warnings of approaching death and destruction burst into life and, punctuated with bursts of revolutionary music, announced the main terms of the Agreement and what they meant. On the main street corners, mountains of the special morning editions melted like snow in the hot sun and the vendor's hands were hard put to cope with the press of customers.

For the next three days it was the 'let joy be unconfined' of officially-declared rejoicing. The stream of returning evacuees turned into a flood-tide. Never had Hanoi residents better cause to celebrate and never had good news come at a more appropriate moment. Tet now provided the occasion for family reunions on a mass scale. Wives and husbands had been separated from each other according to their work, parents from their children, children from each other, schools were evacuated by classes, the tinier children sent to villages remote from communication routes (where possible with their grandparents). It was only by such measures that maximum survival could be assured. Now the long-separated elements of the families were converging for the greatest family reunions the capital had ever known. And the very first lines of the Paris Agreement were the most magnificent Tet gift that any Vietnamese could imagine.

> The United States and all other peoples respect the independence, sovereignty, unity and territorial integrity of Vietnam as recognized by the 1954 Geneva Agreement on Vietnam.

Patriotic Vietnamese had been fighting for this for all their adult lives. Oddly enough the words 'and all other peoples' were not in the October version of the Agreement, but were inserted – obviously with no objections by Le Duc Tho – during the January negotiations. This was typical of the emptiness of the pretensions of Nixon and Kissinger – that the most terrible bombings of the war had been necessary to bring about some fundamental changes in the text. All the essential points, the ones that one must assume Kissinger fought hardest against having included in the original text, remain. The key Article 4, for instance, that 'The United States will not continue its military involvement or intervene in the internal affairs of South Vietnam', is word for word as in the original text. The adding of 'and all other peoples' to Article 1, was designed to imply that the U.S. was not the only one who failed to respect the

1954 Geneva Agreement. Similarly Article 9 (c) states that 'Foreign countries shall not impose any political tendency or personality on the South Vietnamese people', whereas the original text states 'The United States is not committed to any political tendency or to any personality in South Vietnam, and it does not seek to impose a pro-American regime in Saigon.'

The change here, a slight gain for Kissinger, revealed by omission U.S. intentions to continue to impose a 'pro-American regime in Saigon.' 500 waves of B-52s were employed as a red pencil to correct Kissinger's shoddy editing of the original version!

Any objective point-by-point comparison of the Agreement signed in Paris on 27 January 1973, and the summary as published by the DRV government of that to be signed on 31 October 1972, makes it abundantly clear that the changes did not justify the sacrifice of a single human life. The steadfastness with which the original text was defended reflects one more humiliating defeat for the Nixon–Kissinger strong-arm methods. Their aim had been to bomb the original version to smithereens. Instead they had to swallow it whole.

Apart from the military provisions for an end to all acts of war, the dismantling of all U.S. bases, a stand-still ceasefire in South Vietnam and provisions for supervising these arrangements, the Agreement laid down the precise steps to be taken for a political solution in the South, including (Article 11), non-discrimination against individuals or organizations which collaborated with one side or the other and the introduction of broad democratic liberties – freedom of press, association and assembly, freedom to choose one's place of work or residence, etc. All this in an effort to promote 'national reconciliation and concord.' The key article for bringing this latter about was contained in Article 12:

(a) Immediately after the ceasefire, the two South Vietnamese parties shall hold consultations in a spirit of national reconciliation and concord, mutual respect and mutual non-elimination, to set up a National Council of National Reconciliation and Concord of three equal segments.

The Council shall operate on the principle of unanimity. After the NCNRC has assumed its functions, the two South Vietnamese parties will consult about the formation of councils at lower levels.

The two South Vietnamese parties shall sign an agreement on the internal matters of South Vietnam as soon as possible and do their utmost to accomplish this within 90 days after the ceasefire comes into effect, in keeping with the South Vietnamese people's aspirations for peace, independence and democracy.

(b) The NCNRC shall have the task of promoting the two South Vietnamese parties' implementation of this agreement, achievement of national reconciliation and concord and ensurance of democratic liberties.

The NCNRC will organize the free and democratic general elections provided for in Article 9(b) and decide the procedures and modalities of these general elections.

The institutions for which the general elections are to be held will be agreed upon through consultations between the two South Vietnamese parties. The NCNRC will also decide the procedures and modalities of such local elections as the two South Vietnamese parties agree upon.

The PRG concept of a three-way transitional government as proposed by Madame Nguyen Thi Binh on September 11 was thus retained in a somewhat downgraded form of a three-way advisory council. An ominous indication of how the U.S. intended to respect 'self-determination' came in Nixon's broadcast statement of January 23, announcing the conclusion of the Agreement. After stating that final agreement had been reached that day and that this would bring 'peace with honor' to South Vietnam, he stated in part 'The United States will continue to recognize the Government of the Republic of South Vietnam as the sole legitimate government of South Vietnam', a statement which Thieu never ceased to exploit by refusing to implement any of the terms of Article 12, for instance.

However, there was plenty to rejoice over in Hanoi; plenty of reasons for three days and nights during which the streets and parks were thronged with animated crowds, emotional reunions occurring all over the place as friends met who hadn't seen each other during the years of evacuation. The explosions of enormous quantities of firecrackers of all calibres replaced those of the anti-aircraft batteries. Mayor Hung had released thousands of tons of extra food and in the homes of various friends I visited there was no lack of food or the potent 'shum shum' rice alcohol to wash it down. Even in the rubble of Kham Thien Street, amidst pathetic handwritten notices on sticks poked into the rubble that such and such a child had survived and was now with 'Uncle Nguyen . . .' or 'Auntie Minh . . .' at such and such an address, there were also peach blossoms and orange trees planted outside makeshift shelters, thus contriving to soften the desolation. 'The recent past was terrible, the present is difficult, the future is bright – and at Tet we always think of the future' was how a diminutive, elderly woman summed it up, as she stepped back to survey the little orange tree she had just propped up between some bricks outside the ruins of her home – also in the Kham Thien area. Even during the holidays people were at work there, scraping mortar off bricks, neatly stacking them up and in some cases laying them without mortar in between to make walls of temporary dwellings.

What did the Agreement mean to Vietnamese? Firstly, that within 60 days there would be no more foreign troops on Vietnamese soil for the first time since a Franco-Spanish expedition captured Saigon in 1859. The bombings had been stopped and this time it seemed for good. The independence and unity of the country was recognized – and this time, as distinct from 1954 in Geneva – the Americans had put their signature to the Agreement. In whatever way Thieu would implement the Agreement in the South, this time – also as distinct from the 1954 Geneva Agreement – the revolutionary forces stayed where they were, arms in hand, until political solutions were implemented and the armies of both sides were integrated with a large part demobilized. The revolutionary forces in the South had their own government which was being accorded increasing international recognition.

'The Geneva Agreement gave us half the country "red",' explained a peasant from the city outskirts, whom I found gazing with contempt at the B-52 in the Hanoi Zoo. 'The Paris Agreement gives us half the South "red." That took 20 years. It will take much less to make the other half of the South "red".' That was one of the best summings-up I heard.

For the more politically sophisticated – Luu Quy Ky, for example, president of the Vietnamese Journalists Association – the Agreement was a document of the highest importance for the forthcoming struggle in the South. A 'veritable political tribune' he said, 'which provides the legal base for carrying on the struggle at a higher level. Our position and that of our comrades in the South will be for the strictest implementation in the liberated areas, the avoidance of any provocations, a demand for the same strict observance of the Agreement for the Saigon regime.'

There was plenty for a journalist to do and see in those first few days. On the evening of the 28th itself, there was a ceremony at which Vo Nguyen Giap farewelled the advance group of VPA officers who were to go to Saigon as delegates to a four-party Joint Military Commission. The head of the group pledged to Giap that they would faithfully carry out their duty to observe the strict application of the Agreement. It was a solemn and rather moving moment and I was not the only one to have some inner doubts as to how many of them would ever return to Hanoi, in view of the torrent of abuse against the Agreement that continued to pour out of Thieu's headquarters (Vo Nguyen Giap looked remarkably fit, incidentally, considering the report by U.S. intelligence sources in Saigon that he had been blown to bits by a delayed-action bomb in Haiphong just one month earlier). The delegation was held up for 24 hours when they arrived the next day at Saigon airport because the authorities tried to make them fill in forms as if they were immigrants or tourists, whereas, according to the Protocols of the Agreement, they were to have the status of diplomats. Finally they were herded off into a barbed-wire enclosure at the Tan Son Nhut airbase, which was to serve as their residence and headquarters. This was the beginning of harassment and insults which ended only on 30 April 1975.

There was another ceremony to welcome a triumphant Xuan Thuy and his negotiations' delegation on their return from Paris. There were visits to Haiphong (two-thirds destroyed) and the coal mining center of Hongay, on the entrancing Baie d'Along north of Haiphong, which will surely become a major international tourist resort. Hongay had been 100 percent destroyed, not a building left intact. The city's pride, a fine football stadium on the outskirts of the city, had been blown sky-high the very day it was to be formally opened! High quality Hongay anthracite is one of the country's most important export items – much appreciated in Japan amongst other countries – but the grading works and the nearby Campha wharf facilities had been blown to bits.

There was the arrival of Henry Kissinger on February 10, for a four-day visit to discuss, as had been believed, implementation of Article 21 of the 23 Article Agreement. It stated:

The United States anticipates that this Agreement will usher in an era of reconciliation with the Democratic Republic of Vietnam as with all peoples of Indochina. In pursuance of its traditional policy, the United States will contribute to healing the wounds of war and to post-war reconstruction of the Democratic Republic of Vietnam and throughout Indochina.

This incidentally was the exact wording of the original version of the Agreement. Kissinger and his party were accorded all the courtesies of distinguished guests. They were met at the airport by Le Duc Tho. But Kissinger had not come to discuss 'post-war reconstruction' although he would have had to be blind not to see a few hundred million dollars worth of civilian 'wounds of war' just in driving from Gia Lam airport to his guest house! He had come to discuss the size of the bribe the U.S. was prepared to pay in return for a DRV pledge to abandon its compatriots in the South. It was as simple and crude as that, but his hosts continued to treat him and his aides with the good manners of a highly civilized people. No deviation from the official itinerary to drive past Kham Thien Street, nor any invitation to visit the Zoo! The only concrete result of the visit was a decision to set up a Joint Economic Commission 'charged with the task of developing economic relations between the two countries ...' It was an affable, smiling Kissinger who arrived and a sombre, glowering Kissinger who left, four days later (the Joint Economic Commission subsequently held a few fruitless sessions in Paris, then went into indefinite adjournment when it became evident that the United States was interested only in buying the South for X number of billions of dollars). A typical illusion of the U.S. leadership to think that a billion-dollar carrot could succeed where a B-52 stick had failed! President Nixon at one point sent a personal letter to Pham Van Dong pledging 3.25 billion dollars worth of aid to contribute to 'healing the wounds of war!'

On the eve of Kissinger's visit, Premier Pham Van Dong told me 'We will do everything for the integral respect of the Paris Agreement. It is the concrete expression of everything we have won and it opens up new prospects for the victory of the national democratic revolution in the South.' On the question of U.S.–North Vietnam relations, in view of the Kissinger visit, the prime minister said 'We are ready to normalize relations. But some problems have first to be settled. The question of the contribution to healing the wounds of war and aid for reconstruction, must be settled to the satisfaction of everyone. But we will accept no conditions. In all matters, our interests, our right, our sovereignty must always be respected.' Referring to reports that the U.S. Congress would probably not approve the passage of funds to implement Article 21, Premier Pham Van Dong said 'We will demand that the United States fulfill its obligations. If the people of the United States want to salvage their conscience, they will support this. But we will insist on freely disposing of funds that are allotted. We are absolutely determined to remain masters in our own country.' On the overall question of implementing the Agreement, Pham Van Dong commented 'The United States seems to be bent on repeating the same old errors of closing their eyes to reality. The same old mistake of not seeing things that are extremely vital for everyone.'

This was the viewpoint defended during Kissinger's visit to Hanoi and at the meetings of the Economic Commission in Paris. If Kissinger had been expecting to find some 'last gasp' economic situation in Hanoi, with hands outstretched in the sort of dollar-grasping attitude that he was used to in South Vietnam and in so many other of America's beggar-client states, he must have been sorely disappointed. North Vietnam was poor in a material sense, yes, and the United States had done its best to make it poorer by bombing out of existence the little bit the North Vietnamese had. But it was also infinitely rich in national pride and dignity which, if Kissinger and his team had been sensitive, they would have noted. By the mercantile attitude of the U.S. delegates on the Joint Economic Commission – trying to buy half a country on the cheap – it seemed that they had not!

One of Kissinger's aides was discreetly on hand on February 12, to watch the departure of the first batches of U.S. pilot-POW's from Gia Lam airport. First there was a meeting in the bombed-out passenger lounge of members of the International Commission of Control and Supervision (Canada, Indonesia, Poland and

12: *A US jet plane goes to the airplane cemetery, Hanoi, 1966 (photo: Wilfred Burchett)*

Hungary) plus representatives of the Pentagon and the VPA, at which were agreed the modalities of the handing-over procedure. A representative of the U.S. Air Force then took his place at a table under a tent awning, with a list of POW's to be released, flanked at other tables by the ICCS officers. When all were in place, a camouflaged bus drew up and out stepped the pilots. Neatly dressed, sleek – obviously fit – one by one they marched to the desk, saluted, gave their names and units, and were escorted off to silvery Stratoliners waiting to fly them off to Guam.

A distraught-looking Pentagon official tried to catch up with each one and whisper a few words in his ear – presumably on what to say at the receiving end. Among the first to be released was one of the 'Christmas bomber' pilots, his leg in plaster from an unanticipated 'landfall.' They were all in very different shape from the emaciated wrecks from the prisons of the U.S.-Saigon Command, slithering their way to freedom, as portrayed on Western TV, by propelling themselves with their hands – their legs withered and useless from years in chains in the Tiger Cages of Poulo Condor and elsewhere. Yet somehow it appeared in the U.S. press that it was the U.S. pilots that were to be pitied, not the tortured remnants from the U.S.-run prisons or the tens of thousands of orphans, widows and limbless victims of their activities!

As the first gleaming Stratoliner took off with its load of pilots, an old friend, a Vietnamese historian, murmured 'Truly, times have changed. When we defeated the Mongols, we usually sent them back to China on our own horses or boats, with sufficient rations to see them on their way. We then sent delegates to Peking – once with a golden statue of the commanding general who had been killed – always with generous tribute and our excuses for having defeated their armies in regrettable incidents during which they had crossed our borders. "Please spare us this in the future," we said. Now at least there is an invader who sends his own transport to remove the captives, and even sends us an emissary to discuss the amount of *their* tribute.'

[Chapter 12 of *Grasshoppers & Elephants: Why Viet Nam Fell* (Outback Press, Melbourne, 1977), pp. 171–180.]

24

'Something from Nothing' Township [1976]

In the early 1970s, Wilfred Burchett was a frequent visitor to Beijing while writing a book with Prince Norodom Sihanouk of Cambodia (*My War with the CIA*) and covering Nixon's visit to China for America's CBS. He also covered China's re-admittance to the UN in New York and took a break from that to take up the offer of breakfast with Henry Kissinger at the White House, an offer extended by Kissinger as a result of Burchett's reputation as the best-informed journalist in Indochina. So it was logical that he would also want to take a break from war in Indochina to investigate post-Cultural Revolution China, and in the wake of 'ping-pong' diplomacy and Nixon's 1972 visit to the country, the West was demonstrating a growing interest in all things Chinese.

At the same time, tensions were increasing between China and the USSR, with Vietnam caught in the middle. In the summer of 1973, Burchett and his old friend, New Zealand author, journalist and China expert Rewi Alley, set out on a journey across China, each of them covering a particular part of the vast country and a variety of topics: people's communes, oil fields, minorities, women, youth, health, education and so on. The intent was described in the Introduction to the book: 'Our central interest has been to measure the changes that have occurred in recent years in China and to set them in perspective against what we knew of old China. We tried to understand also how ordinary Chinese citizens conceive that much-bandied-about term "quality of life". Their concepts were bound to be different from those who measure human progress by the "gross national product" – a point of view badly shaken in many countries by the "energy crisis" in the latter part of 1973.'

The result of their collaborative effort was one of Burchett's best-selling books, *China: The Quality of Life*.

* * *

That there was no 'oil boom town' atmosphere at Taching, no bars, brothels or night clubs doing a roaring trade as technicians and oil drillers with fat pay cheques swaggered in from lonely drilling sites for a long weekend, obviously did not surprise us. That concept of 'Great Celebration' left for Taiwan with the Kuomintang. It was difficult at first to locate Taching city – an oilfield capital. We found there were three big urban centres, spaced 5 or 6 kilometres apart, in each of which a lot of planned building was going on, and forty more townships, each surrounded by two or three satellite villages, the whole connected with a network of good roads and provided with free bus services. All this came under the general heading of the Taching Municipality.

'When premier Chou En-lai came here in 1962,' explained Li Huei-hsin, of the oilfield's secretariat, who turned out to be an indefatigable and wonderfully well-informed guide, 'he advised us to make this a new type of model enterprise. Industry should be integrated with agriculture, with production and local administrative power. There should be an all-round development of industry, agriculture, stock-raising, fish-breeding, etc. We should become an autonomous community, with production, distribution, education all under 'one roof'. Living quarters should not be concentrated in one spot – they should be scattered according to where the oil is found. Workers' families should go into agricultural production – become producers instead of consumers. This is what we have done. People say that the city looks like the countryside and the countryside looks like the city.'

This explanation, backed up by our further investigations, threw an entirely new light on the 'Learn from Taching' slogan. Taching was to be the vision of an unpolluted future for new industrial development. Green industrial centres! A thing which had struck us before was that huge patches of the grassland had been transformed into fields of ripening wheat and early maize, growing not only right up to the little white well housings but also in the fields where actual drilling was taking place. We had our photographs taken with the shift-workers of Team 1205, up to our knees in a heavy-yield wheat crop, with the drilling rig towering above us 20 metres away. Some of the wheat was knocked down when the rigs were dragged by stubby little tractors to the next site, but this was infinitesimal compared to the rippling ocean of wheat lapping right to the base of the rigs. Obviously the usual forest of derricks and oil-wells could not have co-existed with the grain fields. Only the complete automation of scientifically spaced wells made it possible.

We were invited to visit any of the townships we liked and could not resist Chuan Yeh ('Something from Nothing') township, not only because the name itself was one of the key themes of our investigations, but also because one of the township's satellites was the home village of Hsueh Kuei-feng, the nationally famous female counterpart of the 'Iron Man'. We found her a diminutive, grey-haired woman, modest and gentle. We were the first foreigners she had ever seen and she had to be prompted by her fellow-members of the Chuan Yeh revolutionary committee to relate one of those epic stories so typical of the development of Chuan Yeh. She had come with some members of her family to join others who had left Yumen for the new oil centre.

'We arrived here in April 1962,' she said, 'and the conditions were really tough. We were given some tents but the men drilling some 15 kilometres away were living in improvised huts or holes in the ground, lacking food supplies. We decided we had to do something – grow them some food. So we set out, five of us, with babes on our backs and lanterns in hand – and each with a shovel.' (This episode has entered into the folklore of Taching as that of the 'five-shovel brigade'.) 'We went to the first drilling site – the men had already moved on, but had left some improvised huts. We moved into one of them. It was very cold and terrible; gale-force winds roared over the plains. At night wolves came howling around and some of us were frightened for the babies. The first time they came, we just blocked the door with our five shovels, ready to fight them off in case they got in. Afterwards we got used to them – they are cowardly beasts. One afternoon a couple of them came circling round, getting closer all the time. I took my shovel and beat it on the rocks, howling twice as loud as the wolves, and they soon went slinking off. We had no more trouble with them after that.

'We started digging up the grasslands with our shovels, but the soil was half-frozen and it was heavy going. Later, we were joined by thirteen more wives and we found an abandoned plough. So we formed a team of ten to pull the plough, nine yoked in front and one behind to steer. We were not used to marching in step, so the first rows wandered all over the place. We stopped and discussed the problem and decided: "If men can do it, women can also do it." (By that time the "Iron Man" team had also been at work.) We decided to shout in unison at every step, and in that way got the rows straight, breaking up the big clods later with wooden clubs.' (We suspected that it must have been the traumatic experience of seeing and hearing a twenty-legged creature, roaring at every step, that scared the wolves out of that part of the grasslands for ever.)

In that first, bitter season Hsueh Kuei-feng and her group managed to cultivate 5 acres and sow it with wheat. The next year new reinforcements brought the group to seventy – and they cultivated 18 acres. In 1964, all the wives from the township's 300 households joined in and they put almost 100 acres under crops.

'Things are very different now,' she said, in conclusion, 'we have tractors and harvesters and get more grain every year, and plenty of fruit and vegetables as well.'

If anyone wants to get down to the real essence of Women's Lib. in China, it is difficult to imagine a more appropriate spot than 'Something from Nothing' township. For several hours we sat around talking with the organized housewives and visiting their creations. With glowing cheeks and flashing eyes, they prompted each other to relate how they had tamed the grasslands – and by inference their husbands. The most eloquent of all was Li Chang-yung, a classic peasant beauty who could have stepped straight out of the title role of a film, ruddy-tinged bronzed cheeks, perfect teeth, coal-black, glowing eyes and a husky vibrant voice. As vice-chairwoman of the revolutionary committee she was the most explicit about women's emancipation.

'We can prove our progress in farming with statistics,' she said. 'What we can't demonstrate with statistics is the changed social consciousness of everyone here. Before, we women had only our menfolk, kids and household chores to think about. Now we think about the whole country – the whole world – starting with the oilfield and ending with Tien An Men. There has been a revolution in family relations. A husband may be an advanced oil-worker – but his wife is an advanced farm-worker. What's the difference? Now there is real respect for each other. We discuss each other's problems – the oilfield or the wheatfield – and encourage each other.

We've acquired really equal status. When our husbands come home they help with the cooking and washing-up. They help look after the kids. We're really emancipated, socially, politically, economically. There are no longer any sharp divisions between husband and wife because we have proved by deeds that Chairman Mao was right when he said: "What men can do, women can do".'

Cho T'a-ching, another vice-chairwoman, provided some of the factual background to Li Chang-yung's enthusiasm.

'When we arrived,' she said, 'we were faced straight away with a choice: everyone for herself, or the collective road. At Yumen we had hardly stirred out of our houses. But here it was a different situation. We have gradually increased to 713 households, 2760 people altogether, and by this year we have 500 acres of cultivable land, 391 pigs, 133 cows, 57 horses and 590 sheep. We also have eight tractors and two combine harvesters. Last year we produced 225 tons of wheat, 550 tons of vegetables and 7 tons of meat. By several years of hard work we have brought Chuan Yeh up to the standards suggested by premier Chou En-lai, that Taching should become an integrated industrial–agricultural area. We have maintained the good old tradition of hard work and plain living, but our living standards have improved year by year.' 'Something from Nothing' was a self-contained community, with a nursery, kindergarten and schools, a thirty-bed clinic, hairdressing salon, bank, post office, public baths and well-stocked shops which between them kept open from 6.30 a.m. to 9.30 p.m. There were workshops for producing noodles, soya sauce and vinegar, a bakery, a sewing centre for repairs and tailor-made clothes, and repair shops for bicycles, radios and watches.

Housing and shops had been built by the housewives – the typical single-storied adobe buildings of the north-east, the almost flat, asphalted roofs having enough of a hump for the snow to be pushed off easily.

'We have tried to do everything to free ourselves from useless labour,' continued Cho T'a-ching. 'In the old days we used to waste a lot of time making noodles, for instance. Now, we take one pound of flour to the noodle mill and within a few minutes get back one pound and two ounces of noodles (presumably the water gave the added weight) and pay a fee of one cent.' Two housewives ran the noodle mill, and two more the tiny plant which produced soy sauce and vinegar, both of these extracted in the same process from soy bean, after which the residue was fed to the pigs.

We asked Hsueh Kuei-feng whether she preferred Yumen or Taching. 'No comparison,' she said. 'Taching. In Yumen we had no chance of working in the fields. There are only sand and rocks there. We didn't know then about the experience at Tachai or perhaps we would have done something. We came here to support the battle for oil, to support our menfolk, and we see that we did make a contribution. We feel we have done something new.'

The irrepressible Li Chang-yung broke in to say: 'Of course it's new. This is a rural area, but it's like a small town. We have electricity, telephones in the offices, central heating – everything that a small town has. But we grow grain and vegetables right up to the walls of the houses and raise cattle, pigs and sheep, so although it looks like a small town it isn't. You can say we're small-town dwellers, but in fact we're farmers. Per acre yields may be low but they're rising all the time.'

We visited Hsueh Kuei-feng's village, one of three satellites of Chuan Yeh. The waist-high wheat promised an excellent crop, and there was a great variety of vegetables, tomatoes, red and green peppers, garlic, apple and peach orchards, and even young grapevines. Everything was neat and geometric, the fields bordered by trees for windbreaks, the ground levelled off to facilitate mechanized ploughing and harvesting. It looked like a well-tended market garden, with only the grasslands around the perimeter to recall what had been. From a little knoll overlooking the village, as the sun etched a golden line around the clouds, as far as one could see in every direction in the sea of green were the little white houses over the disciplined wells passing on their quotas of oil to the collection centres twenty-four hours per day.

As the Chuan Yeh people – and this applied to those from the other thirty-nine townships and the satellite villages – had built everything themselves from nothing, it was hardly surprising that all the main facilities were free. Free rent, free lighting, free natural gas – piped into each house for kitchen fuel and heating – free cinema, free bathhouse, free bus rides, free medical care for the oil workers and at half cost for the dependants. The combined earnings of husband and wife averaged between 110 and 120 yuan per month, whereas living costs for a family of four – mainly food – averaged around 15 yuan per head, so that half the earnings could be banked away or spent on such things as sewing machines, radios, watches and bicycles – the four most popular hardware items in rural China today, with cameras and portable TV sets looming over the horizon.

We were invited, as usual, to criticize the imperfections but, surrounded by the 'Something from Nothing' women, glowing with the pride of achievement, it was difficult to find anything to criticize. Thinking over things on the way back to our lodgings, we had some overall critical reflections. The emphasis on the collective, as far as amenities were concerned, was overwhelming, but perhaps a corrective was needed from somewhere higher up. Trees planted in abundance as windbreaks round cultivation patches and along the roads were lacking along the township and village streets or around houses. Asphalt was used generously on the excellent roads linking residential areas with each other and the oilfields, but not on the rutty streets and footpaths which became mud bogs when it rained – as it had done most fiercely just before our arrival. There is no lack of space – the grasslands are state property and the new townships and villages can help themselves to as much as they like for building and for developing agriculture – but township and village streets are relatively narrow and the space between houses leaves little room for gardens which would blend in with the surrounding area. But the current mood in the Taching area, as elsewhere in China, is so much that of 'the family should hold back' that it would need a Chou En-lai to visit the place again and say: 'Well done, but don't forget your own homes, streets and villages! There's plenty of space for all. Make it beautiful as well as functional.'

Such advice, at this stage of China's development, has to come from a topmost level. For anyone to suggest it at Chuan Yeh would be to risk a thorough ideological dressing-down by Cho T'a-ching, Li Chang-yung and their fellow committee-women . . .

In a last talk with him before we left, Li Huei-hsin again stressed the original pattern of development of the oilfield. 'We have completely broken away from the old idea of first building up a city with housing and all sorts of facilities, the family dependants inside the city and the workers away on the distant drilling sites. In our concept, small communities with all urban facilities go parallel with the development of the field.'

Taching had gradually built up to a population of over 300,000, dispersed in three big urban centres, forty townships and over a hundred township–satellites – the latter purely residential but within easy walking distance of the townships and their urban facilities. Serving this community was one higher educational establishment of university level, three specialized technical institutions giving higher secondary education and 269 primary and middle schools. All children of school age, as elsewhere in China, received their schooling free. 'There is no "boom town" atmosphere, because workers receive the same wages as elsewhere and prices in the remotest oil-drilling site are exactly the same as those in Peking or anywhere else in China,' explained Li Huei-hsin – something we had checked for ourselves.

Although the negative aspects of urban conglomeration had been avoided, there were over 160 public health centres and clinics, including hospitals with up to 300 beds in the Taching area.

Whether this impressive de-concentration of population – like the underground oil storage and distribution centres – was also part of the 'be prepared against war' strategy was not mentioned, but Li Huei-hsin did point out that the oilfields 'have the equivalent of a full division of people's militia, the members of which also take part in productive labour. If an enemy ever attacks, everyone will take to arms to defend the oilfields.' Referring to the early sabotage, Li commented: 'The grave miscalculation of Liu Shao-ch'i was that he underestimated the determination of the workers to press on and develop the field. Without that grass roots determination, symbolized by such comrades as Wang Chin-hsi and Hsueh Kuei-feng, nothing could have been done.' As is customary when the time came for us to leave, Li touched on the shortcomings as the oilfield leadership saw them:

'Our drilling equipment – apart from the high-speed bits – is basically what was used in the early 1950s. The level of mechanization and automation in many processes is not high. Per-hectare yield in agriculture is comparatively low; we are lagging behind in re-afforestation. We will have to work hard to overcome these weaknesses, but we are determined to do this.'

At the Taching siding as our train pulled out, the parallel tracks were filled with long lines of cistern-cars being readied for a long haul south and freight trains discharging mysteriously shaped equipment which we assumed was for the new chemical plant. From the train window during a fast non-stop run to Harbin, interspersed with fields of rice, wheat and market gardens close to the urban centres, we saw vast plains in which herds of beef and dairy cattle and droves of horses grazed up to their middles in the lush grasslands and flocks of sheep nibbled at herbage on the fringes of bald patches where wind erosion had lifted off the top soil. It was an extension of the Sung Liao basin, of which Taching was the heart, and one envisaged it in years to come dotted with the same white oil-well housings.

Alongside every railway siding were scores of squat grain silos covered with woven matting, and more were being prepared. At Harbin we were informed that Heilungkiang province, of which it was the capital, had reaped excellent harvests for thirteen years in succession – unaffected even by the natural disasters which smote most of the rest of the country in 1960–62 – and that 1973 promised to beat all records in wheat and soya bean production. The state of the crops along our route from Harbin southwards and the scope of the construction of new grain storage space at almost every railway siding seemed to confirm the estimates.

What a contrast the Yumen field presented as compared to Taching. From a control tower we felt as if we were on the bridge of the flagship of a fleet, supervising the performance of the smaller fry. Below for as far as one could see were the kowtowing pumps obediently nodding their heads, while a computerized tape on the 'bridge' registered their performance.

The Yumen field is at an altitude of over 7000 feet (2300 metres) on the Old Silk Road, along which camel caravans used to pass between Ancient Cathay and the Arab world. The presence of 'black water' – oil seepages – in the surrounding Gobi Desert was noted by early travellers like Marco Polo, and by still earlier Chinese travellers in the eighth century. The American Texas Oil Company was promised by the Kuomintang a majority lifetime interest in any oil found. It prospected in the Yumen (West Kansu) area in the early 1930s but reported there was no oil in exploitable proportions. A Chinese geologist disputed this view in 1938 and small-scale production started shortly after. American specialists predicted then that it would be worked out within ten years. After the People's Republic was set up the field was developed with Soviet help and peak production of 1,200,000 tons was reached in 1959, falling off gradually to 620,000 tons in 1972. Two new fields were being opened up at the time of our visit, with new Chinese-made drilling equipment which must be the envy of the Taching drillers. The more cumbersome and slower Soviet and Romanian equipment is no longer used.

The new fields are to be developed along the lines of Taching, using the water-injection system to maintain stable pressures. Yumen seemed a big field during our early visits to the area. It will produce for about fifty years to come, according to the Chinese engineers on the spot, at a level sufficient to fuel the rapidly growing industry and transport needs in the area. But it is completely dwarfed by Taching.

One of the most valuable functions of this pioneer field is that it trained, and sent out to other fields, some 63,000 technicians and specialized workers and provided over 2000 pieces of oil-exploiting equipment made in the factories built to serve the field.

At the wells where pumps are being used, average production is 6 tons daily. The newer ones, based on stable pressures, average 30 tons daily for an expected five years, after which pumps will have to be used because of the pressure lost during the exploitation of the older parts of the field.

As a measure of China's progress, it was interesting to look in at the old oil refinery and, in one section alone, count machinery from fourteen different countries, none of it made in China. At the new Yumen refinery, as at Taching, apart from some ultra-modern measuring instruments, everything in the petrochemical plant was Chinese-made.

[From Chapter 7 of *China: The Quality of Life* (Penguin Books, Harmondsworth, 1976), pp. 114–126.]

25

Evaluating the Past [1976]

Though *China: The Quality of Life* often lapsed into the laborious advocacy which had marred his books on the Soviet Union such as *Come East Young Man*, as well as the tedium of production figures and long discourses on engineering projects, in this book Burchett again demonstrated a desire to pursue more intangible aspects of the new China, as in this chapter about attitudes to history and the past.

He initiated this with an anecdote about his co-author, a man well-known to contemporary readers. Rewi Alley was a New Zealander who moved to Shanghai in 1927. After the invasion of China by Japan in 1937, he became involved in setting up co-operatives across China in an effort to counter the Japanese blockade of inland China and pursued his interest in education by establishing a school at Shandan. Then following Liberation in 1949 he was urged to remain in China and work for the Communist Party. He produced many works praising the Party, but his reluctance to write about China's problems or to criticise the Party colours the historical value of his work, and influenced the book co-written with Burchett. Although imprisoned during the Cultural Revolution, Alley remained committed to Communism and later travelled the world, usually lecturing on the need for nuclear disarmament. In stark contrast to Australia's handling of Burchett's case, the New Zealand government did not strip Alley of his passport and remained proud of his ties to important Chinese leaders.

In the 1950's he was offered a knighthood but turned the honour down.

* * *

In May 1967, when the Cultural Revolution was at its stormiest, a bullet-headed youngster with a Red Guard armband on his sleeve swaggered into Rewi Alley's Peking apartment. With a jerk of his chin towards the pottery shards, bronzes, ivories, scrolls and other treasures accumulated during decades of work and travel in the back country, where every sandstorm uncovers fresh relics, the Red Guarder said: 'Better chuck all this old junk out.' Roaring 'Down with your pants,' Rewi Alley reached for his belt. An offspring of one of his adopted sons, the lad had come from a remote province to give the Cultural Revolution in Peking a push from behind – intent on applying too literally the campaign against the 'four olds' (old ideas, old culture, old habits and old ruling-class customs). There were enough young zealots around with similar misinterpretations to cause the government to close museums and place ancient monuments under armed guard.

Fortunately, the treasures which Rewi Alley uses to illustrate facets of China's past remained intact. The campaign against the 'four olds' was aimed at the Confucian-inspired sanctity of age and authority behind which Liu Shao-ch'i and his followers sheltered to advance their policies. In a more specific way, the campaign was also used against well-known reactionaries of the old order to uncover illegally hoarded treasures in the form of gold bars and foreign currency, arms, radio transmitters, Kuomintang uniforms and decorations and, far more significantly, title deeds to properties taken over during land reform and detailed records of former tenants' debts, with compound interest calculated in many cases up to the month of the seizure. Like White Russian emigres in European capitals, and the dispossessed in all revolutions, a tiny handful of upper-class Chinese still pinned their hopes on the miracle of a Kuomintang comeback. Confiscated evidence of this was displayed during the Cultural Revolution in special exhibitions in Peking, Shanghai and other former strongholds of the privileged.

It was the period when many students and young people from the cities were taking advantage of free transport and peasant hospitality to wander all over China and discover the countryside, while their opposite numbers from the countryside descended into the cities, doubtless with lurking suspicions that they were dens of iniquity that had spawned revisionism and 'capitalist-roaders'.

In urging an attack against the 'four olds', Mao was laying down a challenge to any automatic obedience to authority based on age, classical learning and custom, a legacy of Confucianism which had permeated the educational system and dominated some approaches to scientific research (it was later seen to have even resisted the cleansing winds of the Cultural Revolution in some fields) . . .

Wherever one travels in China one is conscious of this combination of respect for the old – homage to historical continuity and all that contributes to man's understanding of his own evolution – with a meticulous attempt to separate the progressive from the retrograde.

For example, during a never-to-be-forgotten boat trip from Chungking to Wuhan, through the fabulous Yangtze gorges, an attentive stewardess, when not occupied with the banalities of room and table service, divided her time between pointing out the impressive development of industry and housing on both banks of the Yangtze and indicating the historic monuments past which we glided in a very comfortable passenger steamer. Just before nightfall on the first day, we dropped anchor at Wanhsien, with its lovely grey building leading up from the steep banks, new constructions blending perfectly with the old, in order to pass through the first of the three gorges – the Ch'u Tang – in daylight. During the late afternoon, stewardess Tzu Hung-li, fresh-faced, with stiff, short pigtails and tireless in her attentions, pointed out a succession of curved-roof pagodas, rising one above the other up several hundred feet of steep cliffs on the southern bank to a splendid structure on the summit, a single architectural complex, gleaming white in the rays of the setting sun against the emerald of the tree-covered cliffs. It was the 'Magic Stone' pagoda, Miss Tzu informed us, to mark a Chinese version of the 'Goose That Laid the Golden Egg' morality fable. Legend had it that from a hole in the rock at the summit enough grain emerged every morning to feed a handful of hermit monks who had taken up their abode there. One of them had the bright idea of chiselling out a bigger hole to get more grain. He chiselled away and, like the man who killed the goose to get all the golden eggs at once, found there was no more grain. The pagodas remain as monuments against greediness.

Early next morning, as the broad river started narrowing to squeeze itself into the first gorge, great whorls in the chocolate waters testifying to the inner turbulence that bore us along at speed to a gap where hazy blue mountains stood like giant sentinels, it was to a beautiful sunlit temple on the northern bank that Miss

Tzu drew our attention. It had been built innumerable centuries earlier to the memory of Chang Fei, one of the three main personages in *All Men Are Brothers,* the famous fourteenth-century novel by Lo Kuan-chung. Chang Fei, Miss Tzu told us, had been assassinated by two traitors at the spot where local people had erected the temple.

If Tzu Hung-li was too busy with professional duties, there were fellow-passengers with guidebooks in hand to point out historical or legendary landmarks, or to explain the origins of names of towns and counties (one of the first counties after leaving Chungking had been named Chiang Chou (Longevity) three centuries earlier on the recommendation of an official scholar. Forced to spend the night at the county seat because of bad weather, he had found himself as the honoured guest at a birthday party in which seven generations participated to honour the 150th birthday of an old chap who presided over the ceremonies, downing the wine with the rest of them).

The most famous sight, the notorious 'Come to Me' rocks, however, had disappeared. Situated as they were in one of the narrowest channels – only 150 feet wide – the only way of avoiding being wrecked on them was to steer straight for the rocky outcrops with the huge 'Come to Me' characters painted in white at the summit, so that the rushing waters would bear your craft aside on a course parallel to the rocks. If you steered to avoid the outcrop you were certain to be swept sideways by the current and be dashed to destruction against the sharp-teethed rocks that lined the gorge.

Liu Hung-yin, the captain of our 'East Is Red No. 32' passenger boat, who had been on the Yangtze run for thirty-three of his forty-six years, said he could not remember how many wrecks he had personally witnessed in the Kuei Min Kuan, or Demon's Gate Pass, as the 'Come to Me' rocks section of the gorges was known. 'The most spectacular was when a Kuomintang troop transport with about a thousand troops on board was travelling upstream,' he said. 'The captain steered correctly for the rocks, but the troops must have panicked. They all rushed to the shore-side of the boat, which overturned. Not a single person was saved.'

Rewi Alley, who had made the trip frequently in the old days, recalled that boatmen and travellers wore their oldest clothes and left valuables behind if they had to make the trip. 'Steamers would stop when a junk went down, but you would never see a sign of life – everything was sucked straight under the rampaging current. The trackers who were hired in the old days to pull junks upstream fought their way inch by inch along the towpaths. If anyone missed his footing – and it happened all the time – he was flicked off into the river. Nobody would stop pulling because it was useless and, with one man's hauling power less, the rest of the team and the junk were already in danger. They worked naked, for a tiny pittance – a bitter, dangerous trade with about the shortest life expectancy of any.'

Captain Liu steered our boat comfortably over the spot, through Demon's Gate Pass. In the early days after liberation, P.L.A. men had set to work to widen, straighten and deepen the gorge and blow most of the 'Come to Me' rocks to smithereens. Tackling the bigger rocks first, then the sides of the gorges, they worked away until the navigation hazards were eliminated. Some of the 'Come to Me' rocks still poke their heads above water in the dry season but in calmer and wider waters they were easy to navigate around – at least so Captain Liu assured us, inviting us to make a dry season trip to see for ourselves. The son of a poor peasant tenant-farmer who could not feed his family, Liu Hung-yin started life as a cabin boy at the age of thirteen and later graduated to be an apprentice-sailor. Incredible as it sounds, he had never received a cent of pay in his nine and a half years of boat service before liberation, considering himself lucky to have a deck to sleep on and the leftovers from officers or rich passengers' tables to satisfy his hunger.

'It is difficult for foreigners to understand what our life was like,' he said. 'Apart from the miserable living conditions, relations between officers and men were terrible; the gap between the living standard of the captain and the other officers, and between the officers and men, was unbelievable. Now we all live and eat together on an equal basis and have friendly, comradely relations. I've noticed you taking pictures of the old temples and the pagodas and that's fine. Everyone admires them. They are beautiful and we are proud of them – they were built by man a long time ago. But don't let anyone persuade you that these were "good old days" just because beautiful temples were built. For the mass of the people they were terrible old days. In my village, which is now part of a commune and where my father has a decent house, people say: "In the old society poor people were transformed into ghosts, now they are honoured and educated as real people." Had it not been for the revolution, I would still be eking out a non-life, beaten up by anyone who had a stick handy, kicked around like a dog. It was the revolution that pulled me up on to my feet and gave me the chance to study and learn navigation. I am able to serve the people in a way I know – handling a boat up and down the Yangtze. If I speak like this, it is because we have the occasional passenger who sticks his feet up, admires the views and temples and sighs about the "old days". We know how to honour the old,' he concluded, 'but also how to appreciate the new.'

This was proved to be true when some young zealots who wanted to attack ancient monuments as symbols of feudalism were restrained by the local people. Destruction and damage to ancient monuments in China has usually been at the hands of foreign invaders or local warlords. A typical example is at Changteh, in North Hopei, the summer-resort palace of the early Ch'ing emperors. A magnificent bronze temple, together with priceless images, was destroyed and smelted down for munitions by the Japanese shortly after their entry into the Second World War. They shot the deer which grazed in the walled-in forest for food. Later the Kuomintang quartered a division of troops there for three years from 1946 onward, cutting down the trees to build pill-boxes, smashing up doors and windows for fuel and in general completing the depredations started by the Japanese. Since liberation the few scattered pine trees that remained from what had been a magnificent forest have been reinforced by more pines, poplars, elms and cypress trees, so that it has become once again one of the loveliest spots in China. The most famous of all the Ch'ing palaces, the Yuan Ming Yuang in Peking, was burned down by the Anglo-French expedition at the time of the Second Opium War (1856–60).

Indeed while the 'four olds' were being attacked on the ideological front, excavation works continued in many parts of China to uncover past glories, including the search for the tomb of Ch'in Shih-huang, the first Ch'in emperor. The building of his tomb at Lintung, near Sian (once Changan), the first capital of the

Chinese empire, is said to have involved the labour of 700,000 men for eleven years! Just as elderly Chinese like to contemplate good, solid coffins near their bedsides in their declining years, so the emperors liked to have tombs to contemplate, no less palatial than the palaces from which they reigned. The fabulous Ming tombs, an hour's drive north of Peking, one of the largest of which was excavated after liberation and is now a favourite sightseeing spot for foreign tourists, are a spectacular example of this dual attitude towards the past. The exhibition of the finds is an example of the respect paid by the People's Republic to historical treasures.

One finds this blend of respect for old values and traditions, while rejecting retrograde old concepts, in the approach to arts and crafts. The drive to industrialize is not permitted to bulldoze traditional handicrafts out of existence.

We found an interesting example of the cautious approach to modernizing handicrafts at the famous old ink factory of Hu Kai-wen, at Sihsien, the ancient name to which Hweichow city in Anhwei province has now reverted. The ink used for the brushes which make Chinese calligraphy an art in itself comes in small, oblong slabs, usually with delicate landscapes or historic scenes embossed on both sides. Enough ink is rubbed off on the stone ink slab, to which water is added from a special water pot, to form that jet-black ink so much admired on Chinese scrolls.

China now produces – and exports – excellent fountain pens, and there are all kinds of modern bottled inks to go with them. But alongside this there are the sixth- and seventh-generation descendants of the eighteenth-century master craftsman, Hu Kai-wen, still making ink slabs in the finely carved moulds cut in the days of the old master. Some of the moulds still in use date back to the Ming Dynasty (1368–1644), when an old craftsman named Tsao was famous for his mould-making. The fact that such names have been handed down testifies to the appreciation of superb craftsmanship in general and of the making of ink slabs as an art form in particular.

Machinery was installed to avoid muscle-straining work such as the 2000 strokes with heavy iron bars which pairs of workers used to deal to every mixture, considered essential to obtain the right consistency before the black paste was poured off into the moulds. But essentially the process remains on the old handicraft basis. The fine engraving of wooden blocks to vary the landscapes or other themes is still done by hand, as is the painting of the embossed patterns. The slow natural drying process is still watched over for the month considered necessary to give the slabs the special quality for which the factory is renowned not only in China, but in Japan and among Chinese all over the world. A high proportion of the annual production in fact goes for export . . .

In the Peking Arts and Crafts Workshop, apart from jade and ivory carvings, specialities included carved red lacquer, silver filigree work, small translucent perfume bottles, painted from the inside by the use of mirrors, and very fine brushes and cloisonne work of which Peking has had the exclusive monopoly for a good 500 years. 'It requires very fine, delicate and precise work,' explained Liu Hsueh-ming, a genial member of the revolutionary committee in his late thirties. He initiated us into the intricacies of setting multicoloured fragments of enamel into mosaics separated by hair-thin copper wire fillets. 'We have preserved the traditional art but developed new patterns, colours and paints,' explained Liu Hsueh-ming. 'Until a few years ago, there were only a dozen shades of colours. Now there are a hundred. There is also a big development in pattern and design, some reflecting modern trends, the needs of a socialist society, others preserving forms of the Ming and Ch'ing Dynasties.' As an example of catering to modern requirements he cited the manufacture of prize trophies for the two most recent Asian ping-pong championships.

The faces of the old craftsmen were a study in themselves – their deep concentration when they picked up a piece of raw jade or ivory, turning it round in their hands, eyeing the shape and grain before deciding the object into which the material could best be transformed with a minimum of waste; their pursed lips and frowns and screwed-up eyes – usually behind spectacles – as they critically examined the work of apprentices or young workers; their appreciative nods and smiles when their strict standards were met. We asked one sixty-three-year-old veteran, Chin Shieh-chuan, a wisp of a man with a deep-lined face, what he thought of the younger generation of workers and apprentices.

'These young people have good points,' he said. 'They bring enthusiasm into their work and some new ideas. They "dare to speak, think and act", as Chairman Mao advises. We older workers have a low level of education, but the younger people help the veterans. In technical things we help the younger people. It is a good sort of partnership. When I was an apprentice, if I had dared open my mouth about anything, I'd probably have been beaten to death.' His mouth set in a bitter straight line, even at the thought of the old days. It turned out that he had started work at the age of ten. 'The life of an apprentice was hell no matter what the job was,' he continued. 'But if you were working with expensive materials like jade and ivory, where a mistake caused serious losses, it was even worse. If the master craftsman made a mistake, he would blame the apprentice and you would get a terrible beating from the owner. If you dared open your mouth to tell the truth, you'd be beaten up by the craftsman as well. There were no set hours – from dawn to dusk in summer and deep into the night in winter. No wages at all, no medicine if you got sick. When you finished your apprenticeship, the usual thing was to be thrown on to the streets, as I was. Although I was a skilled filigree worker, I eked out a living as a pedlar until after liberation. By accident I heard that some of the people I had worked with were going to set up a handicrafts co-operative and that the government was going to give it a start with money and materials. I was delighted to get back to my old trade. Later on several other co-ops with different specialities joined together to form this factory.'

Chin Shieh-chuan had the status of 'veteran craftsman' and earned 100 yuan per month. Married late in life, he had one son, to whom he had passed on his skills. 'But he joined the P.L.A.,' the old chap said. 'Young people have a mind of their own these days.'

When we asked if he thought there was any danger of industrialization replacing the handicrafts, he looked at us dumbfounded. 'Never,' he replied. 'Machines are good for making trucks and trains, ships and planes and all sorts of things our country never made before. But when it comes to turning out a nice figure or bit of jade or ivory filigree work, you have to have human hands and eyes.'

To our question whether the young people paid due deference to his age, he replied 'They respect me for what I am, for what I know, for what I can do and for what I can tell them about the past. It's not like the old days of bowing down to people just because they are old. Why should they respect me if I was an old exploiter who got rich by starving and beating up his workers? In this factory young people respect the old for what they are and we respect the young for what they will be and do our best to help them develop all that is best in our old traditions of craftsmanship.'

[From Chapter 17 of *China: The Quality of Life* (Penguin Books, Harmondsworth, 1976), pp. 282–299.]

26

Mercenaries: British Export Model [1977]

On 25 April 1974 a group of Portuguese military officers overthrew the last fascist dictatorship in Europe. Three days later, Wilfred Burchett was in Lisbon meeting with the leaders of what would be known as the Carnation Revolution to find out how sincere they were about granting independence to their African colonies of Angola, Mozambique and Guinea-Bissau, whose peoples were fighting their own anti-colonial resistance wars.

Predictably, once Portugal washed her hands of these former colonies, including East Timor, other forces vied to fill the vacuum. East Timor was invaded by Indonesia while Australia looked the other way. In oil- and mineral-rich Angola and Mozambique, anti-colonial resistance soon turned to civil war, with the USSR and Cuba supporting one faction and China, the US, South Africa, Rhodesia and her former colonial master Great Britain backing another.

In Angola, Cuba sent troops to support the MPLA against a South African-led military intervention. The US and UK covertly sent mercenaries to assist the forces of FNLA–UNITA, backed by South Africa. Most of the mercenaries ended up killed – many by their own side – or captured and on trial in a people's court in Angola's capital Luanda. Burchett's book *The Whores of War*, written in collaboration with Derek Roebuck, an expert on international law, tells their story.

* * *

Only someone made of stone could have sat unmoved through the nine days of the Luanda trial. It was a tense human drama, charged with complexities of human character and emotions – nuances and contradictions of behaviour which would have been difficult to imagine beforehand. What was specially interesting was the evidence showing what kind of person becomes a mercenary.

The thirteen accused were not swashbuckling ex-Legionnaires or SS types, the veteran killers who swarmed through the Congo in the 1960s. Apart from Callan the cold-blooded and Barker the hot-blooded killers, and Gearhart eager for hot or cold killing, they were rather ordinary examples of the underprivileged of Western society. Even allowing for hard-luck stories exaggerated to excuse their actions, there was a reasonable chance that some of them had been tricked into believing they were going to well-paid non-combatant jobs behind the lines. To be mercenaries – yes; killers – no. But even if compassion could be felt for these victims of the society which formed them, there could be nothing but contempt for those who sped them on their way at a 'body count' fee of two or three hundred pounds a head.

It is frightening to take the backgrounds of each of the accused and to consider the mercenary potential in Britain and the United States, indeed in the Western world in general. The reasons most of the thirteen gave for enlisting – unemployment, financial difficulties, boredom of colourless lives, insoluble family problems, yearning to be back in uniform – show that the number could be multiplied by millions. Over 300 replies to that first tiny advertisement in one British newspaper alone! The same sort of response to one small publicity effort by Bufkin. The neat handwritten statement of Acker revealed that while he was waiting to leave for Angola he had stayed for a few days at Bufkin's house in California:

> While at Dave's house he had Lobo and myself set up a file system of all the people who had written to Dave concerning Angola. We listed their names, qualifications and experience, addresses etc. These were only people who would be useful. Those who would not be useful were discarded. At this time we had approximately 120–150 names. Letters were coming from as far as Israel, Hongkong, Belgium, Germany and England. This doesn't include the telephone calls of people interested. Dave also had us start a newsletter to those people who had sent letters and qualified. This letter explained about mercenary jobs in Rhodesia and possible jobs in South America. The letter explained that there was no more money funded for Angola and there would not be for some time . . .

This newsletter, a copy of which was found on Grillo, was undated, but a reference in it to a contact made on 6 January 1976 shows that it was sent out between that date and departure of the American group on 6 February – after the Congressional ban on further funds for Angola.

It is clear that people like Banks and Bufkin realized they were on to a major racket, on a par with drugs, white-slaving and Mafia operations – trading in human flesh on a lucrative per capita basis, with an unlimited market as the liberation struggles in southern Africa and elsewhere got into full stride. Their raw material came from society's rejects and victims of social systems that condemned humans by the millions to unemployment and drab existences on the borderline of hunger and despair.

All thirteen were case studies, as star witnesses not only against mercenarism but against the societies which educated and conditioned them, including in all cases but one, McIntyre, military systems that threw them back into civvy street alienated from the world in which they were supposed to make their living.

McIntyre had left school at fifteen and his first job was as cook's apprentice in a hotel. Later he studied at night to become a nurse, graduating after a three-year course at the Edinburgh Royal Hospital. This is what he told the court.

Between 1970 and 1972 I worked at the Perth Royal Infirmary. In 1972 I left to go to the Orsett Hospital, Essex, and after I had been there six months I began to be ill with my nerves and depression. I went into Warley Hospital, that is Warley Mental Hospital, Brentwood, Essex. I went in and out of this hospital until December 1975. While I was at Orsett Hospital, a friend. . . came to see me to help him to end his drug addiction. I said yes. I helped him and nine months later he was cured.

To do this is forbidden in England because treatment must be done in specialized hospitals and by authorized personnel. However, as his girlfriend was also an addict. . . she came and threatened me, saying she would denounce me if I did not supply her with drugs. As my work meant a great deal to me I had to help her, giving her drugs. Every week she asked for larger quantities. I did not want to give them to her, but it was the only way out I had. My wife finally got to know what was going on, abandoned me, and I stayed with the two children – later they went to my parents. I left the hospital and changed my original name of Wright to McIntyre, which means exactly the same thing, except that one is English and the other Scottish. By doing this I wanted to prevent the girlfriend. . . locating me. I found work in a hotel, the Queen's Hotel, Southend, but a few months later I had to go into hospital again for mental illness. I was discharged on 23 December 1975. Meanwhile I knew that my wife had died, in September. I spent Christmas with my family, and I continued to have difficulty in concentrating and continuing the treatment . . .

As we have seen, Wright–McIntyre was contacted on about 20 January by another 'very close friend', John Cook, who put him in touch with the mercenary recruiters. He was a victim of his own weakness of character and exceptional circumstances. For Banks, he meant another £200 or £300.

At the opposite end of the scale was thirty-five-year-old Derek John Barker, one of several old soldiers contacted directly by John Banks. The following, in Barker's printed handwriting with spelling uncorrected, is his account of what happened:

> I was drinking in a public house in Aldershot with friends when I was asked by a man named John Banks if I would like to go to Angola as an Special Avice Service, SAS! He said we get 600 dollars every two weeks. With this he gave us ten English pounds each and said he would meet us in London hotel named the Tower Hotel, London, next day. I then traveled to London with my friends, McKenzie, McFarson, Saunders and Aves. When we got there, there was ex-army men from some parts of England. We was told we were to stay in the hotel till 8 o'clock that same day when we was to have a talk.
>
> Then at 8 o'clock that evening we was told we was to go to Angola, West Africa, to help train an army of natives whose moral was very low. This army was named ENLA. This talk was given by a man named John Banks. We was told we would not leave the hotel so me and my friends had a talk and we agreed it was a very expensive hotel. 22 English pounds per person for one night only and lots of drinks. We thought this job we was going to do, if it was like this, was OK seeing I was out of work and things was expensive in England . . .
>
> A private coach came at six o'clock Sunday night and we got on to go to Heathrow airport London. On the coach we was given an envelope containing 500 dollars American. We was told we was to get another. 100 dollars when we arrive at the other end which was Kinshasa. It was a six month contract . . .

When he was asked why he had come to fight in Angola against the legitimate government of that country, Barker replied:

> I was wanted by the police for assault in December 1975, and I was on £200 sterling bail. I was released just before Christmas . . .

Asked if he had been in prison before, he replied:

> Yes. I had a prison record before I joined the British army. This was when I was about seventeen year old and was in Borstal for stealing cars, housebreaking – in fact I was a juvenile delinquent. In 1968, I served a nine months' prison sentence for stealing, and a six months' sentence in 1969–70 for assault over a woman I had been living with.

One of the trial's surprises was the playing of the soundtrack of a BBC *Panorama* programme on mercenaries, broadcast on 26 April 1976. It produced varied reactions among the accused. Wiseman, who was in tears when he heard the voices of his wife and children, burst into hysterical laughter when he heard the description of the incident which led to the assault charge against Barker in December 1975. The interviewer, Michael Cockerell, was speaking to Douglas Saunders:

Cockerell: In Angola both Saunders and Barker were immediately promoted to majors. He now works as a hod-carrier – the job 'Brummy' Barker once had. In their time in Aldershot the two men made many enemies. Last November they gatecrashed a party given by their local rivals, the Long family.

Saunders: This man came, picked on 'Brummy' and 'Brummy' had no option but to defend himself.

Benny Long: Barker came up to me. We had a few words and then he lunged at me and before I could realize it he was biting off the end of my nose . . .

It was at this point that Wiseman almost went into hysterics, which only a glowering look from Callan halted.

Michael Cockerell then produced Mary Slattery, a landlady in whose lodging-house Barker had lived for a while and who put up the £200 bail when he was charged with biting off the tip of Benny Long's nose. Mary Slattery expressed the opinion that if Barker 'had a bit of mother's love, he would have been a different boy altogether'.

Cockerell: How disappointed were you when you put up bail for him and suddenly he skipped off to Angola?

Mary Slattery: I was hurt, I was really hurt, because I never dreamed that 'Brummy' would do that on me, never.

Michael Cockerell to Saunders: Did Banks promise you anything apart from £150 per week?

Saunders: He said something about the President, you know, you would be stopping at the Palace, and you wouldn't go short of girls, you know, if you were destitute.

Mary Slattery's Son, Mike Slattery: I think they just thought they were going to fight a lot of backward niggers, you know, fire a few shots and out they would come. But . . . £150 is like the moon, isn't it? And a six months' tour, I mean they had all spent £5000 before they even left Aldershot, you know, in a month.

Cockerell: What do you think was the specific attraction for Barker himself?

Mike Slattery: Well, Barker to me – he just likes fighting. And it's a sort of fight, isn't it, being a mercenary? I mean, if he stands behind a tree and shoots you, that's lovely isn't it? There's no rules, is there, as a mercenary?

Cockerell to John Banks [also on the programme]: John Banks and his associates maintain the main reason why men become mercenaries is not for money, nor to escape the shambles of their personal lives, and they are now writing a book about it.

Banks: Why shouldn't they fight against Communism, whether it be for money or for a cause they believe in? Sure – how many English people want to be a bloody Communist state? I don't – he doesn't! I don't want to be a bloody Communist. People should listen to people a bit more before it's too late . . .

Cockerell: How responsible, John, do you feel for the fact that ten of them are now facing trial, perhaps trial for their lives?

Banks: Every man that left UK for Africa must be extremely naive. He knew he was going to war. Every African war is very, very dirty – very ill-equipped, very dirty wars. They were going to a war, they were not going to play games. They took their chances of being killed, maimed, wounded or captured, the same as any other man.

The ten British in the Luanda courtroom listened to this with suppressed, bitter rage clearly expressed on their faces as Banks spoke his 'serve the bastards right' line. This was the ultimate betrayal. They believed by then that apart from having pocketed his 'head' money – for their heads – Banks had also pocketed the pay which was supposed to be sent to their families. Cockerell's ironic last words were:

> Banks received thousands of letters from would-be mercenaries. He believes that whatever happens to the ten men in Angola, if you are buying mercenaries these days, you are buying British.

Michael Douglas Wiseman, a short man with a round head and a self-assured look, was another who featured *in absentia* in the *Panorama* programme.

Cockerell to Michael Giffin [an old school-friend with whom Wiseman went to live after he left his parents]: Why do you think he did want to go to Angola?

Giffin: He said on more than one occasion that it was for the money, so that he could get back and give to his children what he wanted, believe me, he did think the world of those kids. And he told me that he was hoping to get back with his wife . . .

Lynn Wiseman: He phoned me on the Saturday before he went, to see the children. And I knew next day about his volunteering – it was the way he was looking at the children. On the next day he popped in from work again, in the afternoon, he said: 'I'm off now.' He said 'that's where I'm going.' He had a pamphlet with Angola on it.

Cockerell: Did he ever explain why?

Lynn Wiseman: No, well – presumably for the money. He can't stand black people. I don't know . . .

The other family investigated in the *Panorama* programme was that of Cecil Martin (Satch) Fortuin. Born in South Africa, Fortuin – a well-built, powerful man – has slightly negroid lips and crinkly hair. He had been a bosom friend of Banks and, with two more of Banks's friends in the 2nd Parachute Regiment, they had each other's names tattooed on their arms.

Cockerell to John Banks: And all four of you had that tattoo? Did you keep in touch with Satch Fortuin?

Banks: Yes. Satch was a remarkable guy, always happy. Down in Aden, we used to drive around and say: 'look at those black bastards!' And we used to turn round to Satch and say: 'the pot calling the kettle black', you know?

Cockerell: Fortuin, who was born in South Africa, was himself coloured, but his parents were classified as white.

His parents and a Catholic priest (Father Matthews) spoke of Fortuin's early youth and his regular church attendance, 'a very devout boy' according to Father Matthews.

Cockerell to Father Matthews: There seems to be some contrast between the devout young altar boy and the chap who now ends up as a mercenary on trial for his life in Angola.

Father Matthews: I don't really think so. Myself, I would disagree with that. I think that Christians have always been adventurous people, and there does not seem to be any conflict between devotion to God and an adventurous life.

Michael Cockerell described how Fortuin had served in various parts of the world during five years as a paratrooper; how his first marriage broke up soon after he left the army and that, in 1974, he had married again.

Cockerell: With his second marriage ended after only eighteen months, Satch went on to live with Hilary Roberts who served behind the bar of the New Inn, in Kettering. Can you remember at all what your first thoughts were when you met him?

Hilary Roberts: Well … he was a very smart fella, unusual, had this flair about him that attracted me.

In his written statement to the investigators, Fortuin said: 'I am now living with another woman who has four children and with whom I am very happy.'

Cockerell to Hilary Roberts: What did you feel when he actually went?

Hilary Roberts: I don't really know. A bit numb, I suppose, apprehensive. From the reports out there, the FNLA were losing anyway. I asked him to come home. It wasn't worth staying

out there any more. Told him that I missed him. They went
with the warning of what would happen to them if they were
caught. And now he's been caught so I don't think he should
expect the government or the people of this country to fall out
and help him.
Cockerell: Do you feel any sympathy for him?
Hilary Roberts: No.

Fortuin's face was a study in incredulity as he heard that dry, crisp
'No', from the only person he still thought he had to fall back on. If
he ever had faith in old loyalties, and men on trial for their lives have
to have something to support them, it cannot have survived this
rejection, added to the betrayal by his old comrade-in-arms Banks,
whose name was tattooed on his arm and who had recruited him
by assuring him that he would only be a bodyguard. But under the
first pressure from Callan, Banks had tricked him into the front
line and abandoned him.

Callan had maintained a swaggering, arrogant posture throughout the trial, nudging and glaring at 'his men', still obviously in
command. But his body sagged and his face went livid as he listened first in anger then shock to Cockerell:

> In Angola it was the psychopathic exploits of the mercenary leader,
> the self-styled Colonel Callan, that caused public outrage. Callan, a
> dishonourably discharged paratrooper, ordered the execution of twelve
> mercenaries sent out by John Banks when they refused to fight. One
> of Banks' associates, the mercenary Chris Dempster, witnessed what
> Callan and his henchman Copeland did . . .

At this point, Callan started to wilt and never regained his com-
posure. He had believed he was some kind of hero to the British
public. To hear this from the BBC forced him to give up his self-
deception. From then on his determination to say nothing faltered.
His impersonation of a disciplined army officer carried no conviction. Not only did he lose control of himself: the leadership of the
group passed at that moment to Grillo.

[Chapter 4 of *The Whores of War* (Penguin Books, Harmondsworth,
1977), pp. 52–59.]

27

The Geneva Conference [1978]

Burchett visited sub-Saharan Africa a number of times in the 1970s to observe first-hand the liberation struggles taking place in many of the countries there. *Southern Africa Stands Up* reports on a number of these struggles. For many on the Left, in the second half of the century the region became a grand theatre where the shackles of colonialism were being cast off, and Burchett would have been sympathetic to this view. Superficially, many of the liberation movements achieved their aims in removing corrupt and elite European regimes, though the consequences have usually proved less benevolent than their supporters had hoped. In the 1970s, world attention was largely focused on the struggle for majority rule in Rhodesia and the removal of the white British administration of Ian Smith. In the light of recent events in Zimbabwe, Burchett's support for Robert Mugabe in this chapter may seem misguided, but Mugabe and Joshua Nkomo enjoyed support around the world and across the political spectrum at the time.

* * *

For the first time in thirty-seven years of reporting, including covering innumerable international conferences, I wrote a gloomy first dispatch predicting the failure of a conference before it had even started. I am normally an optimist on such matters, and used to the protracted ups and downs of negotiations such as those at Panmunjom to settle the Korean War (two years), the 1954 Geneva Conference on Indochina (three months), the Paris Peace Conference on Vietnam (four and a half years). But after having visited all the delegations before the Conference on Rhodesia started in Geneva on 28 October 1976, I wrote:

> The Zimbabwan liberation movement is relying on victory through its widening armed struggle and not the conference on black majority rule set to open here October 28. The British-sponsored negotiation effort

will almost certainly fail. Its very agenda is beset with irreconcilable differences between the position of the racist Ian Smith regime and the joint Patriotic Front delegation headed by Robert Mugabe of the Zimbabwe African National Union and Joseph Nkomo of the Zimbabwe African People's Union. The Patriotic Front is negotiating in Geneva on behalf of the Zimbabwe People's Army, which is waging a guerilla war against the white settler regime in Salisbury ... The rock upon which the Geneva Conference appears about to crash is the 'Kissinger Plan,' the 'package deal' product of the Secretary of State's September shuttle diplomacy efforts. Rhodesian Prime Minister Ian Smith says he bought the entire package, which he insists Kissinger assured him had been approved by the five front-line presidents.

Smith asserts he is at the Geneva Conference only to implement the Kissinger deal, a blatant neocolonial scheme in which the armed power of the state would remain in the hands of the white minority. The fact that the front-line presidents (of Mozambique, Angola, Tanzania, Zambia, and Botswana) have jointly repudiated the plan, which also calls for an immediate end to armed struggle and lifting of international sanctions against Rhodesia, is attributed by Smith to a Kissinger double cross.[1]

At that time we did not know that the front-line presidents had not even seen the Kissinger plan but had been vaguely informed that the great shuttler had succeeded in persuading Smith to accept majority rule.

Soon after the conference started, Smith's foreign minister (and former defense minister) Pieter Van der Byl called in the press to present photos of dead and mutilated Africans as 'proof' of terrorist atrocities. A big man with an oversize head and steely blue eyes, Van der Byl was soon ill at ease under a barrage of sharp questions. The sharpest was also the shortest: 'Does majority rule mean one man, one vote?'

'No,' snapped Van der Byl. 'We stand for responsible majority rule.' He refused to define this on the grounds that it might be a negotiable matter at the conference. But in the Rhodesian press room next door there was ample literature on that and related subjects.

'Responsible majority' as in force at the time the Geneva Conference started meant that Europeans, coloureds, and Asians must prove they earned an annual average of 2772 U.S. dollars (in the Rhodesian dollar equivalent) and owned property worth 5544 U.S. dollars. They must have completed not less than four years of secondary education. Africans must prove they earned an annual average of 924 dollars, owned property worth 848 dollars, and had completed not less than two years of secondary education 'of prescribed standard.' The House of Assembly – according to the Constitutional Act approved by Ian Smith's parliament on 17 November 1969 – consisted of sixty-six members, of whom fifty Europeans represented their 280,000 of the population and sixteen Africans represented their 6,000,000. Only eight of the sixteen were directly elected, the remaining half to be nominated by 'electoral colleges' comprised of 'chiefs, headmen, and elected councillors of the African Councils in the Tribal Trust Lands in Mashonaland and Matabeleland respectively . . .' A very original concept of 'responsible majority rule.' The upper house, or Senate, was comprised of twenty-three members, ten Europeans elected by the European members of the House of Assembly and ten African chiefs, chosen by an electoral college consisting of members of the Council of Chiefs. Five of these African Senators are chiefs in Matabeleland and five are chiefs in Mashonaland. What could be fairer? Numerical equality between white and black senators, and between black senators from the two predominant tribal groupings! But just in case the balance did not work, the president was empowered to appoint the remaining three Senators 'acting on the advice of the Cabinet and they may be of any race.'

There was no evidence throughout the Geneva Conference that Mr. Smith had departed from this original concept as to how majority rule could be exercised. In a three-paragraph statement on the first working day of the conference, Ian Smith devoted the first two paragraphs to 'commiserating' with British Chairman Ivor Richard and the British government after all it had done 'not only in Rhodesia but in many other parts of the world in spreading Christian civilization' for the 'insults' of the nationalist speakers who had preceded Mr. Smith with their opening statements. In the third, he stated that the previous month he had announced his government's 'acceptance of the joint Anglo-American proposals to settle the constitutional future of Rhodesia which were put to us by the American Secretary of State. The proposals provide for an early meeting between government representatives and Rhodesian Africans to determine the membership of the Council of State as the first step in establishing the interim government. . . .' Work on this, he indicated, should start immediately.

From the beginning to the end of the Geneva Conference the exact contents of the 'joint Anglo-American proposals,' and the Kissinger 'package deal,' were never disclosed. The conference got bogged down trying to decide whether 'majority rule' would come into force in two years, as Ian Smith maintained Kissinger had proposed, or in a far shorter period, as the nationalist leaders demanded. Never had Kissinger's wizardry in the art of ambiguity and his ability to be 'all things to all men' been used to greater effect in sowing bewilderment among all involved. This is how Ian Smith in a nationwide address on 24 September 1976, presented the results of having been shuttled by Kissinger following the final Kissinger–Vorster–Smith meeting in Pretoria. After referring to the series of meetings and asserting that 'pressures on us from the "Free World" would continue to mount' to introduce 'majority rule,' Smith continued:

> Dr. Kissinger assured me that we share a common aim and a common purpose, namely to keep Rhodesia in the Free World and to keep it free from Communist penetration. In this regard, of course, Rhodesia is in a key position in southern Africa. What happens here will inevitably affect the entire subcontinent . . .
>
> Before I spell out these proposals in detail there are some general comments I should make. The proposals represent what, in negotiating parlance, is usually called a 'package deal' – which means that some aspects are more readily acceptable than others. First, on the positive side, as soon as the necessary preliminaries have been carried out, sanctions will be lifted and there will be a cessation of terrorism. Dr. Kissinger has given me a categorical assurance to this effect and my acceptance of the proposals is conditional upon the implementation of both of these undertakings. In the light of previous experience there will be some understandable skepticism regarding the undertaking that terrorism will cease, but on this occasion the assurance is given, not only on the authority of the United States government, but of the British government as well . . .

Kissinger had had no contact whatsoever with those who directed battlefield operations, nor had he received any such assurances from the front-line heads of state; and the British government mumbled and bumbled to the effect that it had given no such assurances. Kissinger had absolutely no mandate to speak for the United Nations, which had imposed sanctions, but he had apparently mesmerized Ian Smith during the shuttling process.

Having given you the general background, I shall now read the actual terms of the proposals put to me by Dr. Kissinger. Paragraph six, relating to economic aid, is an agreed summary of a longer paper.

1 Rhodesia agrees to majority rule within two years.
2 Representatives of the Rhodesian government will meet immediately at a mutually agreed place with African leaders to organize an interim government to function until majority rule is implemented.
3 The interim government should consist of a Council of State, half of whose members will be black and half white, with a white chairman without a special vote. The European and African sides would nominate their representatives. Its functions will include: legislation; general supervisory responsibilities; and supervision of the process of drafting the Constitution.

The interim government should also have a Council of Ministers with a majority of Africans and an African first minister. For the period of the interim government the Ministers of Defense and of Law and Order would be white. Decisions of the Council of Ministers to be taken by two-thirds majority. Its functions should include: delegated legislative authority; and executive responsibility.

4 The United Kingdom will enact enabling legislation for this process to majority rule. Upon enactment of that legislation, Rhodesia will also enact such legislation as may be necessary to the process.
5 Upon the establishment of the interim government, sanctions will be lifted and all acts of war, including guerilla warfare, will cease.
6 Substantial economic support will be made available by the international community to provide assurance to Rhodesians about the economic future of the country . . . The aim will be to expand the industrial and mineral production of the country . . .

There was much more about international aid and a trust fund which would enable Rhodesia to 'expand the industrial and mineral production of the country'; guarantees of investments and the 'remittance overseas of an individual's liquid resources'; and other thinly veiled measures of a scheme the CIA had been trying to promote for some months prior to the Geneva Conference: the financing of whites who wanted to emigrate. Smith continued:

> In our discussions in Pretoria, my colleagues and I made it clear that Rhodesians were not enamoured of schemes to buy them out – they were looking for a solution which would mean that they could go on living in their homeland. We were assured that the other parties to the proposal strongly supported this contention. Accordingly, whatever plan is produced to assist those who decide to leave, the incentive should be aimed at making it worthwhile for Rhodesians to stay.[2]

So much for what the public was told! The composition of the Council of State which would have the real power during the transition period seemed ominously similar to the existing Senate, and it was unthinkable that the nationalists – even the moderates – would agree to the army and police remaining in the same white hands as those who were doing their best to exterminate them. Or that the guerillas would lay down their arms on a vague promise of a very spurious-looking 'majority rule' within two years. Or that the international community would agree to call off sanctions in exchange for a Kissinger–Smith promise!

At his Geneva hotel headquarters, Bishop Abel Muzorewa, a small, gentle owl-like man, assured me that everything – including the conference – that affects man 'must be God-inspired and God-centered' and that 'all man's needs must be served with Godly concern ... In being a militant, I am also doing God's work ...' More to the point, because of his good contacts in Salisbury from whence he had come directly to the conference, he had brought with him the resume of the briefing given by Ian Smith's deputy, Ted Sutton-Pryce, to the Cabinet, on what had really been agreed with Kissinger and which would be Smith's negotiating position at Geneva. That such a document could be leaked was easily understandable after a few days at Geneva. A former prime minister, R.S. Garfield Todd, released a few months before the Geneva Conference from four years of forced residence for opposing Smith's racist policies, turned up at Geneva as a negotiations' adviser to Joshua Nkomo! A steady trickle of white Rhodesian business people visited him in his room at the Intercontinental Hotel to urge him to stand firm for real majority rule. They had no fears for a future under a black regime. Like Garfield Todd they had excellent relations with many of the militant Zimbabwan nationalists and knew they were not racists.

Although the opposition to Smith within his own government came mainly from the right, there were others who considered he was being unnecessarily pigheaded and was set on a disaster course. It was through such realists that the ten-point document came into the hands of Bishop Muzorewa. It has to be read in the light of the first five points of Smith's public version:

1 The present government will appoint the proposed Council of State which will be kept small, with an equal number of white and black members, with the Prime Minister as chairman.

2 A two-thirds majority vote must be obtained for any change in the composition of the Council of State to ensure that the whites remain in complete control.

3 Justice, Internal Affairs, Defense, and the Army and Air Force Chiefs, plus the Police, remain the same as they are now.

4 The Council of State appoints the Cabinet in which Africans will have a majority and a black chairman, but the Council of State will have to approve anything they want to change. [It is unclear whether this refers to legislative or constitutional changes or to changes in the composition of the appointed cabinet – W.B.]

5 The present government will be suspended during the period of interim government. [Bishop Muzorewa added the comment: 'In fact it will be "on ice".']

6 Sanctions will be lifted as soon as the Council of State is formed.

7 This all means that if after two years we do not agree on a Constitution, we can revert back and the present government will take over again.

8 Terrorism is to cease immediately.
9 Majority rule does not mean *black* majority rule. It is majority rule of the people on the voters' roll, *as it is now*. [Emphasis added]
10 European secretaries of all the ministries remain the same – i.e., European.

When I asked Robert Mugabe whether these ten points corresponded to his own information about the Kissinger 'package deal,' he replied: 'We are simply not interested in it. What has Kissinger to do with our affairs? We have not come here to discuss his ideas as to what is good for our people. Nor to negotiate with Ian Smith. We have come to negotiate with the British not the principle, but the modalities, of the transfer of power.' A calm but forceful and highly impressive personality, Robert Mugabe had also been released from jail in Zambia to attend the conference. In his Geneva hotel room where he received a small group of correspondents shortly after his arrival, he replied with superb scorn to an American journalist from one of the leading newsweeklies who asked 'what price' the Patriotic Front was willing to pay for independence. 'You have the effrontery to ask that we should pay something to be free after eighty-six years of semi-slavery?' he said. The journalist shrank into his seat and mumbled: 'I meant in terms of facilitating the departure of those who want to leave.' 'Why should we want to retain people who won't accept African rule?' said Mugabe. 'Some will stay – many will leave. It's a question of whether they accept whatever legal government emerges.'

The great bombshell of the conference was the formation – announced only a few weeks before the delegations were due to meet in Geneva – of the Patriotic Front. Smith had great hopes of exploiting the old divisions based on personal political rivalries. But he came up against a solid wall of unity between the two most important leaders of the two most important movements. Of the four official Zimbabwan nationalist delegations at the conference, that headed by Reverend Ndabaningi Sithole counted least. Although he pretended to represent ZANU, that organization in fact had explicitly rejected his leadership. Sithole was clearly looking for outside support. I found myself in the same waiting room for an interview with Sithole with a West German correspondent from Johannesburg (who confided to me that Sithole was 'the only real statesman' among the nationalists), a young American from a CIA-funded labor organization, and the Zaire ambassador to Switzerland. During my own interview there was an embarrassing moment when Reverend Sithole handed me a copy of his book, *African Nationalism*. Opening it, I found a eulogistic dedication to President Mobutu of Zaire. It was quickly retrieved and replaced by a 'clean' copy! Mobutu had just 'happened' to be in Switzerland during the early stages of the conference, looking for a role to play in the wings and perhaps for a client willing to serve his interests.

Apart from the ZIPA team and the ZANU–ZIPA reinforcements who came at a later stage, Robert Mugabe and Joshua Nkomo dominated the stage as far as the nationalists were concerned. They represented real power, while Bishop Muzorewa and Reverend Sithole represented positions. Nkomo, a huge man with grizzly, crewcut hair, strikes one as very shrewd, experienced and with a strong personality. He made mincemeat of some journalists who should have known better than to try to put their words into his mouth by means of barbed questions. At our first meeting, he said:

The Patriotic Front has been set up not just to present a single ZAPU–ZANU position at this conference. We set it up, above all, to intensify the armed struggle. It is because of the battlefield successes that the British government and its allies have sensed a threat to their interests in Zimbabwe and southern Africa and have thus been compelled to bring about this conference. We have come here as a result of the sweat, blood, and toil of our people. Our delegation is here to discover whether the message of armed struggle has sunk in sufficiently to ensure the immediate and unfettered independence of the people of Zimbabwe. We consider this conference as strictly between Zimbabwans of whatever colour and race on the one hand, and the colonizers, the British government, on the other... We insist on the fact that Britain never ceased being the colonizer of Rhodesia and therefore must now take steps to march out of Zimbabwe through the normal decolonialization process by the end of the transitional period. The final aim is independence from Britain.

Referring to fears expressed in some sections of the Western press that blacks might seek revenge against white settlers once they had state power in their hands, Nkomo said:

> First, our liberation struggle aims at ending all forms of racism and discrimination because of colour, as well as ending economic exploitation and all forms of social privilege. Second, in the new nation of Zimbabwe colour, race, or tribe cease to be the measure of value in society and, in this connection, any settler who chooses to be a Zimbabwan shall be as much of a citizen as any other. It is not our intention to substitute one form of evil for another.

An embittered Ian Smith left the conference five days after it started, saying he had 'more important things to do at home.' He had not been able to play the game of using one leader against the other and, moreover, Kissinger could not come out into the open and say: 'Yes, Ian Smith's negotiating position is the one we agreed on.' During the dreary weeks following the start of the conference, the attempts to split the delegations proceeded apace. To split the 'moderates' Muzorewa and Sithole from the 'militant' Mugabe and Nkomo, and to split the 'moderate-militant' Nkomo from the 'revolutionary-militant' Mugabe. At one point the ZANU element of the Patriotic Front was kicked out of the Intercontinental Hotel, where it had been installed together with the ZAPU element and Sithole. The pretext was that the bills – which the British government was supposed to take care of – were not being paid. The British found them cheaper lodgings at the Hotel Royal. ZAPU stayed on at the Intercontinental.[3]

On November 29, the Patriotic Front issued a communiqué protesting 'divisive tactics' employed by Chairman Ivor Richard:

> There have been undisguised attempts to 'divide and rule.' On at least two occasions, favoured delegations were shown conference documents which were expressly denied to the Patriotic Front ... More serious perhaps is the way the conference is being conducted. Minutes of bilateral talks have not been recorded as conference documents. As a result delegations do not know what has been discussed in bilateral meetings that do not involve them. We call upon the chairman to hold more discussions in the open forum than in secret. . .

The Patriotic Front leaders, especially those who had only recently been freed from jail, were chafing at the inaction. They wanted to end the farce and get back to the battlefield. They were uncertain as to how their fruitless diplomatic activities were viewed by their comrades in the field. It took the arrival of Mozambique Foreign Minister Joaquim Chissano in Geneva to persuade them not to stage a unilateral walkout. Chissano offered to send a planeload of leading ZANU and ZIPA militants to prove that they had the backing of the front-line combatants. On the night of December 3 there arrived three members of the ZANU Central Committee (including Josiah Tongogara, who had returned to the battlefield after the first week in Geneva) and six ZIPA commanders, including Rex Nhongo, acting commander-in-chief during Tongogara's imprisonment, and Dzinashe Machingura. It was an extremely high-level delegation, with the top military and political leaders of the ZANU–ZIPA element of the Patriotic Front. They were almost all wiped out within a few hours of their arrival. A ZANU communique issued on December 4 describes what happened:

> At 4:15 this morning, Comrade Rex Nhongo woke up and saw smoke and flames advancing from the door toward the center of his room. He bravely groped his way to the door and rushed out, leaving all his belongings behind. The incident was immediately reported to the hotel authorities. The fire brigade arrived after about half an hour and put out the fire which had spread all over the building. One other comrade incurred bruises as the comrades rushed out of their rooms... We have no doubt that it was arson and that the act was calculated to take the lives of members of our delegation, if not to destroy the entire delegation. It was an attempt by the enemy to intimidate us so that we would soften our stand on the question of irreversible transfer of power...

Virtually the whole floor of the Hotel Royal was completely gutted. Had Rex Nhongo awakened a few seconds later, it is highly possible that the entire group would have been wiped out. It was difficult for them to grasp that comfortable hotel rooms in sophisticated, neutral Switzerland could be infinitely more dangerous than battlefield bombs and shells. The Swiss police pooh-poohed the idea of arson, but came up with no convincing explanation for the fire. Ten days later the Geneva Conference was officially 'adjourned' until January 17, although few had any illusions that it would be reconvened. It gave me no satisfaction at all to lead my last dispatch from Geneva:

> The Geneva Conference on Rhodesia has broken down and the liberation struggle must now go back to the battlefield and be intensified. This paraphrases the point of view of leaders of the Zimbabwe Patriotic Front and the ZIPA in exclusive interviews with this correspondent, as they prepared to return to Africa . . .[4]

It was Kumbirai Kangai, mentioned earlier as a member of the ZANU Central Committee, who summed up the results of the Geneva Conference for the Patriotic Front delegates. 'The British say the conference is adjourned,' he said, 'but we think this is a diplomatic way of saying the conference has failed. A failure for the British and for Ian Smith, but not for us. In fact it was a victory for us.' He went on to explain why:

> We consider that at this moment there are two fronts. The battlefield inside Zimbabwe and the diplomatic front at Geneva. Here we claim a decisive victory. A couple of months ago, apparently prodded by Kissinger, who correctly foresaw the danger that Zimbabwe could become a new Mozambique or a new Angola, Smith stated that he accepted 'majority rule.' That was the basis of setting up the Geneva Conference, which Kissinger had not foreseen. He thought that by sleight of hand, Smith could manipulate some tribal chiefs and others known as 'moderate' nationalists and claim that he had the elements of 'majority rule.' Once the Geneva Conference was scheduled we decided to come to see what the enemy had in mind, but also ready for serious negotiations in case of any possibility of peaceful transfer of power. In fact, it was quickly clear that Smith had come to play for time because he was hurting from our battlefield successes. Kissinger thought he only had to wave a magic wand and we – and the front-line heads of state – would be dazzled by his brilliance. In fact, Smith – and thereby Kissinger – was smoked out into the open. Before he arrived at Geneva, Smith said repeatedly he now favoured 'majority rule.' It was quite clear to us that he was lying. He repudiated 'one man, one

vote' as a criterion and talked about 'responsible majority rule.' We managed to isolate him with regard to world public opinion.

Some people criticized us for agreeing to talks. As revolutionaries, they said, we should never have come to Geneva. But other good revolutionaries have talked and fought at the same time. Our Vietnamese comrades talked in Paris while they intensified their armed struggle. That under our constant prodding the British agreed that Zimbabwe had to have its independence, and even set a date for that independence, was a victory for us. World public opinion has accepted this and also that our interpretation of 'majority rule' as 'one man, one vote' is a reasonable one. In fact, we no longer talk about 'majority rule' because this implies a minority to be repressed. We are for the independence of all Zimbabwans and equal rights for all regardless of colour.

We had to participate at Geneva to avoid deals being made behind our backs. We came to prevent the British and Smith from maneuvring to set up a puppet regime, for this was the essence of the Kissinger 'plan.' British annoyance that the plan failed is implicit in the statement made by British foreign secretary Anthony Crossland after the conference broke down. He said that somehow or other it had got 'off course' and that plans for a 'moderate regime' had been thwarted.

In the closing days of the Geneva Conference, there was a revolt within Bishop Muzorewa's ranks. It had been simmering for some time with a number of the Bishop's closest aides wanting to join the Patriotic Front at the beginning of the conference. But they were urged by Mugabe and Nkomo to stay where they were and influence the Bishop in the cause of unity. The revolt had been sparked off by a position paper submitted by Muzorewa on the opening day of the conference in which he accepted elections under the Smith regime on the basis of 'one man, one vote' to elect a new prime minister. Ministries would be allocated on the basis of the proportions of votes received by the contesting parties and the prime minister alone would distribute the portfolios. As the Bishop was the only one of the nationalist leaders who had legal status, while the others were in jail or in exile, it was felt that he was intent on carving out the top position for himself and using the name of the ANC – and even the freedom fighters – to promote his personal cause. Just one week before the Geneva Conference was 'adjourned,' one of Bishop Muzorewa's top aides, the Reverend Canaan Banana, held a press conference in Salisbury to announce the resignation of eleven members of the national executive of the Muzorewa wing of the ANC, sometimes called the 'internal ANC', and finally 'UANC' (United African National Council). Four of them, including Reverend Banana, announced they were leaving for Geneva to reinforce the delegation of the Patriotic Front.

It was against this background that, at the last meeting with journalists before they returned to the battlefront via Mozambique, Kumbirai Kangai was asked to clarify the relations between the Patriotic Front and the African National Council. (In mid-1975 Muzorewa had 'expelled' Joshua Nkomo from the ANC leadership because Nkomo was pushing for a congress according to ANC statutes and Muzorewa opposed this.)

Historically speaking, the ANC was formed by ZANU–ZAPU. When Nkomo was expelled he took most of the ZAPU leadership with him. But because the ZANU element remained and Robert Mugabe could only operate in the semi-liberated zones of Zimbabwe, ZANU could continue to function partially under the ANC umbrella. Then it was discovered that Muzorewa took advantage of this to spread the rumor that he, as head of the ANC, was leader of the armed forces. In fact, he had nothing to do with the armed forces, but as he is the only one who has access and facilities to operate in Rhodesia, he could persuade many members and sympathizers that it was he who was directing the armed struggle. The ANC has no policy, no ideology, no program. Muzorewa's agreement to hold elections, even under Smith's regime, was treachery. He hoped to take advantage of Smith's ban on other leaders to have a monopoly on electioneering. In fact, ANC is practically dead now. Muzorewa will be isolated. The prestige of the Patriotic Front grows every day.

Thus, although the Geneva Conference achieved none of its stated aims, the by-products were of fundamental importance. It provided a forum for consolidation among the real national liberation militants; it brought about the exposure of those who believed it was possible to talk their way into independence and the top power positions. It projected the Patriotic Front into the unrivaled first place and provided a tribune for it to make its aims known to the outside world. Kumbirai Kangai's assessment of Bishop Muzorewa's ambitions was perfectly correct, as was demonstrated some two months later in a dispatch to the *New York Times* from Salisbury by correspondent John F. Burns. Referring to the Patriotic Front's rejection of the Kissinger–Smith proposals, Burns reported:

> Mr. Smith now plans to implement the proposals in a fresh round of talks with moderate black groups, including Bishop Abel Muzorewa's United African National Council. The Prime Minister also plans a referendum among the country's 6.3 million blacks, confident that it will prove Bishop Muzorewa's group to have majority support. But U.S. officials have insisted that the plan will not work, because the Patriotic Front, which claims control of the guerillas fighting the Smith government, will continue fighting.

The whole thrust of the dispatch proves Kumbirai Kangai's other point about the expanding prestige of the Patriotic Front. It was based on Foreign Minister Pieter Van der Byl's reaction to Carter administration skepticism about any settlement in Rhodesia which did not have the approval of the Patriotic Front, a view supported by Secretary of State Cyrus Vance and UN representative Andrew Young, a black who is knowledgeable about the southern African situation. Among Van der Byl's dire predictions:

> Once Rhodesia's gone, you'll have a belt of Marxist states running across southern Africa – Angola, Rhodesia, Mozambique. From there they'll move north – Zambia first, then Zaire, then one by one, further north, until they have the bulk of sub-Saharan Africa.[5]

Oddly enough, he did not mention South Africa!

[From Chapter 19 of *Southern Africa Stands Up* (Outback Press, Melbourne, 1978), pp. 224–243.]

28

How to be a Good Khmer Rouge [1981]

On 17 April 1975 Khmer Rouge units entered Phnom Penh and ordered all residents to leave the city. It was the beginning of Cambodia's nightmare – and one of the worst genocides in human history. Wilfred Burchett, like so many commentators in the West, initially hailed the victory of the Sihanouk–Khmer Rouge alliance and treated with scepticism reports of atrocities in Cambodia. But he was not allowed into 'liberated' Cambodia and his lines of communication with his old friend Sihanouk were cut off.

He first became convinced of the murderous nature of the Pol Pot regime when investigating Khmer Rouge incursions along the Cambodia–Vietnam border. He is still often accused of ongoing support for the Khmer Rouge, but he immediately reported on the true nature of the regime as soon as he was afforded the opportunity to witness the situation with his own eyes – thus maintaining his interest always to report 'on the spot'. He was one of the first Western journalists on the Left to correct the record, and his book on this subject, *The China Vietnam Cambodia Triangle*, demonstrates clearly that he was in fact one of the most important denouncers of the Khmer Rouge regime.

* * *

One of the difficulties in being a 'good' Khmer Rouge was that of knowing the 'right line' to apply or follow at any particular time and place. The Khmer Rouge leadership committed as little as possible to paper.[1] Most policy decisions were handed down orally, and village chiefs were often appointed on the basis of their ability to memorize the contents of what they heard at conferences where policy decisions were announced. As most of them were illiterate, perhaps there was no alternative. It certainly helps to explain the discrepancies occurring in eyewitness accounts of how the system worked in different geographical areas.

Contents of directives were obviously badly assimilated. By the time the village, district, and even provincial chiefs got back to their bases, the directives must have become even more blurred in their minds and application of them must have suffered accordingly. When possible, directives were issued in simplistic, slogan-type form: 'All For Agriculture: Rice Is Everything' . . . 'Self-sufficiency Is The Key To Victory' . . . 'Build Irrigation Systems In Every Province . . .' 'Wipe Out Class Enemies' hardly needed repetition, except when the process had to be stepped up or the category of victims widened.

The all-important rule for a 'good' Khmer Rouge was blind and total obedience. It was also the essential prerequisite for survival. To question orders was implicit criticism of Angkar and, even at the highest level, this was equivalent to suicide. In 'Comrade Ox,' one of his most biting chapters, Pin Yathay delineates the ideal character not only of a citizen but also of a cadre.

The Khmer Rouge often used parables to justify their contradictory actions and orders. They compared the individual to an ox. 'You see this ox which pulls the plough. He eats where one orders him to eat. If you lead him to another field where there's not much grass, he still browses at something. He can't go where he wants because he's guarded. When he is told to pull the plough, he pulls it. He never thinks about his wife or children.' Such a humiliating and insane comparison might once have raised smiles, but smiles now would have to be dragged out of our tears and sweat!

It was based on such reasoning that the Khmer Rouge had let our families, our children die. The ox, docile par excellence, was the model we should imitate. Often in the meetings, the Khmer Rouge spoke of the bovines as humans. They frequently said: 'Comrade ox.' The ox had all the qualities that they demanded from a deportee. The ox never refused to work. It was obedient, never complained and never threw off its yoke. It blindly followed the Angkar directives.

The lesson of the parable was clear to everyone. Even for the rebellious, for the most recalcitrant citizens. We had neither the right to complain nor to reason. We had to put our intelligence to sleep . . . A good revolutionary behaved like a respectful and servile animal, a tamed animal. He had no individualist tendencies, no feelings, no ambitions. The only initiatives tolerated were those judged good by the collective. These initiatives were exclusively practical. The labourer, for example, must know how to repair a damaged plough . . .[2]

It is true, as stressed by Keng Vannsak and other authorities, that two thousand years of monarchies and slave systems of one sort or another in Cambodia had produced a built-in subservience to whomever was in power that could not be eradicated overnight. During Sihanouk's days it was symbolized by the ritual in which anyone approaching him on any matter whatsoever dropped on to one knee and touched the tips of the fingers of both hands together under the chin as a tribute to the Monarchy and Buddhism, the Diumvirate which Sihanouk personified. Oddly enough, it was Lon Nol in Phnom Penh and Ieng Sary in Peking – as I had many occasions to note – who were the most obsequious in this respect!

Blind obedience was particularly difficult for anyone who, like Pin Yathay, had been trained abroad in the exact sciences. When ordered to evacuate Phnom Penh, he had taken with him a few books from his library. They dealt with his specialty, the construction of dams, dykes, and roads. At the first roadblock it had been cameras, watches, transistor radios, and other such objects that Angkar needed to 'borrow.' At the second it was printed material. Pin Yathay pleaded for his technical books, showing diagrams and sketches to prove their utilitarian and non-political contents. In vain! 'These books contain imperialist thinking!' They were hurled onto the road to be ground into the dust and litter by the vehicles which followed.

Ironically, one of the first tasks he and his family were given was to work day and night on an irrigation project in Takeo province. It was the sort of work – digging canals and building dykes – to which most deportees were assigned during the first months of their calvary. 'The big work sites forge ideological solidarity,' they were told. For specialists like Pin Yathay, they were 'rule of thumb' exercises in frustration.

Sometimes physical laws were defied by the Khmer Rouge, dour builders though they were. One cannot define the slope of a field by the naked eye. The Khmer Rouge ridiculed technical help which could have corrected the errors of such guesswork. Vast undertakings were executed contrary to even common sense rules. Each Khmer Rouge leader acted according to his own whims. There was no lack of labour power. Thousands of men and women obeyed the orders of the civilian cadres. The result of this Khmer Rouge amateurism was heart-rending. Canals running in the wrong direction. Dykes destroyed by the first rains, rebuilt and again swept away by the waters . . . The result of all this work, incidentally, hardly seemed important in itself! The essential was to seize how to learn lessons from experience. By learning from such mishaps we should bring our initiative into play to ensure that they would not be repeated . . .

I knew one could not dig canals of up to five kilometres by such rule of thumb methods. But I kept my mouth shut. The Khmer Rouge allotted precise tasks to each brigade of village workers. These limited sections were supposed to fit together, like parts of a puzzle, within the framework of a single, vast project. Such and such a village, for instance, should take care of a certain part of a road, dig its part of the canal, build its quota of dykes . . .

The Khmer Rouge did not like to be bothered with intellectuals and specialists. They maintained that diplomas were useless bits of paper . . . What counted was the concrete work that could be evaluated and approved – ploughing or digging. That was honorable work because it was visible, tangible . . .

Pin Yathay describes how the rains arrived, the rice seedlings were planted out by the women deportees, including his wife, and the water arrived at the required ankle level for the shoots to develop.

Unfortunately, a month after planting out, the fields dried up. Lacking a rational irrigation system the rice plants died. The lack of water ruined all our work. The Khmer Rouge, demoralised by this setback, allotted other tasks to us, varying in their usefulness.

The main point that Pin Yathay makes about this is that in his first few months under the Khmer Rouge he had come to understand that blind, unquestioning obedience, even in matters which went against his professional training and expertise, was the essential ingredient for survival.

I had found the key to survival. Pretend to be deaf! Pretend to be dumb! Understand nothing! Listen to nothing! I tried to feign ignorance and said very little.

He was able to cite innumerable examples of those who did speak up or who dared to question Angkar wisdom and were led off at night never to return.

The next big project in which Pin Yathay participated was the building of a huge dam at Veal Vong at the end of 1975. 'Once again,' he writes, 'the Khmer Rouge were defying the laws of hydraulics and physics.'

But the young 'pure and hard' Khmer Rouge insisted that 'political consciousness' was what counted. They had only contempt for the laws of bourgeois science and for 'book knowledge.' Pin Yathay told me that he knew he was taking part in a disastrous enterprise but he dared not utter a word. To have questioned the wisdom of the methods or even hinted at the possibility of failure would be to commit the most heinous of crimes by suggesting that Angkar was something less than infallible! Security was stricter than ever. For the first time they worked under the surveillance of armed guards. The dam was being built in the dry season across a temporarily empty river bed.

We piled up all sorts of material, which we transported in our woven baskets – earth, mud mixed with grass, leaves, pebbles, branches. Anything went. We threw this debris on to the dam wall, without any security dispositions, any spreading out or compacting. I doubted that this improvised dam would last more than one year during the high water season, even if the dimensions were extremely great – gigantic in fact.

Thousands of men and women expended their energies day and night at this work site. The result was an inevitable bungle of revolutionary fervour. The Khmer Rouge had lost all their critical faculties, all sense of proportion . . . The (new) caste of seigneurs and cadres could take all decisions. They had the right of life and death over us . . .

At the height of the flood season, the Veal Vong dam collapsed. The raging river swept away not only all vestiges of the dam but also the huts and shelters which lined its banks. Over a hundred deportees, mainly old folks and children, were drowned or disappeared.

Below the dam site there was nothing but devastation. Fortunately for Pin Yathay, his work group was established on higher ground above the dam.

One could find the inspiration for most of the criminal absurdities perpetuated by the Khmer Rouge in the worst excesses of the Chinese Cultural Revolution, applied in an infinitely more primitive way. However, although 'Politics in Command' was a favorite slogan of the Cultural Revolution, scientifically and technically sound irrigation systems – including complicated stone aqueducts and tunnels hacked through mountains – were built by the work forces of the Chinese communes. While paper knowledge was officially sneered at during the height of the Cultural Revolution, science and technique – and those who had mastered these subjects – were highly appreciated by the commune members. City intellectuals were sent by Mao Tse-tung to the countryside to be 'educated by the poor peasants.' By and large, they were put to good use by the commune members if they had demonstrable practical skills. Under the Khmer Rouge, city intellectuals were sent to the countryside to be exterminated; they had to exert considerable ingenuity to hide their talents in order to survive.

With unquestioning obedience to Angkar as one of the primary rules for a 'good' Khmer Rouge and for those under his power, there had to be drastic sanctions for the disobedient. These were applied not only to the deportees, who were led out at night to have their heads bashed in, but also to the head bashers if they were imprudent enough to question an Angkar directive. Angkar represented the super-negation of the separation of state powers. Not only was it party, state, and government; it was also executive, legislature, and judiciary, against whose decisions there was no appeal. The local Khmer Rouge chief was the incarnation of all these powers.

In order to ensure that the 'poorest of the poor' would become the new masters, it was often the village 'drop-out' – even by poor peasant standards – who was appointed local Angkar chief (just about any village in the world will have a few such 'drop-outs'; incapable of keeping steady jobs they often lapse into alcoholism, saved from prison or starvation by indulgent relatives keen to uphold family honor!). The Khmer Rouge endowed these village 'marginals' with the powers of life and death over those in their charge. And the latter were not averse to imposing their will by the most murderous means as far as 'new' residents were concerned, nor to settling accounts with 'old' residents whom they felt had humiliated them in the past, nor to helping themselves to any material objects which could be appropriated in the name of Angkar's 'needs.' They were accountable – and automatically executable – only if caught *in flagrante delicto*, appropriating something coveted by a Khmer Rouge cadre of superior status!

A 'good' Khmer Rouge – like all other husbands – had sexual relations only with his wife and only at times and places designated by the local leadership. But there were many pretty, sophisticated young women among the deportees, either unattached in general or separated from their husbands by work projects, starvation, or death. The lumpen-peasant Khmer Rouge chiefs were not indifferent to their charms. And they had the power – even without invoking Angkar – to press their demands. Pin Yathay relates a typical case at the Veal Vong work site.

> A woman was caught by surprise by soldiers when she was making love with a Khmer Rouge. Her son, long before the incident, had been deported to a youth camp and she had been arbitrarily separated from her husband . . . The Khmer Rouge with whom she had been surprised was not just anybody! He was the deputy-chief of Camp Two. During the interrogation to which she was submitted by the Khmer Rouge, she denounced two others. The *chlop* (official spy) and the secretary of Camp Two. The three Khmer Rouge implicated in the affair were real brutes, absolute butchers. They had numerous crimes on their consciences. All four, the young woman and the three Khmer Rouge, were taken into the jungle and executed.
>
> The 'new' residents considered the young woman as an authentic heroine of the passive resistance. She had denounced the *chlop* and the secretary – the most bloodthirsty (cadres) in the camp. Without doubt she had taken revenge for her husband and friends who had been tortured and killed by these two evil characters. We admired her gesture . . . The combination of the ambitions of the chief of the camp and the heroism of the young woman rid us of dangerous elements . . .

One of the ironies of the system introduced by Angkar was that, in the name of establishing a 'pure' and incorruptible society, it created a new administrative class which was just as corrupt in its own way as the old ones had been. 'Power corrupts,' and this could never have been more true than when a cadre at village or work site level had the power of life and death over those under his control. One of the most common forms of corruption under the Lon Nol regime was for high-level officers to draw U.S. dollars to pay and feed non-existent units. Lower-level officers did the same by not striking off the active list those who had died or deserted. Similarly, Khmer Rouge cadres only partially reported the daily deaths, or deferred reporting them for weeks or months, in order to store away their rice rations. Each condensed milk can of rice (the unit of measure by which it was doled out) had its specific value in terms of taels of gold, jewellery, or articles of clothing, this value fluctuating according to the capitalist law of supply and demand. Families like that of Pin Yathay remained alive and together as long as they did only because of the supplementary rations they bought on the black market from the secret Khmer Rouge stores. Of course, these were discreet operations which resulted in instant death for buyer and seller when they were discovered. Transactions were arranged through a middle man, whose life expectancy was short. He was the inevitable scapegoat, as it was on his person that the 'black' rice was found. Occasionally, like the girl in the sexual offense case, he would denounce the principals before he was killed. Usually he kept silent, knowing that his family would be exterminated if he denounced the Khmer Rouge responsible.

Lies and deceit were part of the daily, hourly behavior of a 'good' Khmer Rouge. How could it be otherwise when he was continually passing on lying and deceitful orders given by his superiors? There was no source from which he could acquire morality. The greatest of lies were justified by the cause of Angkar. He killed and stole in the name of Angkar. Pin Yathay relates the case of Uch Sam Sem, chief of the Phnom Penh Customs Service under Sihanouk. In January 1976, when the Angkar leadership announced a new Constitution, he was living alone (having been separated from his family) and was known as an indefatigable worker. One of the articles in the new Constitution stated that citizens were allowed to keep personal belongings. Uch Sam Sem noted that Khmer Rouge cadres started wearing watches. So he started to wear his own. A few days later, a member of the village Khmer Rouge committee said that Angkar 'proposed to borrow' his watch. He replied that he needed it in order to be on time for work. The head of the group came and insisted: 'You've worn that watch for years. You can leave it with me for awhile.' Apparently naively believing in the Constitution – there had been many 'political sessions' at which the Khmer Rouge cadres praised its contents, especially the passage about retaining items of personal property – Uch Sam Sem still held out. Ten days later he was sent into the forest to cut wood and never came back. A week after his disappearance, his watch reappeared on the wrist of a Khmer Rouge soldier. Pin Yathay heard this soldier boasting to his comrades about how he got the watch 'from that traitor who often spoke in the language of the French imperialists.'

The Constitution itself was a lie and every Khmer Rouge cadre soon knew it. Except for the setting-up of Chinese-type communes, none of its articles were ever implemented. Why not continue to lie and steal with impunity? The only one to whom the unfortunate Uch Sam Sem could turn in demanding his constitutional rights was the Khmer Rouge village chief, who had demanded the watch.

'Good' Khmer Rouge cadres learned to suppress any feelings of sentiment or humanity, even toward their own wives and children if they had any. Feelings of pity and friendship, or giving a helping hand to those in distress, were the stigmata of 'individualist tendencies.' They were 'stains of a bourgeois past' and must be suppressed. If a Khmer Rouge couple wanted to be regarded as 'models' they lived apart and met only with the approval of their immediate chief. Family life had to be stamped out as the nucleus of private property, the clan system, and eventually the capitalist state. Normal human sentiments were viewed as expressions of revolutionary weakness and had to be eradicated.

It is interesting to note that the Kuomintang Chinese had been vigilant for any signs of humane feelings among their prisoners, in order to detect which of them were Communists. Spies from the secret police were put in the prison cells to watch for anyone who shared a scrap of food with another, tended his or her wounds, murmured a few words of comfort after a torture session, or did anything which betrayed compassion or solidarity. That person was marked down as a Communist. For the Khmer Rouge, such a person was a reactionary!

The idea of a society comprised exclusively of the Khmer Rouge – that is, the military and civilian organizations of Angkar – was reiterated in numerous utterances from the top level of the leadership down to those who conducted the indoctrination sessions at the base. Only one or two million 'pure and hard' militants would be needed to build this 'new society.' A 'good' Khmer Rouge cadre was aware of this and acted accordingly. The task of the enslaved 'new' residents – who, as they died out, were being replaced by the 'old' residents – was to create the infrastructure of this 'new society' for the master class to enjoy. When the slaves 'old' and 'new' had disappeared altogether, they would be replaced by the 'pure and hard' themselves, who could be counted on to serve a tiny elite who would do their thinking for them. Angkar was the perfect organism to foster and execute such a monstrous concept. Oxen were castrated physically to make them docile and oblivious to their fate. The 'pure and hard' were castrated mentally, spiritually, and psychologically to make them incapable of independent thought. As rigorous guardians of the 'old' and 'new' slaves, the Khmer Rouge cadres were well on their way to becoming slaves themselves.

[Chapter 8 of *The China Cambodia Vietnam Triangle* (Vanguard Books, Chicago, 1981), pp. 111–120.]

29

China Prepares to Attack
Vietnam [1981]

When he finally entered Cambodia – after the Vietnamese 'invaded' Cambodia and overthrew the Pol Pot regime – Burchett witnessed the full extent of the horror and the complicity of China. Instead of peace in his beloved Indochina there were mass graves, and his two 'best friends', China and Vietnam, were at war. Nothing in his decades of reporting had prepared him for this. He simply did not see it coming, and here lies one of his greatest journalistic failures.

This was the time he resigned from the New York *National Guardian*, at the time his only means of material support, because they were toeing the Chinese line and refusing to publish his articles denouncing China's role in the tragedy of Cambodia. Despite the overwhelming evidence of Khmer Rouge crimes against humanity, the US, UK, France, China and other countries backed the Pol Pot regime against the Vietnamese-installed government of Kampuchea. Burchett took the side of Vietnam and was ostracised by many of his friends on the Left and in China. The following chapter's description of life in Saigon/Ho Chi Minh City demonstrates his convictions about the pernicious influence of China on their neighbour to the south.

* * *

Between the end of November and the end of December 1978 I spent a very depressing month in Vietnam, mostly along her south-west border with Kampuchea and her northern border with China. It was a month darkened by the shadows of impending events.

The first evil omen was to learn upon my arrival in Ho Chi Minh-ville that South Vietnam's most popular and talented actress – and one of its true heroines – Thanh Nga had been assassinated four nights earlier. It was no ordinary killing, and the whole city was in mourning. Thanh Nga had received a telephoned warning that she would be killed if she played the title role of the tenth century heroine, Queen Duong Van Nga. Duong Van Nga's husband, the reigning monarch at the time, had been killed by the Chinese occupiers for resisting their rule. The queen continued the resistance and encouraged a young general, who succeeded in expelling the occupiers. The widowed queen then defied Confucian morality by marrying the general. Thus, she was a symbol of national liberation and women's liberation. Thanh Nga ignored the warning and played the role with great success. She was shot dead, together with her husband, as they returned home after a performance on 16 November 1978.

Over a year previously, she had ignored a similar telephoned warning not to play the role of Trung Tac, the elder of the two famous Trung sisters. In the first century AD the Trung sisters had raised an army and, with themselves at its head, expelled the Chinese occupiers for three years. During one performance a grenade had been thrown and a fragment from it had lodged in Thanh Nga's right shoulder.

In both cases the attackers had escaped. When I asked who was responsible, I invariably received one of two replies: 'Ask in the Fifth District' or 'Ask in the North'! The Fifth District of Ho Chi Minhville included Cholon, the heavily Chinese former twin city of Saigon, and was the district with the highest proportion of Chinese residents. The Hoa, as the Vietnamese designate the ethnic Chinese, constituted 65 percent of the population of the Fifth District. The 'North' had by that time become the synonym used in referring to Peking.

I went to see the Chairman of the People's Committee for the Fifth District, Nghi Doan. He was a big, smiling man, an ethnic Chinese who was a member of the National Assembly and also of the Communist Party Committee for Ho Chi Minhville. I wanted to find out how an atmosphere had been created which could result in the two assassination attempts against Thanh Nga. With Nghi Doan were two other members of the Fifth District People's Committee, one of them also currently a member of the city's Party Committee. Their replies were long, detailed, and depressing. Nghi Doan did most of the talking, constantly referring to his colleagues for confirmation of dates and figures.

> The Fifth was the center for Hoa commerce and service trades, also for the big capitalist traders and bourgeois compradores. If one spoke of Saigon in those days, one had to speak of the Fifth District as the home base of the big compradores. One of the main problems of administering Ho Chi Minhville was that all the trade was in the hands of the big Hoa capitalists and compradores. It was the center of the rice trade, with the 'Rice King' May Hy in control. It was the center of banking with over thirty banks and banking services involving U.S., British, French and Hong Kong capital but always with participation by Hoa compradores. To be a bank director, you had to be a high functionary in the administration or a high-ranking officer in the armed forces. It was not necessary to have capital – but rank and authority. The Vietnamese were directors et cetera in name only – they got some financial kickbacks for the use of their names – but the finance was put up by the Hoa compradores and all transactions were controlled by them. They manipulated all financial transactions, the entire import-export trade, the internal trade circuit.[1]
>
> A number of these had relations not only with Taiwan, but also with Peking . . .

Nghi Doan mentioned a certain Tran Thanh, a Taiwan Chinese who had financed a very lucrative sodium glutamate factory in Saigon with 48 percent Taiwan capital, putting up most of the rest himself. Shortly before the liberation of Saigon, Tran Thanh transferred his capital to Peking and returned to his native district in Kwantung province (of which Canton is the capital). There he built a modern highway to impress the Chinese leadership with his 'patriotism' and with the potential usefulness of himself and his co-fraternity in Vietnam.

> Before liberation, there were forty schools (primary and secondary) and six hospitals, all in the hands of Tran Thanh and other Hoa compradores, in the Fifth District. The director of the Trieu Chau hospital was Tran Thanh – naming it after his native village in Kwantung. In this hospital were secret agents of both Peking and Taiwan. Peking – even under the puppet Nguyen Van Thieu administration – sent cadres

to 'help' Tran Thanh run the hospital. It was the same thing with the schools. They were in the hands of people like Tran Thanh. Most of the directors and teachers were from Taiwan, but Peking also infiltrated its agents. The principle was that there could be no expansion of mainland China's influence abroad, if it were not based on the educational system of the young Chinese. For years prior to the liberation of Saigon, Peking started preparing bases among the compradores and traders – but also among the young people. After Liberation, these secret organizations switched over to counter-revolutionary activities against the new regime, under such names as 'Association of Young Chinese for National Salvation' and 'Association for Studying the Works of Chairman Mao.' They started distributing leaflets in favor of Mao. Of course, we had been following the preparations for such activities from the time Peking started exporting the Cultural Revolution in our direction. So we took some measures to limit the damage.[2] But we found agents were being sent in directly from Secret Service organs in Kwantung and other South China provinces. They had identity papers stamped with counterfeit seals. [Nghi Doan handed me a few and demonstrated that very expert scrutiny was needed to distinguish false from authentic documents – W.B.] Young Hoa were sent out of here, given crash courses as secret agents, then sent back again. Fortunately we got on to this quickly.

In March 1978 there had been a nationalization of wholesale and large retail trading enterprises. Some three thousand big merchants were affected, of whom six hundred were Vietnamese and the rest Hoa. Nghi Doan explained that the policy toward Vietnamese and Hoa was identical but as the latter were far more important numerically and financially 'they had to take the consequences.' This action unleashed a flood of protests from Peking, in which 'oppression, persecution, and discrimination' against Chinese 'residents' and 'nationals' were charged.

An 'Association for Struggle of Chinese Residents' surfaced. One of its leaflets urged the Hoa 'to rise up – unify yourselves – be worthy of the task of defending our Chinese Motherland.' Another from the 'National Salvation' group went further and urged 'struggle against the Vietnamese dominating class – the enemy of our Nation . . . Unite for a Radiant Future . . .'

With this type of agitation going on it was easy to whip up the sort of atmosphere of chauvinism and racism in which a Thanh Nga could be murdered.

I then asked Nghi Doan and his comrades from the Fifth District People's Committee what was behind the exodus of Chinese 'boat people.' They replied:

> As for the boat people! We wanted the Hoa people to remain with us. After the socialist transformation of trade, we tried to attract the former merchants to move into productive activities to develop regional – even if capitalist – enterprises. We offered loans, from 10,000 to 20,000 dongs [in terms of what that was worth in state-supplied equipment, it was roughly equivalent to the same amount in dollars – W.B.] to add to their own capital to develop such enterprises. But many of them had the mentality of exploiters – they could not face the prospects of life outside their luxury villas. So they try, by all means, to flee abroad. There is a big network of black marketeers, who formerly lived off the drug traffic but now trade in human beings. It is run by Hoa people who have close connections with Hong Kong and elsewhere abroad – including Peking. When we catch people trying to flee, we reason with them and try to persuade them to lead a normal life. But eventually they succeed, even after several failed attempts. The coastline is very long. For those who are prepared to pay big sums to the 'leaky boat' racketeers, preventing them is very difficult. And we have more pressing problems on our hands than setting up an organization big enough to stop them.

Shortly after the nationalization of the big trading enterprises there had been an unprecedented incident on the Fifth District's Tan Hang Street. On 20 March 1978 cadres had come – as to all other areas of the city – to try to persuade people to volunteer for civic work on Saturdays, a common and widely followed practice in the first years after liberation. They ran into an organized demonstration, with banners and slogans around the theme: 'We Are Hoa – No Obligation To Do Voluntary Work.' The demonstrators waved flags of the People's Republic of China and carried portraits of Chairman Mao. When the cadres tried to explain the need for continuing volunteer labor, they were stoned and bottles rained down on them from upper-storey windows. Police had to be called and Chinese photographers were on hand to record the example of Vietnamese 'oppression' of ethnic Chinese. Following this – and after a suitable propaganda build-up – Peking announced that it was sending two ships to Haiphong and Ho Chi Minhville to start evacuating those they were by then describing as 'persecuted Chinese residents' and 'nationals.'

To grasp the importance of the use of such terms – and of the refusal of Saturday work by the demonstrators on Tan Hang Street because they were 'Hoa' – one needs to know that in 1955 the Chinese and Vietnamese Communist Parties signed an agreement providing for residents in China of Vietnamese origin and residents in Vietnam of Chinese origin to come under the jurisdiction of the Chinese and Vietnamese Communist Parties, respectively, and within two years to become Chinese and Vietnamese citizens. From the time the agreement was signed, they were to have the same rights and obligations as other citizens of China and Vietnam. This had been scrupulously applied in Vietnam and Hoa citizens occupied high positions in the party, the government, and the economy. At a Conference of Overseas Chinese held in Peking at the end of 1977 and beginning of 1978, this concept had been reversed. The delegates from the 20 million overseas Chinese in Southeast Asia were told that if they had Chinese blood in their veins they should remain faithful to the 'Motherland' and contribute their wealth and skills to the campaign for the 'Four Modernizations.'

The Vietnamese government responded to Peking's announcement that it was sending two ships to pick up Chinese who wanted to leave Vietnam by issuing a statement to the effect that it had no objection to the departure of any Hoa who wanted to leave or to the ships coming to ports designated by Vietnam and in compliance with normal international maritime procedures. Hanoi fixed the dates on which the ships could arrive, at Haiphong and at Vungtau (formerly Cap St. Jacques) – 50 miles southeast of Ho Chi Minhville – rather than at Ho Chi Minhville. When the first ship arrived at Haiphong, the captain gave as the reason for entry into Vietnamese waters 'to repatriate expelled and persecuted Chinese nationals.' This was a formula which the Chinese knew the Vietnamese could not possibly accept.

After weeks of negotiations, the two ships hauled up their anchors and returned to China without any passengers. But Peking made a great deal of propaganda about the 'rescue mission' and her prestige among the Hoa people took a nose dive.

I was later told at a high level in Hanoi that the Peking leadership:

> had planned by clandestine means to create large-scale disorders when the boats arrived at Haiphong – and especially at Ho Chi Minhville. The psychological climate had been created and it was planned to move into top gear. But there was 'clandestinity within the clandestinity.' We knew about the planned provocations and the chief provocateurs were 'invited to take a holiday.' The whole affair turned into a fiasco.

This was true. But my impression of the Chinese-dominated sector of Ho Chi Minhville in early December 1978 was that there was an 'explosive' situation and that elements there were just awaiting the igniting of a fuse to spring into action. The compradores had connections with a gangster underworld, as in Shanghai in the 'old days.' They were not likely to take their defeat over the nationalizations lying down. Nor was Peking likely to reconcile itself to the 'mercy boats' fiasco!

[From Chapter 12 of *The China Cambodia Vietnam Triangle* (Vanguard Books, Chicago, 1981), pp. 180–192.]

30
Afterword [1983]

In the early 1980s things looked bleak for the Left around the world. The USSR was bogged down in its own 'Vietnam' in Afghanistan, her leadership sclerotic, her economy static, her satellites rebellious. Vietnam was ostracised and denounced as a totalitarian Stalinist regime by many of her former supporters on the Left – not to mention the triumphant Right. The US, UK and other Western countries were supporting the genocidal Khmer Rouge in the UN and arming them on the ground. The 'free world' had a new leader, Ronald Reagan, who denounced the 'Evil Empire', championed his own 'Star Wars', invaded Grenada and armed the Contras in Nicaragua and assorted death squads in the rest of Latin America. In addition, Burchett was appalled by China's support of the Khmer Rouge and what he considered reactionary forces in Southern Africa.

As mentioned earlier, he resigned from the New York *National Guardian* after being a contributor for 25 years, because they refused to publish his articles critical of China and North Korea (the *Guardian* was running lucrative tours to both countries). With more time on his hands, he wrote his memoirs, *At The Barricades*, and made films with Australian, Italian, British and Swedish independent filmmakers and television companies. And he gave his full support to the anti-war and nuclear disarmament movement.

He finished writing his last book, *Shadows of Hiroshima*, in Sofia, Bulgaria – his wife Vessa's homeland – where he had moved in the last year of his life because of ill-health and financial strain. He finished typing the footnotes for the book, had a stroke, and died a few weeks later on 26 September 1983.

His 'Warning to the World' had made world headlines on 5 September 1945, and *Shadows of Hiroshima* recaps Wilfred Burchett's Hiroshima experience, gives a brief history of the development of the atomic bomb and the cover-ups, talks about the *hibakusha*, the second- and third-generation victims of atomic radiation in Hiroshima, the morality of using the atomic bomb as a political tool and universal threat, and ends on the optimistic note that reason will hopefully prevail over the madness of nuclear obliteration.

* * *

If the nuclear precipice was narrowly skirted in Berlin in 1948/49 and again in Korea, the close calls had little chastening effect on the American presidency. With a recklessness born of hubris, most of Truman's successors have at one point or another in their administrations recoursed to crude nuclear blackmail: notably Eisenhower in his threats to China over the Formosa Straits in 1957, Kennedy over Cuba in 1962, Nixon during the Yom Kippur War of 1973, and Carter with his Persian Gulf Doctrine of 1979. Now the White House is occupied by a regime which exults in its enthusiasm to make nuclear war 'winnable' and in its willingness to 'go to the brink' over any threatened piece of imperial real estate.

It is a state of affairs endorsed by secrecy and exclusion. As we have seen in the case of the Hiroshima cover-up, censorship and official disinformation have been used since 1945 to blunt public awareness of the consequences of nuclear war and to intimidate the voices of conscience from the *hibakusha,* scientists and service-men who have dared remind us of the crimes against humanity committed on the 6th and 10th of August 1945. Likewise, from the top-secret beginning of Project Manhattan in 1941, the development of nuclear weapons and strategic nuclear policy have been put above and outside any democratic process. No one in a 'Western democracy' has, in fact, ever voted on the Bomb or its potential use.

In what the Reagan Administration openly trumpets as the 'biggest public relations campaign in history', NATO is currently spending millions to convince us that they are justified in spending thousands of millions to escalate the new cold war. The all-powerful 'Ministries of Truth' are synchronizing the noise-making to drown out the voices from Greenham Common, Central Park and Hiroshima. Many compliant and hungry journalists will undoubtedly be eager to assist this cacophony of official rhetoric. Others, just as undoubtedly, will dissent and attempt to 'get the story right'.

Meanwhile, as the threat of nuclear war increases with each new task force dispatched to a tropical sea, with each Cruise or Pershing missile implanted in Europe, and with each cheer from the sidelines at Westminister and Bonn, we must guard ever more vigilantly against the misapprehension that nothing can be done to stop such a Leviathan in its tracks. Like Eatherly before he became a resister, we are tempted to give way to despair and helplessness. Yet at times like these – most of all – we must take courage and example from the *hibakusha*.

The 'lesson' of Hiroshima is, in my opinion, actually twofold. On the one hand Hiroshima, like Auschwitz, asserts the existence of a will to genocidal, absolute destruction. We should never cease to meditate on the fact that there has already occurred a first nuclear war, and, because of this precedent, there is little reason to doubt the possibility of a second – particularly if the same constellation of class interests, will-to-power and mind-numbing rhetoric that autho-rized the exemplary immolation of Hiroshima and Nagasaki is again given pretext and opportunity. On the other hand, Hiroshima also represents the indestructibility of human resistance. Despite their ordeals, the cover-ups, even the ostracism from 'normal' soci-ety, the *hibakusha* survivors have fought back, becoming the most stalwart and militant of peaceniks. Through them and their ongo-ing struggle, the *urgency* of Hiroshima is transmitted to all of us.

[From *Shadows of Hiroshima* (Verso, London, 1983), pp. 119–120.]

Notes

1 The Atomic Plague [1945]

1 George Burchett and Nick Shimmin (eds), *Memoirs of a Rebel Journalist: The Autobiography of Wilfred Burchett* (UNSW Press, Sydney, 2005), p. 229.

4 The Trial of Cardinal Mindszenty [1951]

1 Quotes in this introduction are from: George Burchett and Nick Shimmin (eds), *Memoirs of a Rebel Journalist: The Autobiography of Wilfred Burchett* (UNSW Press, Sydney, 2005), p. 258; Wilfred Burchett, *Passport: An Autobiography* (Nelson, Melbourne, 1969), p. 177.

6 The Microbe War [1953]

1 George Burchett and Nick Shimmin (eds), *Memoirs of a Rebel Journalist: The Autobiography of Wilfred Burchett* (UNSW Press, Sydney, 2005), p. 347.

13 Virgin Lands [1962]

1 An industrial centre near Sverdlovsk in the Urals.
2 240 large industrial enterprises, one of which will be among Europe's biggest iron and steel plants at Temir Tau, 24 power-stations, 10,000 miles of high-tension transmission lines, 20 engineering plants.

14 Lilac and Outer Space [1962]

1 Publication of the Young Communist League.
2 Manolis Glezos, hero of the Greek resistance movement who tore the swastika flag from the Athens Acropolis under the very noses of the Nazi occupiers, was convicted by an Athens Court in 1959 on trumped-up charges of being a Communist spy.

3 Leading Soviet satirical weekly.
4 He was right! Gagarin and Titov are both cultivated as well as courageous men.
5 Issue No. 4, 1959.

15   War Against Trees [1963]

1 The fact that Canada is a member of the International Control Commission, whose task it is to see that no war material enters the country, does not seem to have bothered the *Newsweek* reporter.

21   A Spurned Olive Branch [1967/1977]

1 Harrison Salisbury, *Behind the Lines – Hanoi* (Bantam Books, New York, 1967), p. 210.
2 *Yomiuri Shimbun*, Tokyo, 3 February 1967.
3 Harold Wilson, *The Labour Government 1964–70: A Personal Record* (Penguin Books, Harmondsworth, 1971), pp. 444–6.

22   Personal Leader [1968]

1 Referred to several times by Kim Il Sung as that 'notorious bureaucrat.' Ho Ga Yi was in charge of organizational work for the Workers' Party's Central Committee for several years until 1952.

27   The Geneva Conference [1978]

1 *The National Guardian*, New York, 3 November 1976.
2 Prime Minister's address, *To the Nation*, 23 September 1976, Ministry of Information, Immigration & Tourism, Salisbury, 1976.
3 Sections of the British press, notably the *Sunday Times*, 9 October 1977, maintain that ZAPU's hotel bill at the Intercontinental – and various travels of Joshua Nkomo – were paid by Roland 'Tiny' Rowland, head of LONRHO (London & Rhodesian Mining and Land Company), described as Africa's largest multinational company . . .
4 *The National Guardian*, New York, 29 December 1976.
5 Both quotes from *International Herald Tribune*, Paris, 10 March 1976.

28   How to be a Good Khmer Rouge [1981]

1 There were two official journals: the 'Revolutionary Flag,' organ of the Communist Party of Kampuchea, and the 'Red Flag,' organ of the

Communist Youth organization. Both were published irregularly and were not available to the general public. News was obtained – by those with the right to own a receiver – from Phnom Penh radio.

2 Pin Yathay, *L'Utopie Meutriere* (Robert Laffont, Paris, 1980). All the rest of the quotations in this chapter are from this work.

29   China Prepares to Attack Vietnam [1981]

1 In September 1975 Huynh Tan Phat, prime minister of what then was still the Provisional Revolutionary Government (and now the deputy prime minister of the Socialist Republic of Vietnam) told me that his was the first government ever to try to get its hands on the South Vietnamese economy. 'Neither the French, the Japanese, the French in their comeback in 1945, nor the Americans, even tried,' he said. 'It was so completely in the hands of the Hoa that they preferred to work through them.' Our discussion took place a few hours before Huynh Tan Phat signed a decree cracking down on the various 'Rice,' 'Tobacco,' 'Textile,' and other 'kings'!

2 Within a few hours of the liberation of Saigon, French flags began appearing in the windows of French residents, apparently to make the point that they were not Americans. Flags of the People's Republic of China were flying all over the Fifth District and other predominantly Chinese quarters. Both the French and – even more so – the Chinese were mortified when they were ordered to take them down. It was the flag of revolutionary North and South Vietnam which monopolized the scene. It was *their* victory that was being celebrated.

Bibliography

[All titles by Wilfred Burchett, unless otherwise noted.]

Again Korea (International Publishers, New York, 1968).

China Cambodia Vietnam Triangle, The (Vanguard Books, Chicago, 1981).

China: The Quality of Life (Penguin Books, Harmondsworth, 1976).

Come East Young Man (Seven Seas Books, Berlin, 1962).

Furtive War: The United States in Vietnam and Laos, The (International Publishers, New York, 1963).

Grasshoppers & Elephants: Why Viet Nam Fell (Outback Press, Melbourne, 1977).

Mekong Upstream: A Visit to Laos and Cambodia (Seven Seas Publishers, Berlin, 1959).

My Visit to the Liberated Zones of South Vietnam (Foreign Languages Publishing House, Hanoi, 2nd edn, 1964).

North of the 17th Parallel ('Published by the Author', Hanoi, 1955).

Pacific Treasure Island: New Caledonia (David Mckay Company, Philadelphia, 4th edn, 1944).

People's Democracies (World Unity Publications, 1951).

Shadows of Hiroshima (Verso, London, 1983).

Southern Africa Stands Up (Outback Press, Melbourne, 1978).

This Monstrous War (Joseph Waters, Melbourne, 1953).

Vietnam North (Lawrence & Wishart, London, 1966).

Vietnam: Inside Story of the Guerilla War (International Publishers, New York, 1965).

Wingate Adventure (F.W. Cheshire, Melbourne, 1944).

George Burchett and Nick Shimmin (eds), *Memoirs of a Rebel Journalist: The Autobiography of Wilfred Burchett* (UNSW Press, Sydney, 2005).

Wilfred Burchett and Anthony Purdy, *Cosmonaut Yuri Gagarin: First Man in Space* (Panther Books, London, 1961).

Wilfred Burchett and Derek Roebuck, *The Whores of War* (Penguin Books, Harmondsworth, 1977).

Wilfred Burchett and Alan Winnington, *Koje Unscreened* ('Published by the Authors', Peking, 1953).

Wilfred Burchett and Alan Winnington, *Plain Perfidy* (Britain–China Friendship Association, London, 1954).

Index

WB = Wilfred Burchett. Page numbers in bold refer to illustrations and their accompanying captions.

CPSIA information can be obtained at www.ICGtesting.com
Printed in the USA
LVOW12s2323120314

377158LV00001B/44/P